Philip Columbus Croll

Tributes to the memory of Martin Luther

Philip Columbus Croll

Tributes to the memory of Martin Luther

ISBN/EAN: 9783337127237

Printed in Europe, USA, Canada, Australia, Japan

Cover: Foto ©Lupo / pixelio.de

More available books at **www.hansebooks.com**

TRIBUTES

TO THE MEMORY

OF

MARTIN LUTHER.

COMPILED AND EDITED

BY

REV. P. C. CROLL, A. M.

"Great men, taken up in any way, are profitable company."—CARLYLE.

PHILADELPHIA:
G. W. FREDERICK.
1884.

TO
ALL LOVERS
AND STUDENTS OF
LUTHER AND THE TRUTH
FOR WHICH HE WROUGHT AND WROTE,
PREACHED AND PRAYED,
THIS VOLUME IS
DEDICATED.

(i)

MARTIN LUTHER.

That which he knew he uttered,
  Conviction made him strong;
And with undaunted courage
  He faced and fought the wrong.
No power on earth could silence him
  Whom love and faith made brave;
And though four hundred years have gone,
  Men strew with flowers his grave.

A frail child, born to poverty,
  A German miner's son;
A poor monk searching in his cell,
  What honors has he won!
The nations crown him Faithful,
  A man whom truth made free:
God give us for these easier times
  More men as real as he!

                —Marianne Farningham.

PREFACE.

IT is not necessary to offer an apology for the appearance of a book of this kind.   Festivities that
have been so universally and enthusiastically celebrated as the recent quarto-centennial celebration of
Luther's birth, declare that the great Reformer has a
warm place in the hearts of the Protestant world.
The story of his life is known.   It has been told in
hundreds of books, and written in scores of tongues.
This memorial year has greatly multiplied the number
of his biographies, and refreshed the account of his
times.   It might be superfluous to write another Life
of Luther or another History of the Reformation ;
but a collection of tributes, such as we have here
brought together, has never been presented to the
reading public, nor could it have been before the un-
precedented observances of this Memorial Year.   And
while it may perhaps not be as instructive as history
or biography, it will be, we flatter ourself to believe,
equally interesting and even more entertaining.   As
with the ever-changing combinations of the kaleido-
scope, though but reflections from the same crystal,
we feel confident many an admirer will amuse himself
looking over these pages, ever changing, as he will
find them, while the subject is always the same.

It is to preserve in a more permanent and conveni-
ent form many of the thousands of well-said Luther-

encomiums that this volume has been prepared, and is now launched upon the sea of publication.

Amid the super-abundance of material furnished, by almost every Protestant pulpit, and every editor's desk, and every writer's pen, we have experienced no small difficulty in the selection, having been circum-scribed by our purpose and necessarily limited in time, as the publication could, for various reasons, not be long deferred. We discovered that there is no end of panegyric, and our research has established the con-viction that no other man who has ever lived, has re-ceived so much and so general and so just and such discriminating praise.

Part I. is a slight exhibition of what men of note and ability have said during the four centuries since Luther's birth. It is by no means exhaustive of noble tributes, and for further reading on this point we refer the curious and studious to the many "Lives" of the Reformer and the multitude of Church Histories ex-tant, to files of the current periodicals covering the months of October, November and December, 1883, and to such volumes as the "Gloria Lutheri," Leipzig, 1618; "Hūndret Stimmen Namhafter Männer über Luther's Werk and Person," M. C. Bartel, St. Louis, Mo., 1872. Any large library will contain many Luther books. The Mercantile of Philadelphia, has over three hundred volumes treating on Luther. We have made use of it in the compilation of this Part, and received much assistance from Dr. Krauth's "Con-servative Reformation," Dr. Seiss' "Ecclesia Luther-ana," Dr. Rein's "Life of Luther," (as published in English by Funk & Wagnalls, New York,) Wackernagel's "Life of Luther," (Pilger Book Store, Reading, Pa.); "Gloria Lutheri," by M. Caspar Roth; Stork's "Luther and the Bible," etc. The tributes in this part are arranged, as near as possible, in chronological order of their authors.

Part II. contains a few of the many editorials with which periodicals were teeming these past memorial months. We have confined ourself almost exclusively to religious papers in our selection, appending but a few from the secular press. It will be seen that non-Lutheran organs have even surpassed in glowing tribute those of the Lutheran Church. This accounts for so slim a representation of the best Lutheran Journals of our land.

Part III. is a fair showing of what prominent American divines and other eminent men have said in various parts of our land. With but a single exception (that of Rev. C. H. Spurgeon), these last two parts are entirely composed of American tributes. The foreign press dispatch showed what laurel-wreaths could be constructed from the flowers that bloomed this year in Germany, which in the product of Luther-honor was closely followed by all other civilized and Protestant nations. Germany, however, took the lead, where Luther's battle had been fought, and where his glorious Battle-hymn this year "made the rafters roar from Hamburg to Bohemia."

We regret that we were obliged to abbreviate some of the beautiful encomiums sent in, and to omit others altogether, since not bearing exactly on the point for which we had solicited. We regret also having been compelled to break these tributes away from their connection, in which they fitted like jewels in settings of gold. But we have, in most instances, indicated the source from which they were taken; there the reader can find these gems in all their casements of connected thought.

Our thanks are due to many of our ministerial brethren for their encouraging words, etc., in response to our circular. Special mention we owe Drs. Mc-Cosh, C. W. Schaeffer, B. M. Schmucker, J. G. Morris, V. L. Conrad, H. E. Jacobs, Revs. M. Sheeleigh, W. H. Kuntz, G. C. Henry, J. A. Singmaster, A. Stump, J. C. Zimmerman, J. N. Lenker, and Mr. Samuel J. Shanbacher, of Philadelphia, in acknowledgement of assistance received at their hands, either in the loan of a book or paper, or in their direction to such material as we were in search for.

For the make-up of this laurel-wreath we claim for ourself no more than the finding of the hoop upon which the flowers are strung, the gathering of these laurels, and the cord that binds them together. It has proven to be no light task, but it has been a labor of much love, and if it will help to keep alive not only the demonstrations of this "Luther-year," but also to perpetuate the humble faith and the implicit trust in God, the brave heroism and the unflinching defence of right and truth, which has made this "Father of Protestantism," so justly famous and so widely honored, our work shall not have been in vain.

Schuylkill Haven, Pa.   P. C. C.

CONTENTS.

(7)

LUTHER.

BY JOAQUIN MILLER.

Valiant, defiant and free,
  Majestic, impressive and lone,
He looms like an isle of the sea
  That rose to an emperor's throne.

(viii)

PART I.
WHAT SCHOLARS OF THIS AND OTHER DAYS HAVE SAID OF LUTHER.

LUTHER'S HAMMER.

Challenging the license
   To make gain of sin,
Luther nails his protest;
   Listen to the din!

Striking with his hammer;
   How the panels shake!
How the gateway trembles!
   How the timid quake!

Blow on blow resounding,
   Echoed from afar;
How the world is shaken;
   How the Churches jar!

And throughout the ages
   Fraud has felt the force
Of the Reformation,
   As it holds its course.

We to-day are feeling
   Heart and conscience thrill,
And throughout the ages
   Men will feel it still,

Till the death-stroke's given
   To all force and fraud;
For the striking hammer
   Is the word of God.

SCHOLARS' TRIBUTES.

ERASMUS,

A contemporary of Luther, a profound scholar, an able critic of refined taste, and a vigorous promoter of the Reformation is quoted by Jorton in his "Life of Erasmus," London, 1728, among many others, as author of the following estimates of the German Reformer:

"As to Luther, he is altogether unknown to me, and I have read nothing of his except two or three pages. His life and conversation are universally commended; and it is no small prejudice in his favor, that his morals are unblamable, and that calumny itself can fasten no reproach on him."—*Writing to Cardinal Wolsey in 1518.*

"All the world is agreed amongst us in commending his moral character. He hath given us good advice on some points; and God grant that his success may be equal to the liberty which he hath taken." "Luther hath committed two unpardonable crimes: he hath touched the pope upon the crown, and the monks upon the belly."—*In a Letter to Melanchthon in 1519.*

"By the little of Luther's writings which I have rather run over than examined, I thought that I could discern in him natural talents, and a genius very proper to explain the holy scriptures according to the manner of the fathers, and to kindle those sparks of Evangelical doctrine, from which common custom, and the doctrines of the schools upon speculations more subtile

(11)

than useful, had departed too far. I heard men of great merit, equally respectable for learning and piety, congratulate themselves for having been acquainted with these books. I saw that the more unblamable their behaviour was, and the more approaching to Evangelical purity, the less they were irritated against him.__His moral character was recommended even by some who could not endure his doctrine. As to the spirit with which he was animated, and of which God alone can judge with certainty, I chose rather, as it became me, to think too favorably than too hardly of it. And, to say the plain truth, the Christian world hath been long weary of those teachers who insist too rigidly upon trifling inventions and human con-stitutions, and begins to thirst after the pure and living water drawn from the sources of the Evangelists and Apostles. For this undertaking Luther seemed to be fitted by nature, and inflamed with an active zeal to prosecute it. Thus it is that I have favored Luther; I have favored the good which I saw, or imagined that I saw in him."—*In a Letter to Campegius (1520).*

In reply to the pope's agents attempting to win Eras-mus more and more away from favoring Luther, he said: " Luther is a man of too great abilities for me to encounter; and I learn more from one page of his than from all the works of Thomas Aquinas."

PHILIP MELANCHTHON,

"The Hamlet of the Reformation," Luther's most prominent col-league, said during Luther's life:

" Luther is too great, too wonderful for me to depict in words. If there be a ·man on earth I love with my whole heart, that man is Luther. One is an interpreter, one a logician, another an orator, affluent and beautiful in speech, but Luther is all in all; whatever he writes, whatever he utters, pierces to the soul, fixes itself like arrows in the heart—he is a miracle among men."

Again, in his funeral oration at Luther's grave, he said:

" It is also evident that the light of the gospel has been kindled anew through the words and writings of Luther. He must, therefore, be counted among that number of illustrious men whom God has sent to re-establish and build up his Church upon the earth, and whom we recognize as the brightest ornaments of the human race. We acknowledge that Solon, Themistocles, Scipio, Augustus, and the like, who either founded or ruled governments, were distinguished men ; but far inferior are they to leaders like Isaiah, John the Baptist, St. Paul, Augustine and Luther. It is right that we distinguish between merely earthly leaders, and those through whom God preserves and governs his Church.

" But what did Luther do that entitles him to our admiration and praise? Many say that the Church is in a tumult, and that incurable controversies have sprung up on every side. To this I would reply that such is simply the natural course of the Church on earth. When the Holy Spirit reproves the world, dissensions arise on account of the contumacy of the ungodly; but the guilt rests with those who will not hear the Son of God, concerning whom the heavenly Father says, ' Hear ye him.' Luther brought to light

again the true doctrines of God; for it is evident that
the doctrine of repentance, for example, had been involved in the grossest darkness. By dispersing this
darkness he shows what true repentance means; he
points out our sure haven of refuge, and the firm consolation possible for a heart that has been oppressed
by fear of God's wrath. He illustrated Paul's doctrine of ' Justification by Faith,' he marked the distinction between the law and the gospel, between the
righteousness of the spirit and mere external morality
of conduct. He indicated the true way of worshiping
God, and awakened the Church from the heathenish
folly of supposing that God may be rightly worshiped
when the heart is filled with doubt and unbelief, although in such a case the natural heart shuns communion with God.   He bade us pray in faith and with
a good conscience, and led us, indeed, not to images
and dead men, to whom the ungodly in their dark
infatuation pray, but to the one Mediator, the Son of
God, who sits at the right hand of the eternal Father
and intercedes for us.   Other duties and good works
pleasing to God he also taught us, and he adorned
and defended private civil life to a greater degree than
has been done by the writings of any other man.   And
finally he distinguished proper and necessary works
from the childish exercise of human ceremonies, rites
and precepts, that hinder the true worship of God.
And that the pure doctrines of heaven might be preserved to the Church, and handed down to succeeding
generations, he translated the Scriptures into German,
and that, too, in a style of such clearness that this version affords more light to the reader than very many

of the commentaries. In addition to this he was the author of many expositions of the Scriptures, which even Erasmus used to say far surpassed any extant. As it is written of those who rebuilt the city of Jerusalem, that they built the walls with one hand and held the sword with the other, so Luther was at one and the same time warring with the enemies of true doctrine, writing expositions of God's holy word, and comforting the consciences of many by his godly counsels. Many of the truths of the Gospel, as for example the doctrine concerning the remission of sins and faith, seem to be beyond ordinary human comprehension; but we must acknowledge that Luther was specially taught of God, and many of us have seen through what a terrible struggle he passed in learning the lesson that man is heard and accepted by God only through faith. And so throughout eternity devout hearts will celebrate the blessings which God has conferred upon the Church through Luther. They will first give thanks to God, then they will also acknowledge that they owe much to Luther's labors; although the ungodly, who ridicule the whole Church, consider his virtues as merely senseless play or blind infatuation. *   *   *   *   *   *   *

"But if I had purposed praising the rest of his life, which to his sixty-third year he spent in the most severe and earnest exercise of godliness and good works, and the diligent study of the arts, what a grand and glowing eulogy could I not pronounce upon him! No base passions or revolutionary designs were ever observed in him; on the contrary, he was at all times the counselor of peaceable measures. Outside matters he never mingled with the affairs of the Church, to increase his own power or that of his friends. I regard his wisdom and virtue so extraordinary that it seems to me scarcely possible that they were the product merely of human effort. Characters especially earnest, ardent and lofty, such as Luther's was, must be held in check by divine grace.

"What shall I say of his other virtues? Often have I come in upon him when he was praying for the whole Church with streaming eyes. He used to devote some portion of almost every day to repeating some of the Psalms, and with groans and tears he mingled with them his own prayers. He frequently said that he felt indignant at those who either from laziness, or on account of their numerous occupations, asserted that it was sufficient to pray to God merely by a sigh. For that very reason, he says, forms of prayer have been prescribed by divine counsel, that indeed the voice also may confess the name of the God we worship. Likewise, after many grave discussions concerning public dangers had arisen, we observed that he possessed the strength of a great mind, and was in no way fearful of the future. No terrors could subdue his spirit, for he relied upon a heavenly anchor—that is, the word of God—and he did not suffer his faith to be shaken. His mind, moreover, was of so keen an order that he alone of us could determine, especially in dark and complicated circumstances, what ought to be done. He did not, as many think, neglect to consider the affairs of the State, nor was he regardless of the desires of others. On the contrary, he was intimately acquainted with the condi-

tion of the State, and regarded most clearly the sentiments and desires of all with whom he lived. * * * "
—*Translated from the Latin by Rev. C. W. Heisler,
and published in The Workman, Feb. 16, 1882.*

JOHN BRENZ,

The Swabian Reformer.

" Luther alone lives in his writings; we all are in
comparison with him a dead letter."

NICHOLAS VON AMSDORF.

"If all commentaries, ancient and modern, are
collected into one mass, and that which is best be
selected from them, it could not be compared with the
writings of this man. I am not ignorant how boast-
ful this must seem, and to how many such a tribute
must be offensive. But however others judge this
constant assertion, I so affirm, that, since the Apostles,
no one ever has seen or ever will be furnished with
such wisdom, faith and constancy, as we have seen in
Dr. Luther, not without great admiration of God's
gifts; nor have I any doubt that godly posterity will
have the same judgment."—*Preface to Luther's Works.*

MARTIN BUCER,

The Reformed Theologian.

" 1. No one since the time of the Apostles has ever
taught more clearly and faithfully the article of justification. 2. No one has ever opposed the Roman Anti-
christ and his members, even to the last breath, more
courageously, and more clearly exposed its fraud to the

world. 3. None of the fathers has taught with such devotion and according to the mind of the Spirit concerning living good works, viz: those that flow from living faith and advance the welfare of one's neighbor. 4. No one has explained Holy Scripture so purely or more happily, with such energy, and so many penetrating arguments, especially when he professedly undertook to explain any passage. 5. Add his translation of the Holy Scriptures, faithful, terse, and adorned with no small eloquence. 6. So far no one has taught so clearly what are the duties of the civil magistrate in regard to both tables of the law. 7. The incredible success of the greatest works in the Church, an example of which is the Augsburg Confession, in which he aided. 8. The gift of prophecy, so that everything has happened as he has said. 9. He was the author of efficacious prayers, psalms, hymns, chants. As he prayed, so also has he well equipped the church with devout songs and hymns."—*Gerhard's Loci Theologici,* xii., 132.

JOHN CALVIN.

" We sincerely testify that we regard him as a noble apostle of Christ, by whose labor and ministry the purity of the Gospel has been restored in our times. If any one will carefully consider what was the state of things at the period when Luther arose, he will see that he had to contend with almost all the difficulties which were encountered by the apostles. In one respect, indeed, his condition was worse and harder than theirs. There was no kingdom, no principality, against which they had to declare war; whereas Luther could not go forth except by the ruin of that empire which was not only the most powerful of all, but regarded all the rest as obnoxious to itself."

Again : " Luther is the trumpet, or rather he is the thunder—he is the lightning which has aroused the world from its lethargy—it is not so much Luther who speaks, as God whose lightnings burst from his lips."

Again, writing to Bullinger, of Zurich, he says :

"I beg that you may consider how great a man Luther is : with what gifts he has been endowed ; with what power, with what steadfastness, with what address, with what learning, he has been fighting against the kingdom of Antichrist, and for the propagation of the true doctrine of our salvation. I have often said, should he call me a devil, I would yet show him becoming honor, and recognize him as an extraordinary servant of God."

ULRICH ZWINGLI,

The great Swiss Reformer, and Luther's contemporary, and follower in many respects.

" Luther is, it seems to me, such an excellent champion of God, who has examined the scriptures with so great a zeal that he had no equal on earth for thousands of years, (I care not that the Papists call me a heretic also like him,) and in the manly, undaunted spirit with which he attacked the Pope at Rome, no one has ever been his equal, without under-estimating any one, ever since popedom has been established. But to whom may we ascribe such a deed? To God, or to Luther? Ask Luther himself, and I am sure he will answer, to God. Why then do you attribute

other men's doctrine to Luther, when he himself at-
tributes it to God, and submits nothing new but what
is contained in the eternally unalterable Word of God?
This he teaches freely, and points poor, misled Christians to this heavenly treasure; and he does not care
what the enemies of God may plan to oppose, nor
does he care for their rebuke and threats. Yet I do
not want to be called a Lutheran, since I have read too
little of his teachings. Nevertheless, what of his
writings I have read I find to be so well substantiated
and grounded upon the Word of God, that it is impossible for any man to pervert it. * * * * *

"Does Luther preach Christ? So do I; although,
blessed be God, there are unspeakably more souls led
to God through him than through me and others
(whom God endows with superior or inferior talents,
according to his purpose). * * * Hence I hope
it will be understood why I do not wish to be called
a Lutheran, however highly I esteem Luther. * *
Nevertheless, I am not to be compared with him, (in
endowment, etc.").

MARTIN CHEMNITZ,

The great Lutheran theologian.

"A man may tell how far he has advanced in the-
ology, by the degree to which he is pleased with|
Luther's writings."

JOHN GERHARD,

The distinguished Lutheran theologian.

"Our confession does not depend upon Luther's
doctrine or person, but on the unshaken word of

God. We do not ascribe to Luther prophetic or apostolic authority, or absolute infallibility; nor do we make his writings equal to the prophetic and apostolic scriptures; neither without proof from God's word do we believe him asserting anything; but we regard him an eminent teacher of the Church, whom God in these last times has raised up for the profit of his Church oppressed by the papal yoke, and endowed with unique gifts, and furnished with excellent strength of soul, to remove corruptions and abuses from the pure preaching of the Gospel, and to bring back to light the truth, almost covered by the darkness of errors."—*Confessio Catholica.*

JEAN CLAUDE.

"We discover a great many excellent things in him; an heroical courage, a great love for the truth, an ardent zeal for the glory of God, a great trust in His providence, extraordinary learning in a dark age, a profound respect for the Holy Scripture, an indefatigable spirit, and a great many other high qualities."— "*Defence of the Reformation*," English translation, London, 1815, vol. I, p. 289.

JACQUES B. BOSSUET,

A distinguished Roman Catholic theologian and pulpit orator of France.

"In the time of Luther, the most violent rupture and greatest apostasy occurred which had perhaps ever been seen in Christendom. The two parties who have called themselves Reformed have alike recognized him as the author of this new Reformation. It is not alone his followers, the Lutherans, who have lavished upon him the highest praises. Calvin frequently admires his virtues, his magnanimity, his constancy, the incomparable industry which he displayed against the pope. 'He is the trumpet, or rather he is the thunder—he is the lightning which has roused the world from its lethargy; it was not so much Luther that spoke, as God whose lightnings burst from his lips.' And it is true that he had a strength of genius, a vehemence in his discourses, a living and impetuous eloquence, which entranced and ravished the people."—"*Histoire des Variationes.*"

JOHN BUNYAN,

The "Dreamer of Bedford," whose "Pilgrim's Progress" has guided millions of Christians on their way to heaven, speaks thus of Luther's commentary on the Epistle to the Galatians:

" I did greatly long to see some ancient godly man's experience, who had writ some hundreds of years before I was born; for those who had writ in our days I thought (but I desire them now to pardon me), that they had writ only that which others felt; or else had, through the strength of their wits and parts, studied to answer such objections as they perceived others were perplexed with, without going down themselves into the deep. Well, after many such longings in my mind, the God in whose hands are all our days and ways did cast into my hand one day a book of Martin Luther's; it was his comment on Galatians; it was so old that it was ready to fall from piece to piece, if I did but turn it over. Now I was pleased much that such an old book had fallen into my hands, the which, when I had but a little way perused, I found my condition in his experience so largely and profoundly handled, as if his book had been written out of my heart. This made me marvel; for thus thought I, this man could not know anything of the state of Christians now, but must needs write and speak the experience of former days. Besides, he doth most gravely also in that book debate of the rise of these temptations, namely: blasphemy, desperation and the like; showing that the law of Moses, as well as the devil, death and hell, hath a very great hand therein; the which at first was very strange to me, but, considering and watching, I found it so, indeed. But of particulars, here, I intend nothing; only this methinks I must let fall before all men, I do prefer this book of Martin Luther upon the Galatians (except the Holy Bible), before all the books that ever I have seen, as most fit for a wounded conscience."

PHILIP JACOB SPENER,

Founder and father of the Pietists.

"In the days of our fathers, God was pleased again to have pity on His Church, and to give it a new token of His favor, in the blessed work of the Reformation. At that time then did he send forth preachers of the Gospel, in goodly numbers, and endowed with precious gifts, amongst whom was one, a star of the first magnitude, who surpassed all the rest, that venerable man of God, Dr. Martin Luther. Gladly do we embrace the opportunities that are often given to us to speak of him; and by so doing, to record our gratitude to God for the blessings conferred upon the Church, through his ministry. * * * * We can say with perfect truth that seven genuine gifts of the Holy Ghost were imparted to this man in full measure : erudition, eloquence, diligence, fervent love for God and man, an exemplary life above reproach, faith of extraordinary strength, and patience that was always rejoicing."—*Lutherus Redivivus.*

AUCUSTUS HERMAN FRANKE,

The eminent Professor of Halle, and associate with Spener in the Pietistic movement.

" My estimate of the man, Dr. Martin Luther, is that God had not only adorned him with great natural talents, but gifted him also in an extraordinary manner with a true and fundamental theology of His grace, and so richly endowed him with the gifts of the Holy Spirit that he could fill his station as Professor with great influence as well as prove an uncommon and glorious example to his and future times, in his heroic faith and unflinching fidelity and integrity towards God and his fellow-men. * * * * *

" Concerning his Reformation, I hold that God truly raised and led him to the great work of bringing back to light again the pure, evangelical doctrine which had become so beclouded under the papacy; and that no one could have come from God who professed a reformation of the Church contrary to that of Luther. For the pillar of this reformation consisted in the fact that all human work, teaching and tradition was abolished and annulled, and that instead all honor must be given to God the Lord, who has made Christ Jesus

to be unto us wisdom, and righteousness, and sanctification, and redemption. Hence, since I thus hon-
estly regard Luther's doctrine to have been the true,
evangelical, pure and Apostolic doctrine, founded upon
the Word of God, and builded upon such a foundation
on which alone we can come to God and be saved,
and since Luther was saved in this doctrine, I am persuaded as for myself, also to live and die in this faith.
*   *   *   *   *   In like manner do I admire the great and noble gifts, with which God freely
endowed Luther, enabling him thereby, just as in exposition and interpretation of Scripture, so more especially also to translate the Holy Scriptures, to
express the intent of the original in elegant, clear, intelligible, and at the same time, euphonious and impressive German.   *   *   *"—*Monthly Biblical
Notes*, 1695.

PIERRE BAYLE,

The "prince of skeptics" and logicians, in his "Historical and
Critical Dictionary," London, 1736, vol. 3, pp. 934–937, has a long
article in defence of Luther's character against slanders—of which the
following is a brief extract:

" His greatest enemies cannot deny but that he
had eminent qualities, and history affords nothing more
surprising than what he has done: for a simple monk
to be able to give popery so rude a shock, that there
needed but such another entirely to overthrow the
Romish Church, is what we cannot sufficiently admire."

2

FRANCIS ATTERBURY,

The learned Bishop of Rochester, England, living in the 17th century.

"Martin Luther's life was a continued warfare. He was engaged against the united forces of the papal world, and he stood the shock of them bravely, both with courage and success. He was a man certainly of high endowments of mind, and great virtues. He had a vast understanding, which raised him to a pitch of learning unknown to the age in which he lived. His knowledge in scripture was admirable, his elocution manly, and his way of reasoning, with all the subtility that the plain truths he delivered would bear. His thoughts were bent always on great designs, and he had a resolution to go through with them, and the assurance of his mind was not to be shaken, or surprised. His life was holy, and, when he had leisure for retirement, severe. His virtues were active chiefly, and social, and not those lazy, sullen ones of the cloister. He had no ambition but in the service of God; for other things, neither his enjoyments nor wishes ever went higher than the bare conveniences of living. If, among this crowd of virtues, a failing crept in, we must remember that an apostle himself had not been irreproachable; if in the body of his doctrine a flaw is to be seen, yet the greatest lights of the Church, and in the purest times of it, were, we know, not exact in all their opinions. Upon the whole, we have certainly great reason to break out in the language of the prophet, and say, ' How beautiful on the mountains are the feet of him who bringeth glad tidings.' "—" *Vindication of Luther.*"

JOHANN FRANZ BUDDEUS.

"Here, beyond doubt, the highest praise is due to our sainted Luther, who first, when all was lost, all in despair, lifted up the standard of better hopes. Nor could one better fitted for sustaining the truth have been found. Acuteness of judgment and fertility of thought were both his; these gave to him arguments of might, overwhelming eloquence which swept everything before it like a torrent. His was an intrepid soul, which neither power, danger nor threats could turn from the right. The truth indeed fought for him, but no less did he fight for the truth, so that no mortal could have done more to defend it, and place it beyond the reach of its foes. You are forced everywhere to confess the accurate disputer, the exquisite theologian, the earnest defender of the truth. His own writings leave no room for doubt that he argued from profound conviction of the truth, and that he was wholly free from the crime of men, who employ a line of defence, not because they regard it as true, but because it suits their purpose. The abundance of arguments well adapted to their purpose, the copiousness and power of language, alike arrest the attention. He so demonstrates the truth as to leave the errorist no subterfuge; such is the firmness of his grasp, that he seizes the assent of the reader, hurries him, forces him to his conclusion. He asks no favors, makes no effort to propitiate; he compels by the weight of proof, triumphs by demonstration of the truth, and forces the unwilling to do homage to sound doctrine."
—"*B. Isagoge Hist-Theological,*" Leipzig, 1730, pp. 1031, 1040.

JOHANN ALBRECHT BENGEL,

The distinguished theologian and able Swabian commentator.

"Luther was truly a great man. All his colleagues together could not have made a Luther. They had all to stand in wholesome respect of him; and he knew well how to use each of them in the very way in which he could be the most useful. If any of them ever conceived any other or different notions, he prudently kept them quiet until Luther was dead. The death of Luther is an important boundary line in history. After the death of Luther, there was nothing new added to the work of the Reformation."

JOHN WESLEY,

The illustrious founder of the Methodist Church, gives the following account of his entrance into light:

"In the evening, I went very unwillingly, to a society in Aldersgate, where one was reading Luther's preface to the Epistle to the Romans. About a quarter before nine, while he was describing the change which God works in the heart through faith in Christ, I felt my heart strangely warmed. I felt I did trust in Christ, Christ alone for salvation; and an assurance was given me that he had taken away my sins, even *mine*, and saved *me* from the law of sin and death."

JOHANN CHRISTOPH DŒDERLEIN.

"Amidst all that Luther has written, I know nothing more precious than his sermons and his letters. From both of these we can at least learn to know the man in his entire greatness, and in accordance with his genuine character, which superstition and malice, and the

partisan licentiousness both of friends and foes, has dis-
figured; from both beams forth the most open honesty,
the firmness of a courage which never quailed, fearlessness of judgment, and that spirit which knew so
perfectly its aim, which preserved its serenity amid all
calamities and changes allotted by Providence, and
knew how to use to good purpose, sport and earnest.
His letters especially bear the impress of the most
artless simplicity, and of the most naïve vivacity and
. . . are entertaining, rich in instruction, and worthy of
descending to posterity, were there no other purpose,
to show that immortal man speaking, especially with
his friends."—"*Auserlesen Theol. Bibliothek*," Leipzig,
1780, Band I., p. 631.

GOTTHOLD E. LESSING.

The great German literateur and critic, utters his admiration of
Luther in the following striking manner:

" In such reverence do I hold Luther, that I rejoice
in having been able to find some defects in him, for I
have been in imminent danger of making him an object of idolatrous veneration. The proofs that in some
things he was like other men are to me as precious as
the most dazzling of his virtues "

FREDERICK THE GREAT.

" Had Luther done nothing else but liberate the
princes and the people from the servile bondage under which the dominion of the Roman papacy held
them, he would deserve to have monuments erected to
his honor as the Liberator of his country."—*Fleury's
Church History.*

ERNEST KARL WIELAND.

"So great was Luther, in whatever aspect we view him, so worthy of admiration, so deserving of universal gratitude, alike great as a man, a citizen, and a scholar."—(*Characteristics of Luther*—last paragraph.)

JOHANN G. HERDER,

An illustrious German thinker and writer of the 18th century.

" Luther was a patriotic, great man. As teacher of the German nation, as co-reformer, indeed, of the whole of enlightened Europe, he has long been recognized; even people who do not accept his articles of religion, enjoy the fruits of his reformation. He, like a Hercules, grappled with the spiritual despotism which annuls or undermines all free, healthy thinking, and restored to whole peoples the use of reason, and this, indeed, in the most difficult of all things, in *spiritual*. The might of his language and of his upright spirit united itself with sciences, which burst into new life from him and with him, allied itself with the labors of the best men in all departments, who thought, in part, it may be, very differently from him ; and so arose for the first time a popular literary public in Germany and in the neighboring countries. Now, those read, who had otherwise never read, while those learned to read who were otherwise unable to read. Schools and academies were founded, German religious songs were sung, and sermons preached in the German· language. Let us for our times apply and turn to account his manner of thought and his manifest suggestions, and the truths he so strongly and yet so naively uttered."

Again, speaking of Luther as a preacher, he says:
" He spoke the simple, strong, unadorned language
of the understanding ; he spoke from the heart, not
from the head and from memory. His sermons,
therefore, have been the models, especially of those
preachers in our Church who are of stable minds."

WILLIAM COXE,

A noted historical writer.

" Luther possessed a temper and acquirements which
peculiarly fitted him for the character of a reformer.
Without the fastidious nicety of refined taste and
elegance, he was endowed with singular acuteness and
logical dexterity, possessed profound and varied erudition; and his rude, though fervid eloquence, inter-
mixed with the coarsest wit and keenest raillery, was
of that species which is best adapted to affect and
influence a popular assembly. His Latin, though it
did not rise to the purity of Erasmus and his other
learned contemporaries, was yet copious, free, and
forcible, and he was perfectly master of his native
tongue, and wrote it with such purity, that his works
are still esteemed as models of style by the German
critics. He was animated with an undaunted spirit,
which raised him above all apprehension of danger,
and possessed a perseverance which nothing could
fatigue. He was at once haughty and condescending, jovial, affable and candid in public; studious,
sober and self-denying in private; and he was endowed
with that happy and intuitive sagacity which enabled
him to suit his conduct and manners to the exigency
of the moment, to lessen or avert danger by timely

flexibility, or to bear down all obstacles by firmness and impetuosity. His merciless invectives and contemptuous irony, were proper weapons to repel the virulence and scurrility of his adversaries; and even the fire and arrogance of his temper, though blemishes in a refined age, were far from being detrimental in a controversy which roused all the passions of the human breast, and required the strongest exertions of fortitude and courage. Such were the principles and conduct of this extraordinary man, when the enormous abuses arising from the sale of indulgences attracted his notice, and involved him in that memorable controversy with the Church of Rome, for which he seems to have been trained and adapted by his temper, studies, occupation, and habits of life."—"*History of the House of Austria,*" London, Bohn, 1847, vol 1, p. 383.

COUNT VON STOLBERG,

A Roman Catholic.

"Against Luther's person I would not cast a stone. In him I honor, not alone one of the grandest spirits that ever lived, but a great religiousness also, which never forsook him."

AARON BANCROFT.

"Martin Luther, a man of the most powerful mind and intrepid character, who persisted resolutely in his defence of Christian liberty and Christian truth; and by the blessing of God he triumphed over all opposition. His name is identified in every country with the reformed religion, and will be venerated and es-

teemed in every subsequent age, by all who prize religious freedom, and set a value on religious privileges."
—"*Sermons on Doctrines,*" Worcester, 1822, No. xi.

ALEXANDER BOWER.

"In the personal character of Luther, we discern many qualities calculated to enable him to discharge with success the important duty to which he was called. A constitutional ardor for devotion, a boundless thirst of knowledge, and a fearless zeal in communicating it, were prominent characteristics of this extraordinary man. An unwearied perseverance in theological research led him to detect errors, and to relinquish, step by step, many of his early opinions. In all situations Luther is the same, pursuing indefatigably the knowledge of the Word of God, and never scrupling to avow his past mistakes, whenever the confession could facilitate the inquiries or confirm the faith of others. It was in vain that the head of the Church and the chief of the German Empire combined to threaten and proscribe him—he braved with equal courage the very lance of either power, and continued to denounce, with an unsparing hand, the prevalence of corruption. In no single instance did he seek to turn to his personal advantage his distinctions and the influence attached to them. How few individuals would have possessed Luther's power without making it subservient to the acquisition of rank or honors? All these were disdained by him, and his mind remained wholly occupied with the diffusion of religious truth. Even literary fame had no attractions for him. The improvement of the condition of his fellow-creatures was

2*

the object which with him superseded every other
consideration. No temptation of ambition could remove him, in his days of celebrity, from his favorite
University of Wittenberg. While his doctrine spread
far and wide, and wealthy cities would have been
proud to receive him, Luther clung to the spot where
he discharged the duty of a teacher, and to the associ-
ates whom he had known in the season of humility.
The freedom of his language in treating of the conduct
of the great, arose partly from his constitutional ardor,
and partly from an habitual impression of the all-
powerful claims of truth. The lofty attitude so often
assumed by him is not therefore to be attributed to
pride or vanity. In treating of the Scriptures, he considered himself as acting in the presence of God, whose
majesty and glory were so infinitely exalted above all
created beings, as to reduce to one and the same level
the artificial distinctions of worldly institutions. *   *
An independent and manly tone in regard not only to
religion, but to civil liberty, literature, the arts and
sciences, was created and disseminated by his example.
Few writers discover greater knowledge of the world,
or a happier talent in analyzing and illustrating the
shades of character. It is equally remarkable that no
man could display more forcibly the tranquil conso-
lations of religion. Few men entered with more ardor
into the innocent pleasures of society. His frankness
of disposition was apparent at the first interview, and
his communicative turn, joined to the richness of his
stores, rendered his conversation remarkably interesting. In treating of humorous subjects, he discovered
as much vivacity and playfulness as if he had been a

man unaccustomed to serious research."—"*Life of Luther*," Philadelphia, 1824.

ERNST MAURICE ARNDT,

One of the liberators of Germany, and author of that patriotic song, "What is the German's Fatherland."

"Luther was a man of God, a German, who thought more of hearty sincerity than of nonsense, who attached a higher value to truth than to lying, who believed in God and worshipped Him, but fought and despised the devil. Shy and timid he is when first entering upon the course; but the further he advances, the stronger, the grander he grows. His body seems to grow; his heart, his courage, his whole bearing is improved and developed, so that they who had previously known him were amazed to see into what manliness of presence, and what stateliness of mien, the poor little retiring monk had grown. It was possible only for such a stern, fiery, unconquerable spirit as was his, possible only for a man in whom courage, sagacity, eloquence, classical and scientific culture were combined as they were in him, to lay hold of such a gigantic work, and to carry it through. But what could he have done if he had not had the faith that was in him? * * * By means of the most delicate and most ethereal of instruments, fervid with a fire that was sometimes overflowing, by the omnipotent word, for the exposition and diffusion of which his soul was clothed with strength and light, and his lips enriched with the power of faith and of divine assurance, Luther wrought and perfected a work which was, in the highest degree, immense."

DR. REUSS.

" His (Luther's) Bible was, for its era, a miracle of science.   Its style sounded as the prophecy of a golden age of literature, and in masculine force, and in the unction of the Holy Spirit, it remains a yet unapproached model."—" *Geschichte der Heiligen Schrift*," N. T., § 47.

SAMUEL T. COLERIDGE.

"How would Christendom have fared without a Luther? What would Rome have done and dared but for the ocean of the Reformed that ROUNDS her? Luther lives yet—not so beneficially in the Lutheran Church as out of it—an antagonistic spirit to Rome, and a purifying and preserving spirit in Christendom at large."

His son, *Henry Nelson Coleridge*, in his introduction to the " *Biographia Literaria*" of his father, says in defence of his father's religious opinions:

" He saw the very mind of St. Paul in the teaching of Luther on the Law and Justification by Faith.   My father's affectionate respect for Luther is enough to alienate him from the High Anglican party."

Again, speaking for himself, H. N. Coleridge says: "It is an insult to the apostolic man's (Luther's) memory, to defend him from the charge of Antinomianism.   He knocked down with his little finger more Antinomianism than his accusers with both hands. If his doctrine is the jaw-bone of an ass, he must have been a very Samson, for he turned numbers with this instrument from the evil of their lives."

Speaking in defence of Luther's Commentary on

Galatians, he says: "The commentary contains, or rather is, a most spirited siege of Babylon, and the friends of Rome like it as well as the French like Wellington and the battle of Waterloo."

"My father called Luther, in parts, the most evangelical writer he knew, after the apostles."

FREDERICK VON SCHLEGEL,

The scholarly German historian and Romanist.

"It is well known to you that all true philologists regard this as the standard and model of classical expression in the German language; and that not only Klopstock, but many other writers of the first rank, have fashioned their style and selected their phrases according to the rules of this version. * * * In these later times, we have witnessed an attempt to render a new and *rational* translation of the Bible, an instrument of propagating the doctrines of the illuminati; and we have seen too much even in the hands of Catholics themselves. But the instant this folly had blown over, we returned, with increased affection, to the excellent old version of Luther. He, indeed, has not the whole merit of producing it. We owe to him, nevertheless, the highest gratitude for placing in our hands this most noble and manly model of German expression. Even in his own writings he displays a most original eloquence, surpassed by but few names that occur in the whole history of literature. He had, indeed, all those qualities which fit a man to be a revolutionary orator. * * * * * *
As to the intellectual power and greatness of Luther,

abstracted from all consideration of the uses to which
he applied them, I think there are few, even of his
own disciples, who appreciate him highly enough.
His coadjutors were mostly mere scholars, indolent
and enlightened men of the common order.   It was
upon him and his soul that the fate of Europe depended.   He was the man of his age and nation."—
"Lectures on the History of Literature," New York,
1841, p. 348–350.

"That the Reformation did not at its very com-
mencement become a revolution of this kind, we are
chiefly indebted to Luther.   He it was who thus gave
permanency to the Reformation.   *   *   *   *
His personal character in general was excellently
adapted to consolidate and perpetuate his party.   The
great energy which gave him such a decided preponderance over all who coöperated with him, preserved
as much unity as was at all possible in such a state of
moral ferment.   *   *   *   * He was undeni-
ably gifted with great qualities.   Luther's eloquence
made him a man of the people; his principles, however, despite his passionate expression of them, remained, nevertheless, in essentials, both with regard
to political subjects and to matters of faith, within
certain limits; and joined to that circumstance, the
very obstinacy which his friends complained of, consolidated and united the new party and gave it a permanent strength."—*"Lectures on Modern History,"*
London, 1849, p. 169.

"In the first place, as regards the Reformation, it is
evident of itself, that a man who accomplished so
mighty a revolution in the human mind, and in his

age, could have been endowed with no ordinary powers of intellect, and no common strength of character. Even his writings display an astonishing boldness and energy of thought and language, united with a spirit of impetuous, passionate and convulsive enthusiasm. The opinion as to the use which was made of these high powers of genius, must, of course, vary with the religious principles of each individual ; but the extent of these intellectual endowments themselves, and the strength and perseverance of character with which they were united, must be universally admitted. * * * * * It was by the conduct of Luther, and the influence which he thereby acquired, that the Reformation was promoted and consolidated. Without this, Protestantism would have sunk into the lawless anarchy, which marked the proceedings of the Hussites, and to which the war of the Peasants rapidly tended. * * None of the other heads and leaders of the new religious party had the power, or were in a situation to uphold the Protestant religion: its present existence is solely and entirely the work and the deed of one man, unique in his way, and who holds unquestionably a conspicuous place in the history of the world. Much was staked on the soul of that man, and it was in every respect a mighty and critical moment in the annals of mankind and in the march of time."—*"Philosophy of History."*

ROBERT SOUTHEY,

Poet-laureate of England.

"Blessed be the day of Martin Luther's birth ! It should be a festival only second to that of the nativity of Jesus Christ."

F. A. COX.

"Amongst the instruments of this remarkable change, the name of Martin Luther stands pre-eminent. He was not, indeed, the *first* or the *only* advocate of this righteous cause, but he was, in many respects, the *greatest.* Luther possessed a vigorous and fearless soul. He was qualified to take the lead, and to head opposition in a servile age. His mind was incessantly active; his ardor in the pursuit of knowledge and in the propagation of what he knew, inextinguishable; and in the holy war which he undertook, having buckled on the armor, he was impatient for the conflict and assured of the victory. Never scarcely did the 'hand of God form a fitter instrument to do a greater work."—"*Life of Philip Melanchthon,*" 1st American edition, Boston, 1835.

HENRY HALLAM,

A philosophic English historian and critic.

"A better tone (in preaching) began with Luther. His language was sometimes rude and low, but persuasive, artless, powerful. He gave many useful precepts, as well as examples, for pulpit eloquence. In the history of the Reformation, Luther is incomparably the greatest name. We see him the chief figure of a group of gownsmen, standing in contrast on the canvas with the crowned rivals of France and Austria, and their attendant warriors, but blended in the unity of that historic picture. It is admitted on all sides that he wrote his own language with force, and he is reckoned one of its best models. The hymns in use with the Lutheran Church, many of which are his own, possess a simple dignity and devoutness, never before excelled in that class of poetry, and alike distinguished from the poverty of Sternhold or Brady, and from the meretricious ornament of later writers. * * It is not to be imagined that a man of his vivid parts fails to perceive an advantage, in that close grappling, sentence by sentence, with an adversary which fills most of his controversial writings; and in scornful irony he had no superior."—"*Introduction to the Literature of Europe,*" vol. I. p. 197.

HEINRICH HEINE,

A modern German poet and wit.

"He created the German language. He was not only the greatest but the most German man of our history. In his character all the faults and all the virtues of the Germans are combined on the largest scale. Then he had qualities which are very seldom found united, which we are accustomed to regard as irreconcilable antagonisms. He was, at the same time, a dreamy mystic and a practical man of action. His thought had not only wings, but hands. He spoke and he acted. He was not only the tongue, but the sword of his time. When he had plagued himself all day long with his doctrinal distinctions, in the evening he took his flute and gazed at the stars, dissolved in melody and devotion. He could be as soft as a tender maiden. Sometimes he was wild as the storm that uproots the oak, and then again he was gentle as the zephyr that dallies with the violet. He was full of the most awful reverence and self-sacrifice in honor of the Holy Spirit. He could merge himself entire, in pure spirituality. And yet he was well acquainted with the glories of this world, and knew how to prize them. He was a complete man, I would say an absolute man, one in whom matter and spirit were not divided. To call him a spiritualist, therefore, would be as great an error as to call him a sensualist. How shall I express it? He had something original, incomprehensible, miraculous, such as we find in all providential men—something invincible, spirit-possessed."

FREDERICK L. G. VON RAUMER,

A very distinguished German historical writer, in his reply to the charge against Luther by Palavicini, the historian of the Council of Trent:

"To this judgment of Palavicini, after a conscientious testing of all the facts, we cannot assent—but are constrained to acknowledge the truth to be this: A fruitful genius, whose fruits could not all come to a mellow ripeness, because they were prematurely shaken down by storms. A mighty spirit, who helped to arouse the storms; but, had not the building been undermined by fearful abuses, a purification might have been possible without overthrowing it. Only because the builders who were called to the work of reform, not only refused to perform it, but increased the evil, did he become their master; and with success grew his boldness or his faith in his divine vocation, and his wrath against his opponents. In his contest with the papacy he placed in the van evangelical freedom of faith, and this is the source of Protestantism; in the establishment of his Church he often was willing to shackle thought, lost his own clearness of perception, and became intolerant. But his hardest and least becoming language appears mild in comparison with the blood-thirsty intolerance of his opponents, mild in comparison with the headman's ax and the stake. A noble eloquence supplanted the unintelligible prattle of the schools; through him Germany once more learned to speak; the German people once more to hear. He who is displeased with his style, or with his matter, must yet confess that his writings reveal everywhere the inspiration of the fear of God and the power of faith. Luther never dissimulated. Persuasions, promises, threats, had no power to shake his rock-firm will, his indomitable purpose; and the seeming self-will and severity connected with this arose, at least, from no common-place and perverted character. No man ever grasps the whole truth in perfect clearness; but few have more earnestly striven to attain it, and with more perfect self-renunciation confessed it, than Luther. Among his opponents not one can be compared with him in personal qualities; with all his faults, he remains greatest and most memorable among men; a man in whose train follows a whole world of aspiration, effort, and achievement."

THOMAS CHALMERS,

The distinguished preacher of Scotland, in a sermon on Jer. vi. 16, in London :

" A sense of duty acting on an unconquered heart, sent him forth single-handed to encounter hosts of obdurate foes ; and by the bend of his uplifted arm he shook the authority of the high pontificate which kept the earth in thraldom, and brought down the peering altitude of that olden tyranny whose head was raised to heaven and whose base was fixed in the deepest prejudice. His own heart nourished the germ of the greatest revolution the world ever saw. Many hearts caught his enthusiastic ardor, and his voice was echoed from the most distant corners of Europe. He entered the field as a champion of the rights of humanity; his might overcame every difficulty, and he stood forward as the victorious conqueror of ignorance and imposture. Luther did more for the success of a mighty cause than any had before him achieved in the history of the world. From his deep, silent, and meditative spirit, an impulse was given to the mechanism of human society which it never till then received."

BISHOP KIDDER.

"As for Martin Luther, whatever the Romanists say of him now, yet certain it is that Erasmus, who I hope will pass with Cardinal Bellarmine for a Catholic, who lived in his time, gives a better account of him. In his letter to the Cardinal of York, speaking of Luther, he says: 'His life is approved by all men, and this is no slight ground of prejudice in his favor, that such was the integrity of his morals that his enemies could find nothing to reproach him with.' Again, in a letter to Melanchthon: 'All men among us approve the life of Luther.'"—"*Bellarmine's Notes*," p. 312.

C. C. J. BUNSEN,

Formerly Prussian minister to England.

"Luther's life is both the epos and the tragedy of his age. It is an epos because its first part presents a hero and a prophet, who conquers apparently insuperable difficulties and opens a new world to the human mind, without any power but that of divine truth and deep conviction, or any authority but that inherent in sincerity and undaunted, unselfish courage. But Luther's life is also a tragedy; it is the tragedy of Germany as well as of the hero, her son, who in vain tried to rescue his country from unholy oppressions, and to regenerate her from within, as a nation, by means of the Gospel; and who died in unshaken faith in Christ and in His kingdom, although he lived to see his beloved fatherland going to destruction, not through, but in spite of the Reformation. Both parts of Luther's life are of the highest interest. In the epic part of it we see the most arduous work of the time— the work for two hundred years tried in vain by councils, and by prophets, and martyrs, with and without emperors, kings, and princes—undertaken by a poor monk alone, who carried it out under the ban both of the pope and the empire. In the second we see him surrounded by friends and disciples, always the spiritual head of his nation, and the revered adviser of princes and preacher of the people; living in the same poverty as before, and leaving his descendants as unprovided for as Aristides left his daughter. So lived and died the greatest hero of Christendom since the Apostles; the restorer of that form of Christianity which now sustains Europe, and (with all its defects) is regenerating and purifying the whole human race; the founder of the modern German language and literature; the first speaker and debater of his country; and, at the same time, the first writer in prose and verse of his age."

Again, speaking of Luther's translation of the Bible, Bunsen says (*Life of Luther*): "Thousands of copies were read with indescribable delight by the people, who had now access to Him whom Luther had preached to them as the Author of salvation, in their mother-tongue, in a purity and clearness unknown before, and never surpassed since. By choosing the Franconian dialect, in use in the imperial chancery, Luther made himself intelligible both to those whose vernacular dialect, was High German or Low German. Luther translated faithfully but vernacularly, with a native grace which up to this day makes his Bible the standard of the German language. It is Luther's genius applied to the Bible which has preserved the only unity which is in our days remaining to the German nation—that of language, literature, and thought. There is no similar instance in the known history of the world of a single man achieving such a work. His prophetic mind foresaw that the scriptures would pervade the living languages and tongues all over the earth—a process going on still with more activity than ever."

GOTTFRIED THOMASIUS,
Late Professor in the University of Erlangen.

"The most inner nerve of the corruption was still not yet reached, the great word to enkindle the flame was not yet spoken, the man of spiritual might, who, with a prophetic voice, was to sound the cry to the German people, had not yet arisen. In Luther God gave this gift to the church. In him the principle, one may say the spirit of Protestantism, was made incarnate, and in a way so original that he has attained typical importance to the entire church called after him. Even to this day, it bears his signature."

K. F. A. KAHNIS,
Of the University of Leipsic.

"If it be true that the essence of Christianity consists in the communion of the individual soul with God by faith in Christ, and the essence of the German spirit in feeling, we must acknowledge that never have the Christian and the German spirit so thoroughly pervaded any one man as Luther. They only who comprehend the nature of both the Christian and German spirit, can understand the splendid contrasts found united in him. Luther was most thoroughly natural, yet filled with a deep knowledge of his sinfulness and a conviction of his impotence. He was a man of the deepest earnestness, yet just when he was in the very crisis of his fate, he would both speak and write in a humorous tone. He was a man who bore in his heart, as none other did, the interests of the kingdom, and served it with a gigantic expendi-

ture of energy; yet he found time to take an interest
in everything, in the least as well as in the greatest,
to work at his lathe, to mend his own garments, to
play chess, to practice music, to sing, etc.　He was
a man of bold self-consciousness, as is shown by his
last will, in which he calls himself 'a man well-known
in heaven, on earth, and in hell;' yet he knew

> "'With our own might can naught be done,
> Soon were our loss effected.'

"From head to foot he was full of genius; yet he
submitted all his knowledge, will, and affection to the
Word.　He had a heart touched by all the lively affections of humanity, yet a strength of character which
pursued with inexorable steadfastness the narrow path
of truth."—"*Lectures on the Church,*" p. 763, Eng.
Trans.

JAMES M. HOPPIN,
Professor in Yale Theo. Sem.

"Luther plucked up preaching from the mire in
which it had fallen, and reinstated it as the central light
in the house of God.　From its fanciful and allegorical
character, its scholastic and dry and dead forms of
Aristotelian logic, he restored the true idea of preaching, viz., the scriptural homily.　He spoke freely and
directly out of the Word.　It might be said in a word
that Luther's preaching, as well as his writing, sprang
from his profound conception of the Gospel; of the
length and breadth, and height and depth, of the
work and the law of Jesus Christ.　He came more
and more to see the spiritual aspects and inner substance of Christian faith.　Christ was his unceasing
theme."

MERLE D'AUBIGNE,

The great French historian of the Reformation, abounds in his writings
in beautiful tributes to the character of Luther.

"Luther proved through divine grace the living influence of Christianity, as no preceding doctor, perhaps, had ever felt it before. The Reformation sprang living from his own heart, where God Himself had placed it."

"Some advised the Evangelical princes to attack Charles V., sword in hand. But this was mere worldly counsel, and the great Reformer, Luther, whom so many are pleased to represent as a man of violent temper, succeeded in silencing these rash counsellors."

"Luther was the first to profess the great principles of humanity and religious liberty; he was far beyond his own age, and even beyond many of the Reformers, in toleration."

"If in the history of the world there be an individual we love more than another, it is he. Calvin we venerate more, but Luther we love more."—*Dr. Baird's D'Aubigné and his Writings*, New York, 1846.

THOMAS CARLYLE,

The late distinguished literary genius, tells the momentous and far-reaching results of Luther's stand at Worms in his own striking way, as follows:

"The Diet of Worms, Luther's appearance there on the 17th of April, 1521, may be considered as the greatest scene in modern European history; the point, indeed, from which the whole subsequent history of civilization takes its rise. The world's pomp and power sit there, on this hand; on that, stands up for

3

God's truth one man, the poor miner Hans Luther's
son.   Our petition—the petition of the whole world to
him was: 'Free us; it rests with thee; desert us not.'
Luther did not desert us.   It is, as we say, the
greatest moment in the modern history of men—
English Puritanism, England and its Parliaments,
America's vast work these two centuries; French Revolution; Europe and its work everywhere at present
—the germ of it all lay there.   Had Luther in that
moment done other, it had all been otherwise."

In his " Heroes and Hero-Worship," this remarkable
writer characterizes the birth of Luther in these
words:

" In the whole world that day, there was not a more
entirely unimportant-looking pair of people than this
miner and his wife.   And yet, what were all emperors,
popes and potentates in comparison?   There was born
here, once more, a Mighty Man, whose light was to
flame as the beacon over long centuries and epochs of
the world.   The whole world and its history were
waiting for this man.   It is strange, it is great.   It
leads us back to another Birth-hour in a still meaner
environment, eighteen hundred years ago—of which it
is fit that we *say* nothing; that we think only in silence
—for what words are there!   The age of miracles
past?   The age of miracles is forever here!

" I will call Luther a true Great Man; great in intellect, in courage, affection and integrity; one of our
most lovable and precious men.   Great, not as a hewn
obelisk, but as an Alpine mountain—so simple, honest,
spontaneous, not setting up to be great at all; there
for quite another purpose than being great!   Ah yes,

unsubduable granite, piercing far and wide into the
heavens; yet in the clefts of its fountains, green and
beautiful valleys with flowers!   A right Spiritual Hero
and Prophet; once more, a true Son of Nature and
Fact, for whom these centuries, and many that are to
come yet, will be thankful to heaven."

Again: "They err greatly who imagine that this
man's courage was ferocity—no accusation could be
more unjust. A most gentle heart withal, full of pity
and love, as indeed the truly valiant heart ever is. I
know few things more touching than those soft breath-
ings of affection, soft as a child's or a mother's, in this
great wild heart of Luther. Luther to a slight observer might have seemed a timid, weak man; modesty,
affectionate shrinking tenderness, the chief distinction
of him. It is a noble valor which is roused in a heart
like this, once stirred up into defiance, all kindled into
a heavenly blaze."

Again: "As a participant and dispenser of divine
influences, he shows himself among human affairs a
true connecting medium and visible Messenger between Heaven and Earth; perhaps the most inspired
of all teachers since the first apostles of his faith; and
thus not a poet only, but a Prophet and God-ordained
Priest, which is the largest form of that dignity, and of
all dignity."

LEOPOLD RANKE,
A distinguished modern historian of Germany.

"Throughout we see Luther directing his weapons
on both sides—against the Papacy, which sought to
reconquer the world then struggling for its emancipa-

tion — and against the sects of many names which sprang up beside him, assailing Church and State together. The great Reformer, if we may use an expression of our days, was one of the greatest conservatives that ever lived."

M. GELZER.

"If we recall among other great names in German history the Reformers Melanchthon and Zwingli, the Saxon Electors, Frederick the Wise and John the Constant, Gustavus Adolphus and Frederick the Great, or among intellectual celebrities, Klopstock and Lessing, Haman and Herder, Goethe and Schiller, or turn to the great religious reformers of the last centuries, Spener, Franke, Zinzendorf, Bengel and Lavater, they all exhibit many features of relationship with Luther, and in some qualities may even surpass him; but not one stands out a *Luther*. One is deficient in the poetic impulse, or the fullness and versatility of his nature; another wants his depths of religious feeling, his firmness of purpose and strength of character; others again want his eloquence, or influence over his contemporaries. Luther would not have been Luther without these three leading features: his strong faith, his spiritual eloquence, and firmness of character and purpose. He united—and this is the most extraordinary fact connected with him—to large endowments of mind and heart, and the great gift of imparting these intellectual treasures, the invincible power of original and creative thought, both in resisting and influencing th: outer world."—*From Sketches of Luther, accompanying König's Fifty Pictures of the Reformer.*

ARCHDEACON J. C. HARE.

"As he has said of St. Paul's words, his own are not dead words, but living creatures, and have hands and feet. It no longer surprises us that this man who wrote and spoke thus, although no more than a poor monk, should have been mightier than the Pope, and the Emperor to boot, with all their hosts, ecclesiastical and civil—that the rivers of living water should have swept half Germany, and in the course of time the chief part of northern Europe, out of the kingdom of darkness into the region of Evangelical light. No day in spring, when life seems bursting from every bud and gushing from every pore, is fuller of life than his pages; and if they are not without the strong breezes of spring, these too have to bear their part in the work of purification. How far superior his expositions of Scriptures are in the deep and living apprehension of the primary truths of the Gospel to those of the best among the Fathers, even of Augustine. If we would do justice to any of the master minds of history, we must compare them with their predecessors. When we come upon these truths in Luther, after wandering through the dusky twilight of the preceding centuries, it seems almost like the sun-burst of a new revelation, or rather as if the sun, which set when St. Paul was taken away from the earth, had suddenly started up again. Verily, too, it does us good, when we have been walking about among those who have only dim guesses as to where they are, or whither they are going, and who halt and look back, and turn aside at every other step, to see a man taking his stand on the

Eternal Rock, and gazing steadfastly, with unsealed eyes on the very Sun of Righteousness."

Again, speaking of the inseparable union of Luther and the Reformation, he says:

" Dean Waddington, after beginning a history of the Reformation, felt compelled to turn it into a life of the chief agent in that movement. D 'Aubigne's History of the Reformation is little more than a life of the Reformer, and it is the intense interest of Luther's character that has given such wide popularity to that work, notwithstanding the great vices of its style and manner.

" Melanchthon may easily be conceived apart from the Reformation, as an eminent divine, living in other ages of the Church, as the friend of Augustine, or the companion of Fenelon. Even Calvin may be separated in thought from the age of the Reformation, and may be set among the schoolmen, or in the council chamber of Hildebrand or Innocent, or at the Synod of Doré, or among Cromwell's chaplains. But Luther apart from the Reformation would cease to be Luther. His work was not something external to him, like Saturn's ring, on which he shone, and within which he revolved, it was his own very self, that grew out of him, while he grew out of his work."—*Hare's Vindication of Luther.*

JULES MICHELET,

The brilliant (Catholic) historian of France.

" It is not incorrect to say that Luther has been the restorer of liberty in modern times. If he did not create, he at least courageously affixed his signature to that great revolution which rendered the right of examination lawful in Europe. And if we exercise in all its plentitude at this day this first and highest privilege of human intelligence, it is to him we are most indebted for it. Nor can we think, speak or write without being made conscious at every step of the immense benefit of this intellectual enfranchisement."

And he concludes by saying:

"To whom do I owe the power of publishing what I am now inditing, except to this liberator of modern thought?"

WILLIAM RUSSELL.

"Martin Luther, a name which breaks upon the ear like the distant booming of signal cannon, or of a rising sea—so intimately is it associated with impressions of a great conflict—of a mighty rising up of nations against powers and dominions hoary with prescriptive reverence—of the breaking down of strong holds presumedly rock-based, and reaching to the heavens—derives this illustration only from the reliable facts known of the great Reformer's boyhood; that they clearly show that the stormy and dangerous career which he entered upon in mature life was unsought for, undesired by him, and solely prompted by a sudden awakened, imperious sense of duty—strengthened and aided no doubt by an instinctive consciousness of vast mental energy, and inflexible bravery of will, which no peril could disturb, no obstacle, however giant-like and apparently insuperable, bend or turn aside."—"*Extraordinary Men, their Boyhood, etc.*"

JOHN J. I. DÖLLINGER,

The renowned papist and professor at Munich.

"Luther is the grandest man of the people, the most popular character that Germany could ever claim. The Protestant doctrine was developed in the spirit of this German, the greatest German of his age. In the presence of the superiority and creative energy of this genius, the rising and enterprising part of the nation bowed down, in meek reverence and full confidence. Recognizing in him, this union between force and guiding spirit, they acknowledged him as their master; they lived upon his thoughts; and for them, he was the hero in whom the nation itself was embodied, with all its peculiar traits. They gazed upon him with admiration; they surrendered themselves to his control; because they saw that it was nothing but their own most profound experience which was expressed in his writings, more clearly, more eloquently, more powerfully than they could ever have expressed it themselves. Accordingly, for Germany the name of Luther is not simply the name of a distinguished man; it is the living germ of a period in the national life, it is the center of a new circle of ideas, the most direct and apt expression of the religious and moral views that controlled the attention of the German spirit, from the mighty influence of which even they who opposed them could not entirely escape." p. 10.

Twenty years later this same Döllinger says:

"It was Luther's overpowering greatness of spirit and amazing many-sidedness which made him the man of his time and of his people. It may be said with truth, Germany never had a man who so profoundly understood his people, and who was so completely comprehended, so absolutely absorbed, if we may use that term, by the nation, as this Augustinian monk of Wittenberg. He controlled the mind and heart of the Germanic race as the hand of the musician wakes at will the strings of his lyre. No other man in the whole Christian era has given to his race as much as Luther gave to his—language, a manual of faith for the people (the Catechism), the Bible, the hymns; and everything his adversaries tried to put in conflict or in rivalry with him seemed flat and weak and pallid by the side of that eloquence with which he entranced men. His adversaries stammered; Luther spoke. He alone has left the ineffaceable stamp of his own spirit alike upon the German tongue and the German mind. The very men among the Germans who from the depths of their soul abhor him as the terrible here-siarch and the betrayer of religion, are forced to speak in his words and think in his thoughts."—*Kirche ünd Kirchen, Papstthum ünd Kirchenstaat,"* 1861 (*Kurtz Lehrb. d. K. G.* 74.)

ARCHBISHOP TENNISON,
Of the Church of England.

"Luther was indeed a man of warm temper, and uncourtly language; but (besides that he had his education among those who so vehemently reviled him) it may be considered, whether in passing through so very rough a sea, it was not next to impossible for him not to beat the insulting waves till they foamed

3*

again.   Erasmus tells us that he perceived, the better
any man was, the more he relished the writings of
Luther ; that his very enemies allowed him to be a
man of good life ; that he seemed to him to have in
his breast certain eminent Evangelical sparks; that it
was plain that some condemned things in Luther's
writings, which in Augustine and Bernard passed for
pious and orthodox."—*Bellarmine's Notes of Church
Examined and Refuted,"* London, 1840, p. 251.

KARL AUGUST HASE.
An eminent theologian of Germany, in his description of "Luther's
death and public character."

"In the last year of his life, Luther, worn out by
labor and sickness, took such offence at the immorality and wanton modes at Wittenberg, that he left it
(1545), and only consented to return at the most urg-
ent supplications of the University and Elector. He
saw a gloomy period impending over the land of his
fathers, and longed to depart in peace. Over his last
days still shone some of the brightness of his best
years—the words bold, childlike, playful, amid exalted
thoughts.   Having been called to Eisleben to act as
arbitrator in settling some difficulty of the Counts of
Mansfeld, he there, on the night of February 18, 1546,
rested in a last calm and holy sleep. The mutations
of the times, on whose pinnacle he stood, imparted to
his life its stronger antitheses. He had regarded the
Pope as the most holy and most Satanic father. In
his roused passions emotions had stormily alternated.
The freedom of the spirit was the object of his life,
and yet he had been jealous for the letter. In trust

on all the power of the Spirit, he had siezed the storm
of revolution by the reins, and yet on occasion had
suggested that it would be well if the Pope and his
whole brood were drowned in the Tyrrhene Sea. But
throughout he had uttered with an unbounded ingen-
uousness his convictions, and was a stranger to every
worldly interest. With a powerful sensuousness, he
stood fast rooted in the earth, but his head reached
into heaven. In the creative spirit, no man of his time
was like him; his discourses were often rougher than
his own rough time seemed to approve, but in popular
eloquence his equal has never arisen in Germany.
From anguish and wrath grew his joy in the contest.
Where he once had discovered wrong, he saw nothing
but hell. But his significance rests less upon those
acts by which he searched and destroyed — others
could more easily and more readily tear themselves
away from the old church—it rests much more upon
his power of building up, on his earnest full faith and
love; though in hours of gloom, through the temptations of Satan, he imagined that he had lost God, and
Christ, and all together. Especially, in opposition to
his antagonists, did he believe, and declare without
reservation, that he was a chosen instrument of God,
known in heaven, on earth, and in hell. But with
himself, personally considered, he would have nothing
to do; he would recognize no doctrine of Luther, and
his sublime trust in God pointed not to his personal delivery from dangers, but to the faith that God
could every day create ten 'Doctor Martins.' Insipid
objections and narrow vindications are forgotten; such
a man belongs not to one party, but to the German
people and to Christendom."

K. R. HAGENBACH.

" It may be said that Martin Luther became emphatically the reformer of the German Church, and thus the reformer of a great part of the Universal Church, by his eminent personal character and heroic career, by the publication of his theses, by sermons and expositions of Scripture, by disputations and bold controversial writings, by numerous letters and circular epistles, by advice and warning, by intercourse with persons of all classes of society, by pointed maxims and hymns, but especially by his translation of the sacred Scriptures into the German language. It is * * unjust * * to maintain that Luther's profound and dynamic interpretation of the sacrament, which on that very account was less perspicuous and intelligible, had its origin in nothing but partial stupidity or stubbornness. The opinion which each of these reformers (Zwinglius and Luther) entertained concerning the Sacraments, was most intimately connected with his whole religious tendency, which, in its turn, stood in connection with the different development of the churches which they respectively founded." *Compendium of the History of Doctrines*, Edinburgh, 1847, Vol. 11, p. 156.

J. M. V. AUDIN,
A French Jesuitical Historian.

" Luther's translation of the Bible is a noble monument of literature, a vast enterprise which seemed to require more than the life of man; but which Luther accomplished in a few years. The poetic soul finds in this translation evidences of genius, and expressions as natural, beautiful and melodious, as in the original languages. Luther's translation sometimes renders the primitive phrase with touching simplicity and magnificence, and receives all the modifications which he wishes to impart to it. It is simple in the recital of the patriarch, glowing in the predictions of the prophets, familiar in the Gospels, and colloquial in the Epistles. The imagery of the original is rendered with undeviating fidelity; the translation occasionally approaches the text. We must not then be astonished at the enthusiasm which Saxony felt at the appearance of Luther's version. Both Catholics and Protestants regarded it as an honor done to their ancient idiom."— *Life of Luther*, Chap. xxiv.

H. A. TAINE.

"We take the precise man for a religious man. We are content to see him stiff in his black coat, choked with a white cravat, with a prayer-book in his hand. We confound piety with decency, propriety, permanent and perfect regularity. We proscribe to a man of faith all candid speech, all bold gesture, all fire and dash in word and act; we are shocked by Luther's rude words, the bursts of laughter that shook his mighty frame, his workaday rages, his plain and free speaking, the audacious familiarity with which he treats Christ and the Deity. We do not remember that these freedoms and this recklessness are simply signs of entire belief, that warm and unbounded conviction is too sure of itself to be tied down to an irreproachable style, that primitive religion consists not of punctilios, but of emotions."—*English Literature*, I., 384.

STANG'S LIFE OF LUTHER,
Last paragraph.

" We stand before the image of the great Reformer with the full conviction that between the first century, when Christianity appeared in its youth, and the sixteenth, when it obtained the maturity of its riper age, not one of our race has appeared, in whom the ever-creative Spirit of God, the Spirit of light and of law, has found nobler embodiment, or wrought with richer sequence."

ROBERT MONTGOMERY,
An English preacher and poet.

" In the rugged grandeur of his faith, he may well be considered as the Elijah of the Reformation ; while his life, by the stern and solemn realities of its experiences, and the almost ideal evolutions of events, by which it was accompanied, constitutes indeed the embodied poem of European Protestantism.

" Luther, the *Reformer*, is but an outward and visible index of the inward and invisible characteristics of Luther, the *Man.* * * * * Wonderfully and wisely the trials and experiences of his inner nature were providentially overruled, and wrought into experimental connection with those religious achievements which have made the name of Martin Luther immortal.

" CHIEF o'er all the galaxy of lights
Which stud the firmament of Christian fame,

Shone LUTHER forth—*that miracle of men !* "
A Gospel Hero, who with faith sublime
Fulmined the lightnings of God's flaming Word
Full on the towers of superstitions' home,
Till lo! they crumbled; and his withering flash
Yet sears the ruin with victorious play.

"Let grateful reverence long that work admire,
O'er which a seraph's wings might shake with joy,
By Luther, with colossal power, achieved.
There was the Word Almighty, from the grave
Of buried language, into breathing life
Summoned, in saintly glory to arise,
And speak to souls, what souls could understand.
                    The words of truth
Eternal gave their hoary secrets up
While God's own language into Luther's passed,
  *   *   *   * till behold, the voice
Of Jesus out of classic fetters came,
And, like its Author, to the poor man preached.
  *   *   *   *   *   *   *   * "

"And such was Luther, when the clock of time
Sounded the hour for his decreed approach,
He was a mouthpiece of oppress'd mankind,
A great Interpreter of tongueless wants
And pains, which lack'd an intellectual power
Their own profundity to tell, or prove.
Yet, Preludes were there, which portended change,
Some dawning heralds of a deeper life,
Diviner morals and a purer creed,
Ere the lone monk from out his convent poured
Those thunder peals of theologic truth,
That started Leo from a sensual trance,
And shook the Vatican, with such a force
That yet its chambers vibrate with the shock
They gave them! though three hundred years
Have swept their wings o'er Martin Luther's grave.
There was a ripple in the mental tide
Awakened; streams of holier thought began

With sudden freshness, and more sweeping force,
Heavenward and onward through the heart to roll:
Till lo! at length a master-mind proceeds
Forth from the secrecies of convent life,
In whom the Spirit of the age can find
An Incarnation of itself prepar'd
The mind to utter, and its motion wield."

H. FICK,
The historian.

"The difficulties which Luther had to encounter transcended all conception. In the Old Testament especially, these were so great that he often spent four weeks in reflection and inquiry upon a single word, before he was satisfied how it should be translated into German. It is therefore with justice that Matthesius calls this translation of the Bible one of the greatest wonders which God accomplished through Dr. Luther; so that it seems to an attentive reader as if the Holy Spirit by the mouth of the prophets and apostles had spoken in our German language."—"*Life and deeds of Luther.*"

ARCHDEACON CHARLES HARDWICK,
Late of the University of Cambridge, England.

"In that large and sturdy frame, with appetites of corresponding vehemence and passions ever calling loudly for restraint, there worked a spirit such as rarely tenants human flesh—commanding, fierce, impetuous, dauntless and indomitable, while maintaining what he felt to be the cause of truth and righteousness, and yet combining with these manlier elements an awful consciousness of his dependence upon God, and childlike singleness of purpose. * * * He had every quality of thought, feeling and style that characterizes authors who are destined to impress and elevate the multitude; he was homely, practical and always perfectly intelligible; while the cogency of his arguments, the force and eloquence of his appeals and his convulsive earnestness, electrified in almost equal measure both his readers and his hearers. It has been calculated that in one year (1523) as many as 183 books were published in his name." .

JOSEPH B. BITTINGER,

Pastor of Presbyterian church, Sewickly, Pa.

" His name is before the world, somewhat as Schiller's Bell, in that most beautiful of his poems. It has been lifted out of the pit, freed from the mold and burnished. Behold, it rises up greater and grander, until it is lodged in the belfry—way above the turmoil, and strife, and trouble of the world in the streets below— speaking peace and quiet to men ; with heaven for its tent—the blue outstretched heaven—neighbor to the thunder, whose voice it shall echo.' There it hangs; swinging with melodious sound ; wafting it away off to the north, away off to the south, and ringing out in all directions a word of peace, a word of hope, a word of consolation; speaking to the earth below of the heavens above, and drawing all men's hearts from this lower evil world to that upper and better country.

CHARLES HODGE,
Late of Princeton.

"Luther, glorious and lovely as he was—and he is certainly one of the grandest and most attractive figures in ecclesiastical history. * * * No one knows Luther who has not read pretty faithfully the five octavo volumes of his letters, collected and edited by De Wette. These exhibit not only his power, fidelity and courage, but also his gentleness, disinterestedness, and his childlike simplicity, as well as his joyousness and humor."—*Syst. Theology*, iii, 484.

JOSEPH CUMMINGS,
Late Pres. Wesleyan University, Middletown, Conn.

"The instrument selected for the Reformation, bears a name that has become a household word—a name that shines with greater lustre than the name of Milton, of Shakespeare, or of Newten—because associated with more glorious triumphs—a name that has left behind it a legacy of an unshackeled Christianity—an unclasped Bible— a preached Gospel.

"Kings and emperors, have made pilgrimages to the tomb of that monk, and nations cherish in their hearts his imperishable name. Charles V., Frederick the Great, Peter of Russia, and Wallenstein, and, lastly, Napoleon, visited the spot where the remains of the Reformer lie; and even these names, the sounds of which still shake the casements of the world, seem but ciphers beside the dust of Martin Luther."—*Lectures on the Apocalypse*, pp. 122, 155.

CHARLES P. KRAUTH,

Professor in Lutheran Theological Seminary, Philadelphia.

"The greatness of some men only makes us feel that though they did well, others in their place, might have done just as they did. Luther had that exceptional greatness which convinces the world, that he alone could have done the work. He was not a mere mountain-top, catching a little earlier the beams which, by their own course, would soon have found the valleys; but rather by the divine ordination under which he rose, like the sun itself, without which the light on mountain or valley would have been but a starlight or moonlight. He was not a secondary orb, reflecting the light of another orb, as was Melanchthon, and even Calvin; still less the moon of a planet, as Bucer or Brentius; but the center of undulations which filled a system with glory. Yet, though he rose wondrously to a divine ideal, he did not cease to be a man of men. He won the trophies of power and the garlands of affection. Potentates feared him, and little children played with him. He has monuments in marble and bronze, medals in silver and gold; but his noblest monument is the best love of the best hearts, and the brightest, purest impression of his image has been left in the souls of regenerated nations. He was the best teacher of freedom and of loyalty. He has made the righteous throne stronger, and the innocent cottage happier. He knew how to laugh and how to weep; therefore millions laughed with him, and millions wept for him. He was tried by deep sorrow and brilliant fortune; he begged the poor scholar's bread, and from emperor and estates of the realm received an embassy, with a prince at its head, to ask him to untie the knot which defied the power of the soldier and the sagacity of the statesman; it was he who added to the Litany the words: 'In all time of our tribulation, in all time of our prosperity, help us, good Lord;' but whether lured by the subtlest flattery or assailed by the powers of hell, tempted with the mitre or threatened with the stake, he came of more than conqueror in all. He made a world rich forevermore and, stripping himself by perpetual charities, died in poverty. He knew how to command, for he had learned how to obey. Had he been less courageous, he would have attempted nothing; had he been less cautious, he would have ruined all; the torrent was resistless, but the banks were deep. He tore up the mightiest evils by the root, but shielded with his own life the tenderest bud of good; he combined the aggressiveness of a just radicalism with the moral resistance—which seemed to the fanatic the passive weakness—of a true conservatism. Faith-inspired, he was faith-inspiring. Great in act as he was in thought, proving himself fire with fire, 'inferior eyes grew great by his example, and put on the dauntless spirit of resolution.' The world knows his faults. He could not hide what he was. His transparent candor gave his enemies the material of their misrepresentation; but they cannot blame his infirmities without bearing witness to the nobleness which made him careless of appearances, in a world of defamers. For himself he had as little of the virtue of caution as he had, toward others, of the vice of dissimulation. Living under thousands of jealous and hating eyes, in the broadest light of day, the testimony of enemies but fixes the result, that his faults were those of a nature of the most consummate grandeur and fulness, faults more precious than the virtues of the common great. Four potentates ruled the mind of Europe in the Reformation—the Emperor, Erasmus, the Pope, and Luther. The Pope wanes, Erasmus is little, the Emperor is nothing, but Luther abides as a power for all time. His image casts itself upon the current of ages, as the mountain mirrors itself in the river that winds at its foot—the mighty fixing itself immutably upon the changing."—" *Conservative Reformation.*"

BAYARD TAYLOR.

" The man who re-created the German language—I hardly think the expression too strong—was Martin Luther. It was his fortune and that of the world that he was so equally great in many directions—as a personal character, as a man of action, as a teacher and preacher, and finally, as an author. No one before him, and no one for nearly two hundred years after him, saw that the German tongues must be sought for in the mouths of the people—that the exhausted expression of the earlier ages could not be revived, but that the newer, fuller and richer speech, then in its childhood must at once be acknowledged and adopted. He made it the vehicle of what was divinest in human language; and those who are not informed of his manner of translating the Bible, cannot appreciate the originality of his work, or the marvellous truth of the instinct which led him to it.   *   *   *   In regard to the fullness, the strength, the tenderness, the vital

power of language, I think Luther's Bible decidedly
superior to our own. * * * Luther was a poet as
well as a theologian, and, as a poet, he was able to feel
as no theologian could, the intrinsic difference of
spirit and character in the different books of the old
Testament—not only to feel, but, through the sympa-
thetic quality of the poetic nature, to reproduce them.
These ten years, from 1522 to 1532, * * * were
not only years of unremitting, prayerful, conscientious
labor, but also of warm, bright, joyous intellectual
creation. His style possesses strength and nobility,
 * * * but he was equally capable of expressing
the warmth, the tenderness and the bravery of the
original. * * * The letter which Luther wrote
to his little son, is as delightfully artless and childlike
a piece of writing as anything which Hans Christian
Andersen has ever produced. * * * The influence
of Luther on German literature cannot be explained
until we have seen how sound and vigorous and
manysided was the new spirit which he infused into
the language."—*Studies in German Literature*, Chap. v.

CHARLES A. STORK,

Late President of the Theological Seminary at Gettysburg, Pa.

"Part of the secret, then, of the vast influence
Luther exerted, is to be found in his completeness.
He was all around a full, a complete man. Perhaps
to some that will seem a very strange thing to say
about him. In his energy, fire, his torrent outbursts,
he seems a chaotic creature, the very opposite of
the round, completely proportioned man. But by
completeness in a man we are not to understand pol-

ish, symmetry, rounded proportions; but the full
equipment of the nature with all the great distinctive
features of humanity. It is in this respect that we say
Luther was a marvelously complete man. He was
myriad-sided, multiform, carrying in his one individuality all the great types and features of human nature,
at the top of their power.

"It is of course impossible to show this in detail: we
can only suggest its truth with reference to those great
cardinal features which characterize human nature. A
very obvious classification of this sort is that by which
we distinguish men as emotional, intellectual, practical
or active. Every man, we are accustomed to say,
belongs by his peculiar make to one of these classes:
that is, he is predominantly a man of feeling, of
thought, or of activity. To be a great man, is to possess, in an eminent degree, one or two of these qualities; rarely, indeed, do we find that even men who
tower above their fellows unite them all harmoniously.
We have only to call to mind Aristotle the unemo-
tional, Plato the unpractical, Calvin with his cold side,
and Wesley with his lack of intellectual grasp, to see
how great a man may be and yet fall short of the
greatest. In Luther we have the rare spectacle of a
man sent into the world who was complete in his
whole make. Emotionally, intellectually, practically,
he was complete and justly proportioned.

"Take him on his emotional side; and we feel at
once that as a religious reformer he laid that deep
hold in the common human heart, because he himself,
in a most vivid and vital history, had lived through
the divine life of religion he commended to men. He

was not, men felt then and have felt ever since, argu-
ing about God and religion for any mere intellectual
apprehension of them. No, he had lived with God,
loved him, rejoiced in him, and now out of that deep
experience he proclaimed him. It is not without reason that so much stress is laid in every history of the
man on the striking feature of the long struggle he
went through to find God. The sudden death of his
friend, the thunder-storm, the monastic exercises, the
experience at Rome, all these are the lightning flashes
which let us see the rugged way by which he climbed
out of the pit up to the cross of Christ. Then he
spoke to men of what he knew. The Old and New
Testaments he had lived through in his own experience before he translated them. His preaching and
theology had a fire in them and a strong warmth of
life because they came from God through a burning
experience in his own bosom. Through his denun-
ciations of the Pope, his exhortation to Christians, his
controversies with the theologians, rang the thrilling
voice of one who could say, 'I have believed; therefore have I spoken.'

"It was said of him that in society he would often
drop his conversation with those near and be silent;
when questioned, he explained that he stopped to con-
verse with God: so real and near was his heavenly
Father to him. He had a great, living, hungering
heart, which nothing but God could fill; and after God
he sought as a hunter seeks for game. When he found
him he lived in him. Through all he says and does,
that is continually present. When Luther speaks we

seem to feel God close by; his intense emotional life in the love and service of this unspeakable friend makes of God a wonderful reality. It is this that enabled him to grasp the heart of Europe of his day, and to hold it through all these centuries.

"But that is not all. Others have had the deep, warm religious experience of Luther; but they never revolutionized men's thinking and living as he did. They lacked the intellectual element.

Luther, in addition to his deep piety, was a great theologian. His robust intellect was not content to be put aside or into the back-ground when the question of God and his service came up. He loved God not only with all his heart and soul and strength, but also with all his mind; and having found him as a Father, he never wearied of seeking to solve him as a problem. The more he loved God the more he wanted to know of him, and could not rest till what he had experienced of his grace he had put into philosophic form. Phillips Brooks, in his speech in New York the other day, denied that Luther was a theologian, affirming that his force lay only in the moral and mystical elements of his character. That seems a strange statement to make of the author of the commentary on Galatians. True, he was not a theologian in the logical sense in which St. Augustine and Calvin were. But that he was a theologian, and a most profound one, can never be questioned by any one who has pondered his discussion on the Incarnation, that central dogma of Christianity. * * * * We need not hesitate to declare that it is that magnifying of the Person and work of Christ that has helped theologi-

4

cally to make Luther the power he has been in the world.

"We have only one element more to consider, and that is the active nature of the man. Luther's fervid, emotional experience, and his profound study of truth, issued in making him one of the most practical of men. He did not begin by propounding theological propositions, nor by exhorting men to embrace the joy of a new divine life. His first religious act as a Reformer was to attack an abuse—an abuse so palpable that every man could understand it. He attacked the sale of indulgences: how characteristic of the man that was! His religion, so ardent and mystical, so profound in its cogitations, comes out on the world's stage and sets itself at the business of reform. What slavery, intemperance, political corruption, have been in our day, that was the sale of indulgences then. And so the practical man strikes at once at the living, rampant evil. Through his whole life we see the same mark. In his early life he attacked the Pope: it was because the Pope then was the great abuse that needed to be reformed. At a later day the same practical instinct makes him turn his energies on the image-breakers, the extremists, the fanatics in the church. They were then the abuse needing reformation. At one time he is the ardent preacher of freedom, that no man is to stand between God and man, and that every man must be free to interpret the Bible for himself. But when freedom ran to license, we see him in the Peasants' War teaching men their obligations to submit to the powers of government. He is the defender of law and order.

"Always he is the man who sees how the great principles of truth and righteousness are to be applied to common life: he is intent on having the New Testament ideal of life wrought out in the affairs of everyday. And this made him a power. Too many men are like a furnace and boiler where mighty forces are generated for use, but in whose structure there is no provision for connecting the force and the work to be done. Not so here: what Luther felt, what he saw, that he understood to apply immediately to life.

"Of course, all that has been said here is the barest suggestion of what might be said in detail. But it serves to outline the direction in which we must look to understand the revolutionary force with which Luther wrought on the world. To feel deeply, to see clearly, to apply skillfully: these make up much of the secret of his power. And what is all this but to say, he was a round, complete man? Loving God with all the energies of his soul, pondering the mysteries of the divine being and his working till they grew clear and luminous, applying the sense of the divine presence and love to the every-day work of life—this is Luther."—*Lutheran Observer*, Dec. 7, 1883.

PHILIP SCHAFF,

Of Union Theol. Seminary, of New York, member of Amer. Com. on New Version of Bible, and author of many and learned works, in an article on "Luther as a Husband and Father."

"In this fourth centennial of his birth, all sides of his (Luther's) character and influence are revived and brought to the remembrance of the present generation. He figures in history as the great Reformer who set in motion the mighty struggle for religious and civil liberty throughout Europe; as the founder of the Lutheran Church, which is one of the largest Protestant denominations, and second to none in every department of sacred and secular learning; as the prince of Bible translators, whose version still has the strongest hold upon German-speaking Christendom, and is used Sunday by Sunday and day by day in every Lutheran Church and household; as a hymnist whose 'Ein Feste Burg ist Unser Gott' inspired the advancing armies of the Reformation, and struck the key-note to the richest hymnology of the world.— Truly, greatness enough to insure the immortality of half a dozen men! And this hero was the son of a peasant—a humble monk, and then a professor of theology, with no advantages but his genius, his will, and his faith in God. There is no man in history after the incomparable St. Paul, who accomplished more for his race than Martin Luther.

*   *   *   *   *   *   *   *

The domestic life of Luther has far more than a private biographical interest. It is one of the factors of modern civilization. Without Luther's reformation, clerical celibacy with all its risks and evil consequences would still be the universal law in all Western churches. There would be no married clergymen and clerical families in which the duties and virtues of conjugal, parental and filial relations could be practised. It has been proven that a larger proportion of able and useful men and women have been born and raised in households of Protestant pastors during the last three hundred years than in any other class of society. Viewed simply as a husband and father, and as one of the founders of the clerical family, Luther deserves to be esteemed and honored as one of the greatest benefactors of mankind."—*The Critic*, Nov. 10, 1883.

Speaking of Luther's Battle-hymn (Ein' Feste Burg) Dr. Schaff says:

"It is the great Marseillaise of Protestantism—its words and notes thrill on the heart like bugle-blasts from Heaven."

G. L. PLITT,
Late of Erlangen University, Germany.

"In the history of the Christian Church, next to the Apostles, there is no such prominent a personality as Martin Luther, and no event in the church has cut so deeply as the Reformation."

J. M. BUCKLEY,
Editor of the Christian Advocate, New York.

"Some men have the power to reach nations, and project their thoughts into successive generations. They possess a certain magnetic quality, and impulsive force of brain, by which they become the world's citizens. Martin Luther was just such a character as this. He belongs as fully to the nineteenth century as to the sixteenth, and he will be as much at home in the twenty-fifth as he now is in this century. We do not wonder that all Protestant Germany has been celebrating the four-hundredth anniversary of his birth; that even Döllinger, the founder of Old Catholicism, has lately eulogized Luther as an ornament to the

German race; that in Erfurt, where the young monk first saw the great black-letter Bible which shone into his soul, they have just had special festivities in the Reformer's memory; and that the Germans of every land are rearing monuments, establishing special funds, and organizing great public services, in loving memory of the greatest German mind from the time when Germania was only a savage Roman province down to the Empire of the present time.

" There are strong grounds for our American respect for the great name of Luther.   His birth preceded the discovery of this country by Columbus only nine years; but the most of the following century, the 16th, was occupied with Catholic colonization, especially in South America.   When, however, the Reformation became an established fact, both on the Continent and in Great Britain, North America was thrown wide open for Protestant immigration and ecclesiastical propagation.   The Canadas were largely French, and the Jesuits were prosecuting their lines of missionary work along the Mississippi, the St. Lawrence, the lake chain, and the Pacific coast.   But there was, with the opening of the seventeenth century, a sudden incoming of Protestants from every part of the Continent, and from the Church of England, which turned its persecuting l.and against all non-conformists.   The Puritans were not persecuted by Roman Catholics, but by so-called Protestants, and were fugitives, first to Holland, before they sailed in the *Mayflower* for the Massachusetts coast.   The Germans who came to this country were Protestants, and had received their spiritual light through Luther and his immediate successors.

Wherever they went they carried with them the fervor and courage that distinguished the heroic son of the Saxon miner. Even William Penn's colony of Quakers had a large Lutheran coloring, for Penn had been some time in Germany, had offered special inducements to Germans to emigrate to America, and even had his head-quarters at Frankfort-on-Main for helping Germans to these provinces. He was the founder of the first thoroughly German colony in this country. When the Swedes, together with the Danes, came in large numbers to this country, and settled in New York, in New Jersey, and all along the Delaware, giving their language and national type to many sections of country, they also brought with them the spirit and influence of Luther, who had given his theology to the whole Scandinavian peninsula. No better qualities were ever transferred to this country than came over with the families who, either willingly or by force, had derived their theology and religious experience from Luther.

"This can be seen in the Revolutionary war. The Lutherans, represented by many such heroes in council and on the battle field as the Muhlenbergs, helped us from the beginning to the end. The Keystone State, with its large element of Protestants of the Lutheran type, has been largely and heartily identified with the national life, all the way down from the time the bell rang out freedom from the old belfry of Independence Hall, to the battle of Gettysburg which decided the death of the rebellion.

"As to the Lutheran theology in this country, it has generally taken shape from that of Germany, but never falling to the skeptical depth that we have seen in the Fatherland. Here it has been conservative, always learned and searching, but confined in large measure to the German mind and language. Its general influence has been pure and helpful to our general religious development.

"As a nation, then, we have ample reason to revere the memory of Luther. He was the Reformer of all the reformers of his century. Without him they had not been. He has been our heroic Protestant as fully as if he had been born on our shores, for his children came hither, and have helped us to fight all our battles and rear this new western civilization.

"So as the Germans of the old country think in these days of their grand Luther, and gather about the hearthstones of the Reformation, and rejoice over the incoming of the Protestant era, American Christians have ample ground to rejoice with them, and be thankful, too, for what it has done for us. The central battle-field was Germany, and the victory everywhere depended on the victory there. Luther was too large for one continent, or for one century. Very beautiful was the way the multitude made their filial offerings to his memory in dear old Wittenberg a fortnight since. Two thousand Protestant ministers, gathered from every land, were there. The very houses were covered with reverent visitors, who spoke many tongues. The streets and alleys and market-places were crowded with guests. The aged Emperor Wilhelm deputed his son, the Crown Prince "Fritz," to represent the imperial family, and so that son took with him from Berlin an immense laurel wreath, and proceeding to the church in whose floor lies Luther's dust, laid the wreath upon the slab. The organ pealed out the great warrior's battle-hymn, "A strong tower is our God." The vast audience took it up, the multitude in the streets caught the notes, and the singing echoed far out beyond the walls into the surrounding country. It was a fitting tribute of the royalty of birth to the higher royalty of goodness and worth. It is only a part of the old story: 'Do the right, in the noonday or the midnight, and the world will honor the deed, and not forget the birthday of the doer.'"

A. W. THOROLD,
Bishop of Rochester, England.

"A great man's memory rises like a pillar over the sea, flashing a revolving light. The light is always there, but not always visible on every side. So to the different nations in turn, and at intervals, when they are receptive of the lesson, the dead heroes speak. Men rule their fellows, not only by the vividness of their personality, but by its many-sidedness. St. Paul was many men in one. So was Luther. In this they agree, that they were intensely human.

"In Luther's history there were several epochs, familiar to every schoolboy, milestones not only in his personal development, but in the progress of the world. His conversion into the vital and spiritual apprehension of God; his public burning of the Papal bull; his nailing of the theses to the church door; his public trial at Worms; his friendly imprisonment in the castle of Wartburg; his domestic life—all know these. Who

4*

quite knows their significance?   To understand a man,
and his life, we must take into account what physiolo-
gists say are the two main factors in conduct, heredity
and environment.

"Luther's parents were plain people of the laboring
class, but God-fearing and appreciative of education.
All round him was the Catholic Church, fast sinking
into an epicurean paganism, and Germany in the grasp
of Italy.   The English historian, Froude, who enthusiastically admires Luther, and ungrudgingly commends
him, does not hesitate to say that he changed the face
of Europe.   What an Europe to change!   See what
he possessed and also combined.   Fearless and audacious to a degree, he had his awful moments of reaction
and despondency, which help us to come nearer to him,
and learn of him through that nearness.   Rugged and
abrupt, he was infinitely tender, and there was a well
of beautiful love in his heart.

"It will always be a matter of controversy whether
or no he helped the Reformation and materially aug-
mented his personal influence by his marriage.   It is
certain that he thereby vindicated the freedom of marriage of the clergy, and bequeathed an exquisite ideal
of conjugal and parental love.   He almost recon-
structed the German language by his greatest achievement, the translation of the Bible into his native tongue.
A classical scholar, he was a constant student of Scripture, and all theologians may learn from him that the
Bible is the true storehouse of divinity.

"His hymns are the inheritance of the Church ; his
Table-Talk is the 'heart affluence of discursive talk,'
which has a lesson of its own to a people who are be-

coming almost proverbial for their taciturnity, and whom some think to be too apt to hide from strangers, eager to enjoy their humor, and to borrow from their experience, the kindliness that has too easily, perhaps sometimes in self-respect, come to shroud itself under a very Englishman's reserve.

"As a preacher, he did not aim at rhetorical or emotional self-display. He had an eye to the multitude of young people, children, servants, all round him. Less shrewd than Erasmus, less gentle than Melanchthon, perhaps less logical than Calvin, certainly less divested of sacramentarian error—he towers above them all as George Washington towers over the heroes of the revolution.

"To him, as has been well said, Rome owes her resurrection—to him, it may be said with equal truth, millions of souls their salvation. England loves his memory, for what has not he done for her national and religious life? The free millions of the United States may well rise up and do him honor, by cherishing his example, pondering his history, and maintaining his creed."—*Phila. Press* of Nov. 10, 1883.

GEORGE BANCROFT,
The celebrated American historian.

"Luther was more dogmatical than his opponents; though the deep philosophy with which his mind was imbued repelled the use of violence to effect conversion in religion. He was wont to protest against propagating reform by persecution and massacres; and with wise moderation, an admirable knowledge of human nature, a familiar and almost ludicrous quaintness of expression, he would deduce from his great principle of justification by faith alone, the sublime doctrine of freedom of conscience."—*History of the United States*, Vol. I., p. 274.

Again, in a letter of regret at his inability of attending the Luther Memorial Services held under the auspices of Princeton College and Seminary, he said:

" I agree with those who rate his (Luther's) importance to the world at the highest, and look forward with great pleasure to read what will be done in his honor on his birthday, in a place crowned with memories like Princeton College."

EGBERT C. SMYTH,

Professor at Andover, Mass.

"'The world for two hundred years has hated no one as it hates me,' Luther said, reviewing his life. To-day Roman Catholic as well as Protestant Germany does him honor, and the civilized world ranks him among its chief benefactors. A man so great and mighty deserves something very different from blind admiration. He had great faults. He cannot be regarded as a perfect exponent of the Reformation which he introduced. It is more important carefully to study the man and his work than to eulogize him. Yet we believe that the deeper the insight gained into his character, the more justly his actions are weighed, the more perfectly his nature is understood, the grander he will seem. There was more of humanity in him than in any other man of his time. Therefore he had more power than any other. Melanchthon was a better scholar, Zwingli a calmer and more sagacious reasoner, Calvin had a more systematic and organizing mind, Charles the Fifth is more renowned for his knowledge of men, especially their weaknesses; but no one ranks with Luther in his understanding of human nature, its needs and capacities, its ruin and its glory. No one touched men at so many points, helped them so much, entered, so profoundly into the deepest secrets of their hearts, opened to them such sources of strength.

"It is impossible to explain him by his times, however conditioned and limited he was by them. That the son of a miner, a peasant in a line of peasants, should stand above learned scholars and doctors, cardinals and popes, statesmen and princes, as a leader of thought, a controlling force in human affairs, is a historical fact worthy in our day of profoundest thought. We know of no way to account for it, which can stand a moment's careful scrutiny, that excludes the admission of a divine equipment, a divine call, and a divine mission of particular men, now as truly as in the days of Moses or Paul.

"We do not narrow his place in history, but rather explain why it is so large, when we conceive of him almost exclusively as a religious reformer. Only we must not be misled by the word 'Reformer.' Like the word 'Protestant,' it may have too negative an interpretation. Luther's work was constructive. He was a great builder, not so much in the realm of outward institution, of ecclesiastical polity, or even of theology, as in that which underlies all true divinity and useful church organization, in the realm of spiritual life. He smote the Rock from which flowed living

waters.   He turned men from a religion of ceremony
to worship in spirit and truth ; from the weary rounds
of a legal service to the glad obedience of gratitude
and love; from bondage to liberty and lordship.

" The providential preparation of Luther for his work
was as marked as that of Moses or Paul.   He was
educated into a perfect knowledge of the system to
whose overthrow his energies were to be devoted.   In
the family, the parish school, the university, the convent, he tested to the full the religious resources of
that system.   He believed in it, and he tried it in good
faith and thoroughly.   His personal experience is a
demonstration of its insufficiency.   His one aim was
righteousness.   He could not gain it under the conditions prescribed by the Romanism which he finally
rejected.   Not that the Roman Catholic Church does
not produce saints.   Not that Luther found the peace
and triumph he gained without help from that Church.
But this : the legal system which confronted and ruled
him, from his early training by his parents till he
learned the lesson that the just shall live by faith, did
not and could not yield the fruit of righteousness for
which he longed.   Immediate access to God, reception
of full and assured forgiveness through Christ by personal faith in him, consequent peace of conscience and
motive-power for a Christ-like benevolence—this was
Luther's method of righteousness, and one which put
him at once at variance with the theory of a sacerdotal church and with its practical discipline.   Therefore
he not merely protested against the proceedings of
such a scapegrace as Tetzel, not merely nailed his
theses to the church-door in Wittenberg, not merely

appealed to the German nobility against the usurped authority of Rome, but also wrote his treatise 'On the Freedom of a Christian Man,' proclaiming anew the old evangel with which Paul confronted the legalism of Judaism and the selfish moralities and immoralities of paganism. No so inspiring a treatise on religion or ethics had been written since the age of Apostles. Like the profoundest and most quickening instructions of sacred Scripture, its form is a paradox: " *Christianus homo omnium dominus est liberrimus, nulli subjectus ; Christianus homo omnium servus est officiosissimus, omnibus subjectus*" (A Christian man is the freest lord of all things, and subject to no one; a Christian man is the most obliging servant of all, and subject to all); or, as it runs in his native tongue: 'Ein Christen mensch ist ein freier Herr über alle Ding, und Niemand unterthan; ein Christen mensch ist ein dienstbar Knecht aller Ding, und Jederman unterthan.' There is not a wavering line or note in the whole march and progress of this tract. The ninety-five theses have been aptly described as the cry of an oppressed conscience—a cry, it should be added, of revolt as well as of anguish. The treatise "On the Freedom of a Christian Man" is a song of peace, a pæan of triumph. When we think of Luther at Erfurt, fainting in terror as the consecrated elements were borne about, dismayed before a crucifix, writhing on the ground as a story of Jesus' mercy is read from a Gospel, and then turn to the pages of this treatise, the contrast is overwhelming. It is more than the antithesis of slavery and liberty; it is the freedom of a soul—calm, natural, full of life and strength, breathing its native air, wielding the powers of an inalienable sovereignty. The outcome of a faith which immediately unites the soul to God in Christ is a royal, a God-like love. Service to our fellows, however severe, disturbs no inward peace. Rather it becomes the form and expression of the highest freedom. Myconius saw in the little, rude cloister-church in which Luther first preached the principles of the Reformation, a resemblance to the manger of Bethlehem. It is not too much to say that through Luther, Christ was, as it were, again born into the world. And it is in this coming again into the world of human thought and life of its Redeemer and Lord, that modern history, in all that is most inspiring and encouraging, in all that is most nobly characteristic, finds its source and living impulse. As a new century of this history opens, Luther still witnesses, and with increasing power, to the liberty of the Gospel as against every form of legalism, to the majesty and glory of Christ as revealed in his condescending love, to the worth of the individual soul, to the source of its righteousness and the victory of faith."—*Christian Union*, Nov. 8, 1883.

F. N. ZABRISKIE,
Dutch Reformed.

"Luther's sweet contentment with his worldly condition—a hard one at best, but rendered far more so by his conscientious independence and his generous regard for others—and his tender thoughts of thankfulness to God for every little gift of His providence, were constant and beautiful traits of his character. He would sit down to his frugal table, and his heart would overflow with gratitude which could not be limited to the formal "blessing." He seemed to enter into God's own joy in giving him these things. On one occasion when they were all enjoying their dessert of fruit and nuts, he broke out: 'What do you think the great God in heaven says to our sitting here consuming His gifts? Why, He created them for this very purpose. And all He asks of us is that we enjoy them, with gratitude and genuine acknowledgment of them as His gifts.' At another time he calls attention to the fact that God's very lavish bestowal of gifts is apt to deaden us to their appreciation; whereas, 'if we were all born with one leg or foot, and only in our seventh year received the second leg, at fourteen one hand, and at twenty the other, we might recognize more the worth of the gifts for a time withheld, and be more thankful.'   *   *   *   *   *

"If ever a man was called to be what Bunyan styles a Greatheart, it was this 'little monk' who led his age against the supreme powers of the world, the papacy, the empire, and the devil. Therefore we must not wonder to find his writings and reported conversations bristling with sword-thrusts in the hearts of the King's enemies. His favorite Psalm was the Second. 'I love it,' he said, 'with all my heart. It strikes and flashes valiantly amongst kings, princes, counsellors and judges.' But Luther's sword was a double-edged one, and was as sharp against a godless world as against a corrupt Church, against rationalism as against superstition. The world, in his eyes, is exceedingly ungodly and wicked, and few will be saved.

If left to himself, man 'would willingly throw our
Lord God out at the window.'   Christ would give to
the world the kingdom of heaven, but they will have
the kingdom of earth, and here they part.   He had
little patience with the attempt to weigh God or His
Word in the scales of the human understanding.
Quoting St. Augustine's reply to the question, 'Where
was God before heaven was created?'—viz: that He
was in Himself—he says: 'When another asked me
the same question, I retorted, He was building hell for
such idle, presumptuous, frivolous and inquisitive
spirits as you!'

"All this, of course, was but one side of the man.
He was naturally as gentle and as genial as a child,
and as true a Greatheart in conducting and comforting his flock as in fighting their foes.   It was the
result of a passionate devotion to truth, hardly paralleled in the history of man.   This was the key to all
his words and acts, and that which made him the iron
and unconquerable champion of a free Gospel that he
was.   He was no whit less stern in dealing with his
own heart.   He was as brave in bearing the cross, as
in brandishing the sword.   'I bear upon me the
malice of the world, the hatred of the Emperor, the
pope, and all their retinue.   Well, on in God's name!
Seeing I am come into the lists, I will fight it out.'
Nothing ever bowed his heart except the possibility
of not being in the way of truth and duty.   The devil,
he says, would sometimes tempt him with the thought
that he might be wrong 'till the sour sweat drizzled
off' him.   But when assured of being right he was
unconcerned and full of cheer, though sick of body

and worn out of mind, and overwhelmed with care all his later years. 'When I write against the Pope, I am not melancholy, but fight with joyful courage.' 'I have ·set Christ and the Pope at odds; though I get between the door and hinges and be squeezed, it is no matter; Christ will go through!' Other men had witnessed against the defects of popery, but 'to this I am called: I take the goose by the neck and set the knife to its throat.' He did not reproach others who went not so far as he. 'Not all can bear tribulations alike; some are better able to bear a blow of the devil—as we three, Philip Melanchthon, John Calvin, and myself.' But nowhere is the innermost spirit of this man—his terrific struggle with his own weakness, his sense of overwhelming responsibility, his indomitable fidelity, his sublime trust in God—more impressively exhibited than in the marvellous prayer which he was overheard to utter during the Diet of Worms. Summon before you the situation—this one man against the world—and I think I am not irreverent in saying that nothing has been equal to it since Gethsemane.

"'Almighty, Everlasting God, how terrible this world is! How it would open its jaws to devour me. And how weak is my trust in thee! Oh, thou my God, help me against all the wisdom of this world.) Do thou the work; it is thine, not mine. I have nothing to bring me here. I have no controversy to maintain—not I—with the great ones of the earth. I, too, would fain that my days should glide along, happy and calm. But the cause is thine. It is righteous; it is eternal.) Oh, Lord, help me!—thou that art faithful,

thou, that art unchangeable! It is not in any man I
trust (O, God, my God, dost thou not hear me? Art
thou dead? No, thou art hiding thyself, O, Lord my
God, where art thou? Come, Come! Thou hast
chosen me for this work! I know it. O, then, arise
and work! Be thou on my side, for the sake of thy
beloved Son, Jesus Christ, who is my defence, my
shield, and my fortress. I am ready—ready to forsake
life for thy truth—patient as a lamb. Though the
world should be full of demons; though my body
should be stretched on the rack, cut into pieces, con-
sumed to ashes—the soul is thine. For this I have the
assurance of thy Word. Amen. O, God, help thou
me. Amen . . . (and then, as if in soliloquy) Amen,
Amen—that means, Yes, Yes, this shall be done!'"—
Christian Intelligencer, Nov. 7 and 14.

J. T. HEADLEY,

Noted as a Historian and voluminous Writer.

"Luther was born for action. He was one of those
determined spirits that are at home in strife and danger; opposition and rage steadied him. For a long
time held in bondage, not from fear of men, but because
he could not find the truth, he no sooner discovered it
and announced himself its champion, than he became
a different man. Instead of the menial monk, school-
ing his iron nature into slavish submission, he is the
bold reformer, shaking the pillars of empire.   *⚡ *
Luther's courage had a firmer basis than his own
will—it rested on truth.

"With one thus anchored, and who has no thought
or wish beyond the truth, the common motives that

sway men have no influence. He has nothing to do with compromises, diplomacy, or results. The word of the living God is ever before him, reducing monarchs and dignitaries to the level of the meanest subject, while no consequences can be so awful as the wrath of the Almighty. Here was the secret of Luther's strength.   *   *   *   *   *

"However men may differ respecting Luther's views, or the mode he took on many occasions to accomplish his ends, all acknowledge him to be an honest man and a true Christian. Whether we behold him stretched on the floor of his cloister, struggling for deliverance from spiritual bondage, or unfolding the truths of the Bible to listening thousands; whether we see him on his way to danger and perhaps death, composing and singing, 'Eine feste Burg ist unser Gott;' or listen to his thrilling prayer for help, or hear his deep 'Amen,' at the Diet of Worms, we feel that we look upon a man whom no bribery can corrupt, nor flattery seduce, no opposition overcome or cause to waver from the truth."—*Headley's Luther and Cromwell.*

WILLIAM G. T. SHEDD,
Union Theological Seminary, New York.

"Luther's mission and function was a practical rather than a scientific one, and we do not find his mind strongly interested in any portion of human science.   *   *   *   As Luther did undoubtedly, in his inmost soul, completely submit his reason to that divine revelation, whose normal authority over the church and tradition he was such a mighty instrument of restoring; so in his sober judgment he did recognize the importance of a true and proper science of theology, and of a true and proper science of the human mind, to be employed in building it up out of the matter of revelation."— *A History of Christian Doctrine. See "Philosophy of Reformers,"* p. 90.

T. DE WITT TALMAGE.

"It seemed to be a matter of no importance that Martin Luther found a Bible in the monastery; but as he opened that Bible and the brass lids fell back, they jarred everything from the Vatican to the farthest convent in Germany, and the rustling of the wormed leaves was the sound of the wings of the Angel of the Reformation."

JOHN W. NEVIN,
Of German Reformed Theological Seminary, Lancaster, Pa.

"To understand the Lutheran Reformation, it is necessary, first of all, to understand Luther himself. As the great genius of the movement, he was, in one sense, the product and birth of the general historical force which was comprehended in it. So it is, we are often told, with all grand movements in the history of humanity. They create in a certain sense their own organs, the representative men by whose agency they are brought to pass. But the individual significance of such men, their personal weight as independent forces in what has taken place, is none the less to be acknowledged for this reason. So Luther stands before us as himself the germ and pattern of the new order of life he served to introduce into the Christian world

* * * * Luther himself, of course, had no conception of his own character or work, in becoming thus
the organ of the German Reformation.   There was no
forethought or plan in what he did.   This unpremedi-
tated character of the relation in which he stood to
his work, comes everywhere into view.   * * * *
The whole sense of the Reformation lay in his own
experience.   He had lived himself, with mighty birth-
struggle, into its utmost principle, and felt the presence
of it as a new creation in his soul before he became
unwittingly the organ of God's Spirit for proclaiming
it, and heralding it to the world at large."—*Mercers-
burg Review* of April, 1868.

ISAAC A. DORNER,
Of Berlin University.

"Luther did not set himself up to be a saint, but he
became of model, world-historical significance for the
German mind, and far beyond, by being a man who had
wrestled to find inward peace and direct communion
with God, and had not wrestled in vain.   Having thus
gone through conflict and victory in his own spirit, he
committed his experiences, with eloquent faith, to the
heart of his people, and so won among them the place
of a competent and trustworthy leader in things per-
taining to eternal salvation.   True, he is a hero of the
German *national* spirit, whose image even yet is of
magical force for all circles, high or low; but not by
his natural individuality as such, nor yet by his word
as doctrine merely, has he made himself so enduringly
felt; the secret of his power lies in all that served to
form him to the type of an Apostolic disciple, and to

an example, we will not say of the Christian life generally, but of conscious personal Christianity advanced to the ripeness of manhood—above all, in his clear, free apprehension of the way of salvation through Christ. His faith it was, emphatically, that gave him strength."

GEORGE WILLIAM CURTIS.

"Luther's hearty and affluent nature sympathized with the joyousness of the Christian spirit which did not scorn the flowers of the field, and found Solomon less royally arrayed than the wild rose and the lily.

"None of the traditional external characteristics of the Puritan are associated with Luther. He attacks the common enemy not with austere severity, but with cheerful vigor. His healthy soul was resolved with Charles Wesley that the devil should not have all the good tunes. The sunshine with which God bathed the world, should shine into his heart and be reflected in his life. And he who began the continuous organized movement of Protestantism, remains to this day the most comprehensive and satisfactory type of its spirit—a purifying and elevating, but not ascetic force, rich in all human sympathies and affections, as in all divine aspirations; a lover of children and of sweet and simple pleasures, of flowers and harmless sport; whose voice rings down to us through the four centuries since his birth, now in hearty laughter at a merry jest, now in the soft strain of a sacred song. Luther's name is the synonym of jubilant strength, of cheery health, of unquailing courage. The pioneer of the spiritual emancipation of the modern world, his simple childhood but resistless faith and energy, like Goldsmith's village pastor, 'allured to brighter worlds and led the way.'"—*Harper's Monthly*, December, 1883.

A. CLEVELAND COXE,

Bishop of the Protestant Episcopal Church, in his speech on " National Perpetuity," at Roseland Park, Woodstock, Conn., July 4, 1883.

"Luther sounded his tremendous trumpet, and waked such echoes as were never heard before from the Wartburg to the Odenwald, and along the highest Alps and Apennines, to the Vatican itself; nay, to the world."—*New York Independent* of July 12, 1883, p. 6 (870).

JAMES FREEMAN CLARKE,
A Unitarian.

"The character of Luther had a mountainous grandeur. When near Mont Blanc you perceive its ragged precipices and shapeless ravines: but as you recede, it appears to tower higher above its neighboring summits, until its features are softened by the intervening atmosphere and melted into strange tints and beautiful shadows, and it stands the object of reverence and wonder, one of the most sublime objects in nature, and most beautiful creations of God. So stands Luther, a hero, growing more and more the mark of reverence through succeeding centuries—the real author of modern liberty of thought and action, and the giant founder of modern civilization and pure religion."
—"*Religious Epochs of the World*," p. 256.

5

J. C. LONG,
A Baptist.

"It has been four hundred years since the birth of Luther, nearly one-fourth of the whole Christian era. The new world was not yet discovered. The Moors were yet a power in Spain, and the Turks in Europe. Looking backwards from that time, our eyes rest upon the old world; looking forwards, all seems new, strange, great. The struggles of Catholic and Huguenot, the Thirty Years' War which was to destroy the old Germany and make way for the new; Louis the Fourteenth, and his wonderful reign in France; Oliver Cromwell, the English Commonwealth, the English Revolution of 1688, the French Revolution, the American Revolution, the War between the States, a new theology and a new physical world, were all in the future. Of all these things, Luther was a part; if he had never been, they had never been. There is scarcely a spot on earth which has not felt and does not now feel his influence. He is a part of the United Germany of to-day; England stirs with the energy of his thoughts and spirit; and so does America. He went with Carey to India, with Livingstone to the heart of Africa. Everywhere, recognized or unrecognized, he moves among men. He is one of those great figures that come to stay and grow: to stalk down the ages and answer *Here!* at every roll-call of the centuries.

"It was Luther's sensitiveness to all the forces of his age that made him what he was, and that made him different from the great men about him. There is a sense in which Leo X. and Erasmus were also products of their age. That is, each was the product of one of the age-forces of the *Renaissance*. Leo was born of the classic spirit, and drew his inspiration from art and culture; he was a sort of baptized Mæcenas. Erasmus was the apostle of learning. He was a critic, seeing but not feeling or caring for the antagonisms about him. It was different with Luther; he was the child not of a part, but of the whole of his age. Leo and Erasmus were spectators of the fight; he was in the arena, and the world's battle was his battle as well. As he had grown up in and out of Germany, as he was Germany, his was the only hand that could write the ninety-five Theses, and nail them to the chapel-door. When he stood before the Diet at Worms, he felt, and everybody else felt, that it was not Luther, but awakening Germany that was to stand or fall. Did anybody feel, or could anybody feel, that there was any national or world interest wrapped up in the life of Erasmus or Leo. X?

A PRODUCT, AND A CREATOR.

"At one time, I was in the habit of saying that there are two kinds of great men—those who mold, and those who reflect their age; that is, those in whom the feelings and energies and thoughts of the age are, as it were, focalized or embodied. I would then have assigned Cæsar and Augustine and Bacon to the first and higher order, and Luther to the second class. A closer scrutiny has convinced me that the classification is wrong. No man has ever been a leader and molder of his age without being part and parcel of it; and no man has ever gathered up within himself the spirit and forces of his age, without, at the same time, exerting a formative influence upon it. By living in their age, in every day and hour of it, by breathing its breath, and feeling its heart throbs, and seeing its needs and seizing its opportunities, they have grown and ruled. Thousands stand waiting for opportunities, and opportunities come and go without being recognized at all, or else too late. The man of power does not fail to see them. He gathers from straws and pebbles and wayside flowers, materials with which to build and adorn his fortune. He who sits and dreams of greatness will never be great. He who holds his present position cheap, except as a stepping-stone to something higher, may find it long before he takes that higher step. Luther was great, was the master spirit of the 16th century, because, indeed, he was conscious of all the forces at work about him, but not less because he was ever faithful to duty in its hour and order.   *   *   *   *   *   *   *

"In saying that Luther followed the suggestions of the occasion, I mean no more than that, when the occasion came, it found the man ready for it. In saying that he grew up in, and expressed the feelings and aspirations of his age, I do not mean that the work he did was of such a kind that it would have been carried forward by the age-forces without his aid. I do not believe it would. The sixteenth century is the only one of all the centuries in which there could have been a Luther; but, without Luther, it could not have been what it was. The identity of lightning and electricity would have been proved if there had never been a Franklin; the safety-lamp would have been in-

vented if Sir Humphrey Davy had never lived; if
Columbus had never been born, America would still
have been discovered. In these cases, many were
moving together towards an end, and it was only a
question as to who should reach it first. But if
Elijah had not rebuked Ahab and overthown the
priests of Baal, there was no one else to do it. If
Washington had not achieved American independence,
it does not appear that any other man of the times
could have done it. In Luther's day, no one so truly
as he did saw the Reformation idea, and grasped and
represented it, and made the world feel that he represented it. There was, as far as appeared, absolutely no one who could do what he did. Now and
then an age accumulates energy to bring forth a great
man to meet a great emergency ; but rarely or never
has any age brought forth more than one. When the
age brings the opportunity, if at the same time it brings
no man to seize it, the opportunity passes by, like
some vagrant comet, and returns no more until another
cycle is completed. The sixteenth century brought
an opportunity, and with it a man, and that man was
Luther."—*National Baptist*, Nov. 15, 1883.

HENRY E. JACOBS,

Norton Professor of Systematic Theology in Phila. Luth. Seminary.

"But the chief excellence of Luther's work is derived from the spiritual sense of the translator that so
quickly and thoroughly penetrated into the meaning
of the text, and expressed itself with that rare facility
that is the fruit only of living in the Holy Scriptures.
This manifests itself, too, in the scrupulous avoidance

of the language of the learned, and in the desertion of
all literal idioms that would obscure the meaning of
the sacred writers from the common people.   In all
the world, there has never been a book which can
claim so properly to be a book of the people as
Luther's Bible.   Through it the ancient prophets descend from the stateliness of oriental imagery, and,
entering the home of the German peasant, express
their profound thoughts, without sacrifice of dignity,
in the language of most tender familiarity.   'O Lord,'
he once said, 'what a troublesome and great work it is
to force the Hebrew writers to speak German!   They
resist, since they are unwilling to leave their Hebrai-
city, and to imitate German barbarity.'   But the
charm of the work is, that the German barbarity that
seemed so insuperable is also completely avoided, and
we find what is as elegant and eloquent as it is plain
and simple—the work of a true master, who could
have produced this result only by a special divine
assistance, an inspiration, though, of course, of a lower
and entirely different grade from that of the sacred
writers themselves.   It illustrates Luther's own remark:
'Translation is a special grace and gift of God.'"
Bible Society Record, of December 20, 1883.

S. IRENEUS PRIME,
Editor N. Y. Observer.

"What then does the world owe to the man and
the men who realized the standard of revolution, organized the rebellion against the direst despotism with
which earth was ever cursed, and led the forces of
truth and righteousness to victory and independence!

"It is estimated that in the year 1500, out of the 52,000,000 square miles which measure the earth's area, the Romish church covered nearly 4,000,000. The remainder was held by Pagans and Mohammedans. To-day the Romish church is dominant over 9,000,000 of square miles, and the Reformation principles control the thought of the people on 14,000,000 of square miles! And we cannot adequately estimate the value of that Reformation, without taking a careful survey of the moral, intellectual and physical condition of the people that dwell on the square miles dominated by Romanism and by the Reformation.

"What makes the difference between Spain and England? What makes Scotland better than Ireland? What makes Germany stronger than France? What has kept Italy in mental and moral debasement, and what has infused new life and hope into her since the downfall of the pope? What would this Western world be to-day, if the church of Rome had not been shorn of its strength before its settlement by Europeans? What causes the difference in all the elements of greatness, and of happiness, between North America and South America? Compare Mexico with Ohio, and explain the contrast. What has Roman Catholic principle done for the legislation of civilization? Pagan Rome contributed far more to the just jurisprudence of modern nations than Rome did in the whole ten centuries while papal wisdom and learning were dominant forces in Europe. What but the Reformation has given impulse to letters, to art, to science, to invention, to all that elevates, enriches and gladdens mankind?

"He is blind who does not see the hand of God in history; and in no one event in the whole world's history is that mighty omnipotent hand more distinctly visible, than in the overthrow of papal power and the exaltation of that Protestant principle which now permeates society, and is filling the earth with knowledge and freedom. For this let us acknowledge God. The right of every man to think for himself, subject only to God—this is the core of the Reformation. No other lord of the conscience, no priest between the soul and its great high-priest, the eternal Son of God, no power to forgive sin but God only; these are central truths which Rome denies, and which the Reformation made the vital forces to deliver the human race from mental and moral slavery. This is a victory and the liberty which we celebrate when we thank God for the birth and life of Martin Luther. The Protestant world will recognize these facts when on the continent of Europe, in England and Scotland, and all over free America, the tenth day of November, 1883, is distinguished by meetings, prayers, orations and songs of praise, to celebrate the day when a child was born who grew to be the master man of the Great Reformation. Every Protestant church in Christendom ought to crowd its gates with thankful songs; give glory to God in the highest, and bless his holy name."

REUBEN WEISER,

Denver, Colorado.

"We say without fear of successful contradiction that the labors of Martin Luther made it possible for such a government as ours to exist. The truths that

were announced by our fathers in 1776 as 'self evident'—that all men are created equal; that they are
endowed by their Creator with the inalienable rights
of life, liberty, and the pursuit of happiness, would not
have been published in Philadelphia, if Luther had not
first proclaimed them at the Diet of Worms. He was
the pioneer of human liberty and free government,
and as such he is fully entitled to the gratitude of all
who respect the sacred rights of conscience.

Our Catholic fellow-citizens ought, therefore, not to
find fault with us for our zeal and enthusiasm in celebrating the 400th birthday of Luther. Let them bring
out any other man who has done as much for the promotion of liberty and freedom, and we will most cheer-
fully join them in doing him honor. But until such a
character is presented, we will continue to rally around
the immortal Reformer, and hold him up as the great
High Priest of human liberty, and one of the greatest
benefactors the world has ever seen!"

WM. J. MANN,

Professor in the Lutheran Theological Seminary, Philadelphia, Pa.

" Indeed he was a very peculiar man, that man Martin Luther. Original he was, and like a book of which
only one copy was printed, and towering up above all
the houses of the large town, and standing solitary and
looking down from the majestic height like the spire
of Strassburg cathedral. They were amazed at this
phenomenon, at this meteor, unexpectedly marching
across the horizon and setting the world on fire. They
were horrified at this German monk, bidding defiance
to the pope, then the ruler of all rulers, the jailor of

5*

millions upon millions of Christian intellects. I wonder not that the pope excommunicated him; that all
priests execrate him, all Jesuits curse him, all Roman
Catholics hate him. If I was a Roman Catholic, I
would hate him too. I could not do otherwise. I
would see in him simply the Vandal, the destroyer.
Think of it, what an amount of harm that man has
done to that holy of holies, that 'Holy Church,'
and how little respect he had for all her authority and
powers, and glories and titles, and masters and servants, and how boldly he came out and said things and
proclaimed truths that shook the old walls to their
very foundations, and broke forth like a burning
volcano, upheaving a whole continent, and sending
showers of red-hot boulders upon the land all around.
Was it not as if he was going to turn the world upside
down? There was not a trace of fear in that man.
Not a foot of ground had he to love—not one farth-
ing to gain. The battles of God he had to fight and
he rejoiced in doing it. God's cause was his cause,
Christ's honor his honor. The more enemies rose up
against him, the more he felt like fighting, and gloried
indeed 'to run a race, like a bridegroom coming out
of his chamber.' Of course he was no respecter of
persons. Miserable King Henry, of England, who
sacrificed life after life to his lust, when he meddled
even with theology, Luther thought he was simply an
ass with a crown between his long ears, and this he
called him before all Europe. And how the monk
handled the pope! All Christendom stood aghast at
the unceremonious way in which he scorned all that
halo around the 'Holy Father,' and denounced him

as the very ' Hellish Father.' Whilst his vocabulary in this direction was not easily exhausted, he held his conscience in serene condition, and there was not a shade of self-reproach in him. He had to give men and things their right names. Would to God, such a man would come in our times! He felt never happier, than when his full indignation would blaze out like a bundle of lightnings against that miserable sham under the tiara, which shamelessly pushed itself between God and his Redeemer. All the upholstering around the throne at Rome, could not dim or deceive that eagle-eye, divinely enlightened. Luther knew, that that self-appointed Vicar of Christ was Christ's worst enemy, was the anti-Christ.

"Do not offer that man a bribe, provided he will shut up his mouth and keep the peace. To you it may appear expedient: not so to him. He will knock you down beyond the hope of resurrection. Thousand gold mines will not buy him to say one word less than what he thinks ought to be said, because God says it. Of course, they accuse him: He often was rough in his manners, uncouth in his ways, rude in his language. He was so, and so he had to be. Let that grand soul be as it is. He had a rough bark like an old solid German oak, that raises its venerable head up to the sky and greets old Sol and braves a thousand storms and outlives a long array of icy winters. There is solid, hard, tough, sound wood behind that rough bark. The mighty roots of that old oak go down between the rocks and split them, and fathom the unknown depth and drink the hidden springs. Thus did Luther strike root down into the depth of God's word, power of love and eternal truth, and drink new life. He stood firm and thundered forth his world-shaking words, and in him there was a host of heroes.

"Never was nature more natural, never grace more graceful, than in Luther. In him there was not a trace of affectation. He gave himself just as he was. No man was ever greater. No man did ever care less about his greatness than he did. He knew not of a seeming, hypocritical humility. He rejoiced in the fact that his name was known on earth, in the heavens, and even in hell. He undertook to rise against the dragon that made the blooming land a desert. With the muscles of a Samson he raised the rusty gates of the old ecclesiastical fortress. Europe stood in amazement at the boldness of this agitator. It was a new era that spoke through him. His heart throbbed with the pulsations of generations to come. Yet he went on in shaking the old and honored establishment and uprooting it, as if he were simply doing a duty, totally sinking his own self in his work, and being merely a hammer in the hands of Providence, to form the crude and useless material of the past into the refined, new form of the future.

"Indeed he was a wonderful man! Behold him, as he comes radiant with joy of victory from the fierce battle, throws off his armor, puts his sword in the sheath and takes up his harp to sing the praises of the God of battles, or lulls with sweetest song his dear little children to sleep, or plays like a child with those dear ones and tells them of the golden apples and of the diamond crowns in God's eternal and better home.

Mark him, as he shoots his fiery arrows in holy indignation at those who touch the honor and glory of his God, or sits majestically in judgment against those who, with their own soul-destroying inventions, deny the saving power of Christ. But now you see him bending his knees, humbly bowing down before Him who alone is great, stretching out his hands, raising up his arms, pouring out his soul to the great God, that He would have mercy on him and His people and His church on earth and send forth His mighty Word and Spirit and break the power of Satan and comfort with sweetest love His dearly bought children, and make the light break forth from darkness.

"Revolutions change the relations between men, upset political establishments, and from a new starting point produce a new division of this world's honors, powers, rights and possessions. A Reformation changes the relations of men to their God. No task is more difficult than to bring about a change in a single individual's religious persuasion and habits. Luther caused a vast radical change in the religious feelings, convictions, habits, and interests of uncounted millions. He found the lost foundation-stone of the Church, and with a giant's arms he put the old structure upon it. In him, a new star rose up on the canopy of the heavens, to guide us with its brilliant rays through the stormy sea of time to the happy shores of eternity, to bask in the light of the Sun of Righteousness. To the radiancy of that star, this day and coming centuries will give new lustre."—*Workman*, Pittsburgh, Pa., Nov. 10, 1883.

R. HEBER NEWTON,
Episcopal Rector, New York City.

" It is a rarely rich personality on which the gaze
of Protestantism is fixed at this time—a sturdy peasant's son, who makes himself the friend of princes and
a worthy foe for the two proudest potentates of civilization; a classical scholar and philosophic lecturer
whose spiritual experiences convulsed Europe; a man
of large affairs who so translated the Bible that his
version became a standard of idiomatic German; an
eager controversialist, and a writer of hymns as sweet
as ' Fairest Lord Jesus;' a world-reformer who sends
to his little Johnny that inimitable letter about 'the
beautiful garden;' a saint who was the jolliest of com-
panions, and whose burly humor rolls through his
letters to his ' Rib Kate,' and bursts forth boisterously
amid the most solemn discussions.

" Wholesome the renewed study of such a powerful
personality must prove to our generation, gone daft
upon the idea of impersonality; wholesome alike in
the culture of individual character, in the fashioning
of a philosophy of history and of a philosophy of
nature—another and a deeper matter than science.
Such a study cannot fail also to give us the key to the
religious movement of which he was the masterful
leader. As in other historic instances, the person of
the Founder of Protestantism holds the norm of the
religion he inspired; and an understanding of his spirit
will interpret the nature and destiny of the mighty
movement he initiated. The Genius of Luther is the
Genius of Protestantism. Catholicism will have it that
Protestantism is a spirit of destructiveness. Was

Luther a destructive? He certainly did have considerable pulling-down to do, and he did such work, as all else that he set his hand to, heartily; but his life reveals a thoroughly conservative nature, which shrank instinctively from all excess; from the ecclesiastical extreme of Carlstadt, from the theological extreme of Zwingli, and from the social extreme of the Anabaptists. An iconoclast when any venerable image was crumbling to pieces and threatening ruin upon those who stood below it worshipfully, he took nothing out of the old temple that he thought could stand safely. He was, writes one of his biographers concerning his action in establishing the reformed worship, 'as usually, conservative.' He believed himself to be doing a real piece of conserving. He surely was as truly a conserver as the architect who, to save an old minster, tears down and rebuilds the walls that were settling rapidly, and were threatening total destruction to the venerable pile. He was not 'the spirit that denieth,' as pictured by his fellow German. He was, in his way, an 'everlasting yea' His voice gave new affirmation to faith; an affirmation which rings still through the soul of Protestant Christendom, wakening the echoes of belief. * * * *"—*The Critic*, Nov. 10, 1883.

JAMES A. FROUDE,

The eminent English historian, depicts the memorable scene at Worms in the following words:

"The appearance of Luther before the Diet on this occasion is one of the finest, perhaps it is the very finest, scene in human history. Many a man has en-

countered death bravely for a cause which he knows
to be just, when he is sustained by the sympathy of
thousands, of whom he was at the moment the champion and representative. But it is one thing to suffer
and another to encounter, face to face and single-
handed, the array of spiritual and temporal authorities
which are ruling supreme. Luther's very cause was
yet unshaped and undetermined, and the minds of
those who had admired and followed him were hang-
ing in suspense upon the issue of this trial. High-
placed men of noble birth are sustained by pride of
blood and ancestry, and the sense that they are the
equals of those whom they defy. At Worms there was
on one side a solitary, low-born peasant monk, and
on the other the dreaded power which had broken the
spirit of kings and emperors—sustained and personally supported by the Imperial Majesty itself and the
assembled princes of Germany, before whom the poor
peasantry had been taught to tremble as beings of
another nature from themselves. Well might George
of Freundsberg say that no knight among them all
had ever faced a peril which could equal this. The
victory was won. The wavering hearts took courage.
The Evangelical revolt spread like an epidemic. The
papacy was like an idol, powerful only as long as it
was feared. Luther had thrown his spear at it, and
the enchantment was broken. The idol was but
painted wood, which men and boys might now mock
and gibe at. Never again had Charles another chance
of crushing the Reformation."

"Luther's mind was literally world-wide: his eyes
were forever observant of what was round him. At a

time when science was scarcely out of its shell, Luther had observed nature with the liveliest curiosity. He had anticipated by mere genius the generative functions of flowers. Human nature he had studied like a dramatist. His memory was a museum of historical information, of anecdotes of great men, of old German literature and song and proverbs. Scarce a subject could be spoken of on which he had not thought, and on which he had not something remarkable to say. His table was always open and amply furnished. Melanchthon, Jonas, Lucas Cranach, and other Wittenberg friends, were constant guests. Great people, great lords, great ladies, great learned men, came from all parts of Europe. He received them freely at dinner; and, being one of the most copious of talkers, he enabled his friends to preserve the most extraordinary monument of his acquirements and of his intellectual vigor. On reading the *Tischreden*, or Table-talk, of Luther, one ceases to wonder how this single man could change the face of Europe."—*On Luther's Mind*.

Mr. Froude closes his monograph on Luther as follows: "Philosophic historians tell us that Luther succeeded because he came in the fullness of time, because the age was ripe for him, because forces were at work which would have brought about the same changes if he had never been born. Some changes there might have been, but not the same. The forces computable by philosophy can destroy, but they cannot create. The false spiritual despotism which dominated Europe would have failed from its own hollowness. But a lie may perish, and no living belief may rise again out of the ruins. A living be-

lief can rise only out of a believing soul; and that any
faith, any piety, is now alive in Europe, in the Roman
church itself, whose insolent hypocrisy he humbled into
shame, is due in large measure to the poor miner's
son, who was born in a Saxon village four hundred
years ago."—*Contemporary Review.*

W. H. JEFFERS.

"There were, perhaps, greater theologians than he,
both among his contemporaries and in the generation
which succeeded him. There were men of more profound and accurate scholarship. There were those
whose talents were no less consecrated to the cause of
Christ and the promotion of His truth. There were
men who were not his inferiors in controversial ability.
But Luther possessed that rare combination and bal-
ance of qualities which fitted him above all others for
leadership in the great spiritual movement of the sixteenth century. He was eminently a representative of
the common people, was acquainted with their spiritual condition, sympathized with them in their wants
and aspirations, and knew perfectly how to touch their
hearts and kindle their enthusiasm. In his preaching,
his tracts, and his translation of the Bible, he availed
himself of the language of everyday life, and so skillfully did he mould this to his purpose, that the German
tongue still retains the character which he impressed
upon it. He aimed always at 'the instruction of the
rude, common man,' rather than the gratification of
scholarly tastes. He was a man of unflinching courage. Perils from which others shrunk, served only to
quicken his energy and rouse his determination. 'I

hear,' he writes, in concluding one of his treatises, 'that bulls and other popish devices have been prepared, in which I am urged to recant or be proclaimed a heretic. If that be true, I would have this little book serve as part of my recantation.' He was a man of untiring industry and singular endurance. It requires a good portion of a lifetime simply to read the twenty-four quarto volumes which contain his writings; yet during the twenty-eight years in which these were produced, he was burdened with incessant cares, and almost constantly engaged in preaching and teaching. Some of his treatises were thrown off hurriedly; but there is evidence that his more important works were elaborated with great care. Parts of his translation of the Bible were subjected to no less than fifteen careful revisions before being sent to the press. In connection with these exalted qualities he possessed in singular degree the characteristic of humility. It was through no craving for personal distinction that he assumed the attitude of reformer. He took the first step only when compelled, in faithfulness to his charge in Wittenberg, to utter his protest against the shameful traffic in indulgences; and every subsequent step was taken in obedience to what he recognized as the voice of conscience and the voice of God."—*Westminster Teacher*, November, 1883.

O. B. FROTHINGHAM.

" It is not strange that the birthday of Luther should be celebrated in the land of his nativity and the places made glorious by his achievement; that new biographies of him should be published; that portraits of the man should be distributed; that his books should be reprinted; that essays and discoveries by eminent men should be given to the public; that fresh estimates of his character and work should be made by distinguished thinkers. The marvel is that the whole Protestant world does not indulge in enthusiastic encomium of its great founder, does not magnify the author of the new dispensation of spiritual liberty in faith and worship. For this is his significance as a historical character—this is his conceded position among Protestant believers. The people commemorate persons, not principles. They like concrete realities; they crave personal contact; they must have flesh and blood; a little dirt, a rank smell, a coarse fibre, a touch of vulgarity, is to their taste; overmuch delicacy, refinement, sensibility, scholarship, critical nicety, repels them. Nature itself seems to abhor an excess of cultivation. We cannot breathe pure oxygen, or drink unadulterated spirits, or eat ethereal food. Even ignorance, stolidity, mental inertia and spiritual short-sightedness, are sheaths that preserve the sword of the Spirit from rust, prevent its wounding the wrong person; in a word, keep its activity within limits. It may be quite true that the same results would have been attained had Luther never been born. The drifting vessel may in course of time reach the same goal with the steamship, but it will be much longer about it, and it will pursue a devious track, with frequent stoppages, with retrograde motions, with incessant interruptions from winds and currents. The steamship has all the winds inside, disregards the eddies, ploughs a straight furrow, goes steadily forward, arrives quickly

and surely at its destination, uses the elements which keep the sail-boat back, while it takes advantage of every favorable circumstance of time and tide. But then, the steamship has its inconveniences. There is the noise of machinery, the forced action of the boat against the waves, the unyielding pressure of mechanical agency, the heat of the furnace, the smell of oil, the din of stokers shovelling coal or discharging ashes, the nuisance of cinders, the danger of fire, the risk of explosion, the peril of collision. The general electricity of the earth does not dispense with telegraph wires or render magnets valueless. Without it they could lend no service, but without *them* it certainly would not perform the tasks that man requires. So Luther might have been nothing without his age, but what would that have been without Luther? In him the tendencies of the generation, the elements which were abroad in the XVIth Century, came to a head, culminated as personal power. * * * *
—Luther was a rough, rude man, with all his genius and all his gentleness—a wholesale, terrestrial man; and to this roughness, rudeness, earthiness, his victory was due. To this was owing the warmth of his sympathy, the heartiness of his humor, the native force of his spoken and written thought, the racy heartiness of his scholarship, and his homely rendering of the Scriptures into the language of popular speech—even his courage so largely made up of indomitable wilfulness, and his tenderness, so full of simply human emotion. His love of music was homespun and plain —not soaring or seraphic. He was a child of the soil. He lived near the ground. He thought in masses. He

felt broadly and naturally. Religious he was by nature and by education, but his religion—the parent of modern naturalism—was of the untutored heart, the untrained impulse, the impassioned instinct. His marriage, the motives that led to it, the circumstances that attended it, the domestic happiness that resulted from it, all declare what manner of man he was—an honest, downright, stubborn, cordial, rustic man, muscular and brave, with blood in his veins, capable of getting mad, and of enjoying practical jokes. His furious rage against the Anabaptists at Münster, as well as against all who would carry his principles to extremes, shows how little addicted he was to formal logic—how ready he was to consult the dictates of common sense.

"Providence mingles a good deal of alloy with the fine gold of which the characters are wrought that are to make a broad mark on the world. Emerson, in his famous lecture on Napoleon I., whom he ranks among Representative Men, speaks of the terrible drawbacks on his moral disposition, which made possible his extraordinary achievement. But Emerson himself, one of the cleanest, most seraphic men that ever lived, fails to make a great popular impression on his time, by reason of his fineness and purity. He wielded a different weapon, was what Napoleon would have called an 'ideologist.' His influence may be more lasting; but it is *influence*, the effect of the highest genius on the best minds. Theodore Parker owed his astonishing power less to his vast reading, his capacious memory, his immense industry, than to his practical talent, his ability to state current thoughts in picturesque language, his sympathy with the ruling interests of his day and nation. His friend George Ripley was in some respects a more extraordinary man, of nicer critical faculty, or more evenly balanced intellect, but few comparatively ever heard of him. Melanchthon was, on the whole, a finer intellect than Luther; but he is scarcely more than a name, while Luther is a leader of multitudes. We hardly ever hear of Melanchthon except as Luther's opposite, and to his disparagement. He would, in fact, be quite forgotten but for his relation to the great reformer, who clove his way to the goal while the other was considering the difficulties that beset the path. What kind of a reformer would Montaigne have made, or any skeptic? A distinguished minister once said that he should have done something as a writer if his hands had been less delicate. He was too fastidious of touch to grasp tools by the handle. He shrank from contact with labor. The 'cast of thought' is 'pale;' it 'sicklies o'er' the objects it contemplates.

Luther was not separated from his fellow-men, or lifted above them by any accident of fortune or disposition. He was destitute of private ambition to lead a movement, establish an institution, build up a family, or sit upon a spiritual eminence. He was homely in his tastes, unpretending in his manners, plain in his whole exterior. Probably no man could have been more surprised at his fame than he, for he neither sought it nor gave thought to it. He did not desire money. He lived and died poor. While others made gain from his writings, he made none. He was content with a humble lot, happy in his wife and children, honest of speech and conversation. His great task of translating the Bible was undertaken with simple fidelity to human wants; its prime excellence of speech was simply due to his determination to be intelligible to ordinary people, not to any affectation of plainness of style as a beauty in itself. He was not conscious that he was engaged on an immortal work, nor did he plume himself on his ability to render Hebrew and Greek into idiomatic German. In truth, he plumed himself on nothing that he had or was. * *

"The real genius of Protestantism is not now under debate. Be the decision what it may, one thing is certain, that the character of Martin Luther is no failure; that the more closely it is studied the more honorable it will appear; that years will but add to its intrinsic nobleness. He was a living soul, and none but living souls rule in the spiritual world. Humility, simplicity, sincerity, unconsciousness, obedience, faith, command the future. It is safe to predict, moreover, that his ultimate thought, though altered in expression, will rule over philosophy as long as Christian Theism with its endeavor after communion with God through Christ, is professed among men. The Protestant idea will ever be associated with his name, though interpretations may change and expositions may vary. Protestantism and Martin Luther are synonymous terms."—*The Critic*, November 10, 1883.

EDWARD LeM. HEYDECKER,
Of New York City.

"The nations of Europe which have accepted Luther's principles and embodied them in their public acts—Germany, England, and the United States, the greater nations; Switzerland, Holland, Sweden, and Denmark, the smaller ones—stand foremost in the world in political, social and moral development; while the nations where Loyola's influence has been strongest, Spain and Portugal, are the last in the list of European nations, if we exclude Turkey, which is not Christian. The Jesuit influence is strong in South America, and those nations are the laggards in the march of progress.

The principles of Luther—the principles of Freedom, Truth and Justice—have won their way over the despotism of rulers and the prejudices of aristocracy, and have won the grand results which modern historians record.

Luther's influence on men is uplifting, ennobling, calling forth all the higher qualities of man's nature; the influence of Loyola's teaching is to call into play man's baser passions, to excuse and defend his vices and crimes, and to make him a mere creature, obedient to his master, the pope. The spirits of these men still live and teach, and the end is not yet.

> 'O! vos qui cum Jesu ites,
> Non ite cum Jesuites.'"

—Lutheran Quarterly, Oct., 1883.

GEORGE P. FISHER,
Professor of Church History in Yale Divinity School.

"Luther emancipated himself from the legal and ascetic conception of religion. He attained to the freedom of the children of God. He came to look on this

6

world, not as an abode of gloom, a place of exile, but as a temporary residence of man, given by his Heavenly Father—a residence not wanting in beauty and attraction, though it be only the vestibule of a higher state of being. In his broad sympathy with man as a denizen of this world—sympathy with the avocations, the diversions, the social institutions, of this mundane existence, all of which are to be leavened by the spirit of religion—he showed that he had advanced beyond the point of view of the mediæval saint.

"The largeness of Luther's mind is evinced in the blending in him of the spirit of freedom and of faith. The Rationalist looks to Luther as to his intellectual father. He was a pioneer in the practical assertion of mental liberty. But along with this courage of intellect, there was a profound spiritual life, so that by the side of him, the Rationalist is seen to be but half a man.

"What is it in Luther that, after four hundred years are gone, stirs the heart of the Protestant nations? It is not any one quality by itself. It is not any single function that he exercised — as that of theologian, teacher, author, translator. It is the man behind all. It is the great heart and the great mind, united together. He had very conspicuous faults. But, after all, most of the assaults upon him are like blaming a pillar for being of the Doric order and not of the more graceful Corinthian style. Whoever visits Great Head on Mount Desert Island, does not look for a cliff of polished marble. He is satisfied with the massive crag which lifts itself on high, against whose rugged

side the angry waves have spent their strength in
vain."—*New York Critic*, Nov. 10, 1883.

Again, in an article on " Luther's 400th Birthday,"
he says :

" Had he done nothing more than to make his translation of the Scriptures, it might have been deemed
enough for one man to do. But this work, costing
though it did a great amount of toil and of thought,
was only a fraction of the labor which he performed.
His catechisms, his sermons, his printed comments on
portions of Scripture, his spirit-stirring hymns, his
controversial treatises and tracts, productions, all of
them, called out by the exigencies of the time, and
most effective for their ends, constitute a copious literature. Well does he deserve the exalted rank which
he holds among the leaders of men. No man ever
had reason to doubt his profound sincerity. No man
ever did seriously question his courage. His intellectual power has been fully conceded by the ablest of
his adversaries. The depth of his piety is evident to
all who study his writings and his conduct, with minds
free from sectarian prejudice."—*Congregationalist*, Nov.
8, 1883.

Again, on Luther's translation of the Bible:

"Of all Luther's gifts to the German people, his
translation of the Bible is, no doubt, the most valuable.
In nothing are the resources of his intellect and the
vigor of his character more manifest than in his ability, in the midst of literary warfare with a hundred
antagonists, to undertake most important works of a
positive character, involving a great amount of thought
and toil, for the upbuilding of the Church.

The translation of the Bible cost him a world of labor. He recognized the necessity of taking counsel in such work. Besides the regular help of Melanch-thon, Jonas, and his other coadjutors, he would discuss words and phrases at his own table, with his friends and guests who happened to be with him. Imbued himself with the vernacular of the people, he still did not neglect to inquire of common men, in cases where he was doubtful, as to the right term to be chosen, or as to the precise significance of a popular phrase. For he meant to make a translation which should come home to the understanding and heart of the common man. It should be a *German* Bible that he would give to the people. Not that he undervalued accuracy; he claimed that in cases where precision was necessary he had secured it, sparing no outlay of thought and inquiry to achieve this end.

"Still, he was determined to issue, not a colorless version, or a version enervated by idiomatic peculiarities of the Hebrew and Greek, or a pedantic version, intelligible and interesting only to the cultivated, but rather a translation which should make the Bible appear to have been written in German. He gives some amusing accounts of the struggle it cost him to make the sacred writers 'speak German.' In dealing with Job, especially, his patience was well nigh exhausted. No one could understand what it had cost him to make Job '*reden Deutsch*,' but he succeeded. In his version the apostles and prophets '*reden Deutsch*'—the Deutsch of the shop, the market and the hearth-stone.

"Luther's Bible is a living book. The juicy language of Luther's version, its sinewy vigor, its racy

idioms and the rythmical charms which it has in common with the authorized English version, are literary
merits which it is impossible to estimate too highly."
—*Century*, October, 1883.

VICTOR L. CONRAD,
Of the *Lutheran Observer.*

"There is not an interest or reform affecting human
welfare in modern civilization—whether educational,
social, industrial or political—upon which Luther did
not shed the light of his great intellect and soul, enlightened by the Word and Spirit of God. He taught
that it was the duty of the state to educate all the
children of the people, in order that they might become
intelligent and useful citizens; and thus he was the
pioneer advocate of universal education nearly four
hundred years ago. In quelling the outbreak of com-
munism in Germany, known as 'The Peasants' War,'
he declared it to be the duty of all to be subject to
'the powers that be,' and to acquire property, not by
the plunder and robbery of others, but by industry,
frugality and honesty. In an address to the princes
and nobles of Germany, he taught the reciprocal duties
of rulers to their subjects and of subjects to their
rulers, suggesting the fundamental principle that governments, though 'ordained of God,' 'derive their
just powers from the consent of the governed.'

"Thus the genius and inspiration of the Monk of
Wittenberg furnished the germ truths or principles of
all true reforms in church and state, in government
and society, that make up the Christian civilization of
the present day."—*Frank Leslie's Sunday Magazine*,
November, 1883.

WILBERFORCE NEVIN.

"Summoned by the Emperor to answer for his obduracy at the imperial council at Worms, the priest (Luther) in bold defiance of even his friends, set out and confronted secular and sacerdotal majesty in the form of the Emperor and the Pope. Paul before Agrippa, John before Herod, Joseph before Pharaoh, Daniel before Belshazzar, were supported by supernatural aid. But Luther, a man in all that is human, in heart and brain only above these conditions, confronted the packed Diet, and 'God helping' him, refuted bluntly and triumphantly the imposing paradoxes, whose only strength was in the blades of the empire and the militant church. We call men great, and set forth their puny doings in red-wrought eulogiums. We exhaust the vocabularies of praise to deify the sordid deeds of military captains; we celebrate events by long-continued ecstacies of national self-abandonment and popular delirium. But what are all of these that have passed during four hundred years compared to the courage, devotion and inspiration of this poor monk, arming himself by alms and rejecting the kingdoms of the princes of the world because he read aright—knew that he read aright—the mystical key to the Word that abides."—*Phila. Press*, Oct. 31, 1882.

CHARLES ADAMS.

"A great name is that of Luther—a name to be carried down the generations, and which will be conspicuous forever. Let us, out of multitudes, gather up a few precious sayings of this great name, that the young and the struggling, and the irresolute and the desponding, as well as the more sanguine and aspiring, may review them and catch inspiration as they meditate, and rally strength as they inwardly digest."— *Words that Shook the World.*

J. J. VON OOSTERZEE,
Reformed Church of Holland.

" Who would not gladly have seen and heard this preacher, with the true German head and the overflowing Christian heart, when he first appeared in a little chapel, which would accommodate hardly twenty persons, presently to become by his powerful word, for thirty years in succession, a source of blessing to millions ?"—*Practical Theology*, p. 117.

GEORGE SMEATON,
Free Church of Scotland.

" Luther's treatise in reply to Erasmus, bearing the title *De Servo Arbitrio*, undoubtedly one of the most powerful treatises ever written on the subject on which it treats, overthrows the open Pelagianism of Erasmus, who knew little of theology, and the semi-Pelagianism of men less extreme in their opinions than Erasmus. * * * Almost the only thing that one regrets about this noble production is not its vehemence, which was the natural utterance of the writer, nor the strong statements about man being under the power of Satan, nor the representation of the will as resembling the motionless inaction or immobility of a stock or stone; for these, though lamented by some, will not appear extravagant exaggerations to one enlightened as Luther was—but the title of the book."

MRS. ELIZABETH R. CHARLES.

" He brought over some of the best old hymns into the new worship, not word by word, in the ferry-boat of a literal translation, but entire and living, like Israel through the Jordan, when the priests' feet, bearing the ark, swept back the waters."—*Christian Life in Song*, p. 222.

EPHRAIM MILLER,
Lutheran pastor, Shrewsbury, Pa.

" No one possessed a kindlier nature than Luther. With all the craggy ruggedness of his character, with all the stormy elements of his spirit, his heart overflowed with the gentlest affections. He was one of the most brotherly of men. No man ever touched all humanity at a greater number of sides. So large-hearted was he that he had room for all the strong affections of humanity, and all the weak ones too. So many-sided was he, that nothing human failed to interest or attract him. So broad and deep and lively were his sympathies, that nothing good or strong, joyful or sorrowful, appealed to him in vain. If he was a man of strong intellect, he was a man of equally strong sensibility. If his courage and decision were so manly that he could not be moved by personal dangers, yet was his heart so womanly, that he was easily moved by the sorrows of others. If he cared little for his own misfortunes, yet his heart bled for the calamities of his country. So that if there was an assailable side in this many-sided man, it must be sought in the region of his emotional nature."

Speaking of the spirit that animated Luther in the Marburg Conference as none other than that of pure and conscientious Christian love, the author continues:

" If there were lightnings and thunderings and hail and fiery tempest in his speech, if his movements sometimes were the movements of the storm-cloud or the billowy tumult of the ocean, if he sometimes resembled the volcano pouring down streams of molten wrath, yet over them all was spread the warm sunshine of a fervid Christian love. And it was precisely that love that generated his stormiest discourse. Are not the wildest winds, as well as the gentlest zephyr, the cyclone and the evening breeze, alike the children of the sun? Is it not the sun that lets loose the lightnings? Is it not the sun that silently lifts the vapors of the sea upwards, and then pours them in torrents and floods and snows and hail over the land? Is it not the sun, the genial sun, that converts the quiet air into a desolating force, rending the abodes of man in its uncontrollable march? So it was the strength and fervor of Luther's love, that imparted such annihilating energy to his words, when he was dealing with those who maintained any of the many forms of error that set themselves up against the work of the Lord. It was the same love that led him to submit to the greatest hardships, and face the greatest dangers for the truth, and that impelled him to make his most deadly onslaught on the enemies of the truth. It was the same love that animated him with a calm heroism at the Diet of Worms, and that sustained him with a circumspect decision at Marburg. Without such love, Luther could never have been the Re-

6*

former that he was, never would the multitudes have followed him as they did, never could he have thrilled the heart of Europe as he did in his day, and as he has continued to thrill that heart through so many years even down to the present, when America joins Europe in commemorating the work of this man of God and man of the people, the man who loved the people, and whom in turn the people loved and delighted to honor."—*Lutheran Quarterly*, Jan. 1884, pp. 134, 144.

SCHAFF-HERZOG ENCYCLOPEDIA.

"Luther stands forth as the great national hero of the German people and the ideal of German life. Perhaps no other cultivated nation has a hero who so completely expresses the national ideal. King Arthur comes, perhaps, nearest to Luther amongst the English-speaking races. He was great in his private life as well as in his public career. His home is the ideal of cheerfulness and song. He was great in thought and great in action. He was a severe student, yet skilled in the knowledge of men. He was humble in the recollections of the designs and power of a personal Satan, yet bold and defiant, in the midst of all perils. He could beard the papacy and imperial Councils, yet he fell trustingly before the Cross. He was never weary, and there seemed to be no limit to his creative energy. Thus Luther stands before the German people as the type of German character. Gœthe, Frederick the Great, and all others in this regard, pale before the German Reformer. He embodies in his single person the boldness of the battle-field, the song

of the musician, the joy and care of the parent, the
skill of the writer, the force of the orator, and the sincerity of rugged manhood, with the humility of the
Christian.   *   *   *   'Ein' Feste Burg,' is
Luther in song. It is pitched in the very key of the
man. Rugged and majestic, trustful in God, and confident, it was the defiant trumpet-blast of the Reformation, speaking out to the powers in the earth and under
the earth, an all-conquering conviction of divine vocation and empowerment."—Vol. II. Conclusion of Article on Luther.

McCLINTOCK AND STRONG'S CYCLOPEDIA OF BIBLICAL, THEOLOGICAL AND ECCLESIASTICAL LITERATURE. (*Dr. C. P. Krauth.*)

" *The Character of Luther* lies so open in his life
that it is hardly necessary to trace its lines. He was
so ingenuous that, if all the world had conspired to
cover up his faults, his own hand would have uncovered them. His violence was that of a mighty nature,
strong in conviction, waging the battle of truth against
implacable foes. The expressions which jar upon the
refined ear of the modern world were natural in a
rough era, and from the lips of one who was too pure
to be prudish. The coarsenesses of the mendicant life
can hardly fail to leave their traces on any man who
has been subjected to them—the taint of a system in
which filthiness is next to godliness, or rather is a part
of it. The inconsistencies charged upon Luther's
thinking are those of a man of great intuitions, who
grows perpetually, and who will not stop for the hopeless and useless task of harmonizing with the crudities

of yesterday the ripeness of to-day. His widest diversities, after the sap of the Reformation began to swell in his veins, are like those of the tree which bends with mellow fruit of autumn, careless of consistency with its first buddings in the cold rains of March. That Luther was unselfish, earnest, honest, inflexibly brave in danger, full of tenderness and humanity, the ideal of Germanic strength and Germanic goodness; that he was one of the great creative spirits of the race, mighty in word and deed, matchless as a popular orator, one of the very people, yet a prince among princes, a child of faith, a child of God—this is admitted by all.

"There is scarcely another instance in history in which an individual, without secular authority or military achievement, has so stamped himself upon a people, and made himself to so great an extent the leader, the representative, the voice of the nation. He has been to Germany what Homer was to Greece. 'He was the only Protestant reformer,' says Bayard Taylor, 'whose heart was as large as his brain.' * * * His physical life was largely one of suffering. His habits were abstemious, and his enjoyments at the table were social, not epicurean. His voice was not loud nor strong. Melanchthon's happy phrase touching Luther's words is, that they were 'fulmina,' not 'tonitrua'—it was their lightning, not their thunder, by which their mighty effects were produced. The papal system, the upas of the ages, which they struck, is not dead, but it is riven and blasted from its crown to its root."—Vol. v., p. 569.

THE LIBRARY OF UNIVERSAL KNOWLEDGE.

"Luther's character presents an imposing combination of great qualities. Endowed with broad human sympathies, massive energy, manly and affectionate simplicity, and rich, if sometimes coarse humor, he is at the same time, a spiritual genius. His intuitions of divine truth were bold, vivid and penetrating, if not comprehensive; and he possessed the art which God alone gives to the finer and abler spirits that he calls to do special work in this world, of kindling other souls with the fire of his own convictions, and awakening them to a higher consciousness of religion and duty. He was a leader of men, therefore, and a reformer in the highest sense. His powers were fitted to his appointed task; it was a task of Titanic magnitude, and he was a Titan in intellectual robustness and moral strength and courage. It was only the divine energy which swayed him, and of which he recognized himself the organ, that could have accomplished what he did. Reckoned as a mere theologian, there are others who take higher rank. There is a lack of patient thoughtfulness and philosophical temper in his doctrinal discussions; but the absence of these very qualities gave wings to his bold, if sometimes crude conceptions, and enabled him to triumph in the struggle for life or death in which he was engaged. * * Upon the whole, it may be said that history presents few greater characters—few that excite at once more love and admiration, and in which we see tenderness, humor, and a certain picturesque grace and poetic sensibility more happily combine with a lofty and magnanimous, if sometimes rugged sublimity."—Art. " Luther," Vol. IX. p. 243; see also article " Bible.".

REES' ENCYCLOPEDIA.

" Luther introduced, not into Germany only, but into the world, a new and most important era; and his name can never be forgotten, while anything of principle remains that is deserving of remembrance."— American edition, Philadelphia, vol. xxii.

THE CYCLOPEDIA OF THE SOCIETY FOR THE DIFFUSION OF USEFUL KNOWLEDGE.

" Luther ranks high among German writers for the vigor of his style, and the development which he imparted to his vernacular language. Schrœck, Melanchthon, and others, have written biographies of Luther, and Michelet has extracted a kind of autobiography from his works. From these passages the character of Luther is clearly deduced, for there was no calculation, reserve or hypocrisy about him. He was frank and vehement, and often intemperate. But he was earnest in his vehemence; he really felt the importance of the topics he was discussing; and whether he was right or wrong in his peculiar opinions, he was a sincere and zealous believer in the Christian Revelation. Luther considered religion as the most important of man, and because he considered it as such, he wished to ascend to its very source, unalloyed by human authority. He contended for the right of every man to consult the great book of the Christian Law. The principles of free inquiry, which he introduced, led to further results, and gradually established that liberty of conscience which now exists in the Protestant States of Europe. But Luther, himself, whilst he appealed to the Scriptures against human authority, did not for a moment admit of any doubts concerning the truth of Revelation. * * * Those who judge of Luther's disposition merely from his controversial style and manner, greatly mistake his character. He was a warm-hearted German, kind and generous; he abused and vilified his antagonists the more in proportion as they were powerful; but he could feel for the unhappy, and he even tendered some consolation to his bitterest enemy, Tetzel, when, forsaken by his employers and upbraided as the cause of all the mischief, he was in the agonies of death and despair. Luther gave that impulse towards spiritual philosophy, that thirst for information, that logical exercise of the mind, which have made the Germans the most generally instructed and the most intellectual people in Europe. Luther was convinced of the necessity of education, as auxiliary to religion and morality; and he pleaded unceasingly for the education of the laboring classes, broadly telling princes and rulers how dangerous, as well as unjust, it was to keep their subjects in ignorance and degradation. He was no courtly flatterer; he spoke in favor of the poor, the humble and the oppressed, and against the high and mighty, even of his own party, who were guilty of cupidity and oppression. Luther's doctrine was altogether in favor of civil liberty, and in Germany it tended to support constitutional rights against the encroachments of the imperial power. Luther's moral courage, his undaunted firmness, his strong conviction,

and the great revolution which he effected in society, place him in the first rank of historical characters. The form of the monk of Wittenberg, emerging from the receding gloom of the Middle Ages, appears towering above the sovereigns and warriors, statesmen and divines, of the sixteenth century, who were his contemporaries, his antagonists, or his disciples."
—Vol. xiii.,pp. 206, 207.   (London, 1839).

ENCYCLOPEDIA BRITANNICA.

" Nothing can be more edifying than the scene presented by the last days of Luther, of which we have the most authentic accounts. When dying he collected his last strength, and offered up the following prayer: ' Heavenly Father, eternal, merciful God, thou hast revealed to me Thy dear Son, our Lord Jesus Christ. Him I have taught, Him I have confessed, Him I love as my Saviour and Redeemer, whom the wicked persecute, dishonor, and reprove. Take my poor soul up to Thee.' Then two of his friends put to him the solemn question: ' Reverend Father, do you die in Christ and in the doctrine you have constantly preached ?' He answered by an audible and joyful ' Yes;' and repeating the verse: " Father, into Thy hands I commend my spirit,' he expired peacefully."—Vol. xv., p. 84.

PART II.

WHAT THE RELIGIOUS PRESS HAS EDITORIALLY SAID OF LUTHER THIS MEMORIAL YEAR.

LUTHER AT THE WARTBURG.

Inscribed to the Printing Press in this 400th Year of the Reformer's Birth.

BY JOEL SWARTZ, D. D.

At Wartburg still the ink they show
  Which Luther at the Devil threw.
In these last days we've learned to know
  He fought more wisely than he knew.

For this far more than flaming tongue
  Filled popes and devils with affright:
The inkstand by the printer flung
  Has put the Prince of hell to flight.

Now silent lies great Luther's tongue,
  And palsied is the hero's hand;
But that black thunder-bolt it flung
  Still rolls and smites from land to land.

The martyr's stake and prison cell,
  The tyrant's yoke and scourger's rod,
And other enginery of hell,
  It smites as with the wrath of God.

E'en where consenting captives lay
  In Superstition's ghostly halls,
This bolt has thrown the light of day
  Between the thunder-riven walls.

With Argus eyes, Briarean hands,
  And myriad tongues to curse or bless,
There walks the earth's enlightened lands
  One king of all—the PRINTING-PRESS.

His royal form is wrought of steel ;
  His spirit is the steam's hot breath ;
Before him Power and Genius kneel ;
  His smile is life. his frown is death.

(139)

The harnessed lightnings are his steeds;
  His hands are on the curbing wires;
Each courser every whisper heeds,
  And checks or loosens all his fires.

His hand is on the telephone;
  The light electric burns his path ·
He speaks his thought from zone to zone
  In tones of love or peals of wrath.

If sometimes with a backward fling
  He smites when he should help instead,
Yet mainly aims this noblest king
  His inkstand at the Devil's head.

His Wartburgs crown a million hills;
  The walls are all of paper made ;
His ink, which countless measures fills,
  Is on these walls most deftly laid.

And whether by his hot breath blown,
  Or seized with all his hundred hands,
The whole around the world is thrown,
  To bless and brighten all its lands.

King of the inky sceptre, hail!
  We own thy sway, court thy control;
Thy power shall more and more prevail
  Until it spread from pole to pole !

EDITORS' TRIBUTES.

THE NEW YORK INDEPENDENT,
Rev. W. H. Ward, D. D., Editor, in its issue of November 8.

"Throughout this month the churches and countries of Protestant Christendom celebrate the completion of the fourth century since the birth of Martin Luther. It would be easy to say much about that grand, masterful, passionate, simple, heroic reformer; but it is not necessary. Christendom is his monument; for Christendom is now predominantly Protestant. It has accepted his interpretation of Christianity. The Roman Church, which, when Luther climbed the sacred stairway on his knees, was imperial and imperious, has lost its supremacy never to regain it. The mighty independence of private judgment and personal conscience, asserted against all dictation of Pope or Council, cannot but make manhood such as must rule. A man has a bigger will-force when he thinks out for himself what is right than when he depends on somebody else to decide for him what is right. History has passed its verdict on Luther's theses; and that irreversible verdict is giving the world to the aggressive, liberty-loving Protestantism of Luther, which depends on nothing less and submits to nothing less than God and his word. Protestant Christendom is his monument, with its vigor, earnestness and faith.

(141)

Roman Catholic Christendom is his monument, with its decay, impotence and unbelief.

"Luther was not a perfect man; certainly he was not a man of gentle speech. But what of that? He had rough work to do, and a great deal of it. So he went about swinging an iron flail, fighting with a giant's strength and some of a giant's rudeness. But who dares rebuke him? Certainly not those who remember what was Tetzel, and what the court of Leo X. If he had a voice of thunder, it was raised against corruption and oppression. He had a very gentle voice and a very tender German heart for his own home, and for those who were seeking for the truth.

"Not least ought our Roman Catholic friends, if they cannot join in this celebration of Luther's memory, to give it the tribute of respectful silence. The Catholic Church is a vastly better Church than it was when Luther was thundering against it; all intelligent Catholics know that. And they cannot fail to see that Luther's moral nerve is in a great measure the cause. The Catholic Church has not disdained to learn something from its enemy. Nowhere is that Church so worthy of respect as where Luther's influence has been most felt. So let us all, with uncovered heads, pass before the monument of the man who led Europe out of the darkness of the Middle Ages into the civilization of modern times. He was greater than poets or emperors, as religion is higher than literature or government. His monument—it is all about us; it is in us."

THE NEW YORK OBSERVER,

Rev. S. Ireneus Prime, D. D., editor, in its issue of Nov. 1.

" Luther rises before us out of the dark and level of his times like some great mountain, sky-piercing and rock-ribbed, yet whose slopes are clad with woods and grain fields and orchards, fed with rushing streams and bright cascades from invisible heights; with a background of radiant and prophetic sunrises and sunsets; reposing normally in peaceful and tender light, but capable of clothing itself in passing shadows, thick and stormy vapor, and terrific thunder-clouds; perhaps developing volcanic fires, for the relief of a laboring earth and the destruction of polluted Pompeiis and Herculaneums. Says Richter: ' Luther stood in the midst of the electric tempests which he had enkindled, and for us cleared and unfolded them into pure air.'

*   *   *   *   *   *   *   *   *

" It was not as a man of men—one of a thousand—that he succeeded, but as a man of God. He says himself: ' Obedience, and keeping to the articles of war—this is victory.' His was the obedience of faith. And ' this is the victory that overcometh the world, even your faith.' By faith the walls of Rome fell down, as well as the walls of Jericho. Luther's ram's-horn could not have done it, nor even the Ark which the Reformers bore with them. Theirs was the faith which is simply the electric response of the human to the divine heart and mind and will. They were mighty through God to the pulling down of strongholds, because they were men of God. *   *   *

" In this also consisted Luther's assertion of manhood for men. It is a shallow error to claim him as the champion of the mere Liberty, an unqualified and universal 'natural right' to independence. This destructive and nihilistic temper is the child of Lucifer, and not of Him who is the Light of the World. It was not the spirit or dream of Luther, any more than of the Puritan and the Netherlander and the Huguenot, and all who have built up the towers and bulwarks of modern freedom and civilization. There will be a great effort this year to claim Luther as the champion of an unconditional and even atheistic liberty. Let it not be lost sight of that Lutherism stands for *Freedom in the Truth*, not *from* it. His nature, like that of all genuine and beneficent radicalism, was essentially and intensely conservative. He was the slave of truth, of the light as he saw it. He was altogether heliotropic. Put him anywhere—in the law school, in the convent, in Rome, in Wartburg, at Wittenberg, at Worms, at Spires, at Augsburg, and not less in dealing with anarchic revolts of peasant and noble—he always set his firm and eager face toward the light, and could not be turned aside by fear or favor. To him truth meant 'as the truth is in Jesus.' And in him was fulfilled the promise, 'The truth shall make you free,' as interpreted by the parallel declaration from the same divine lips: 'If the Son shall make you free, ye shall be free indeed.'

"And this it was that made him free from all beside —from self-seeking, from the fear of man, from flattery, from bribes, from care for worldly preferment, from counting his life dear to himself. And this deadness to the world, in its turn, made him life to the world, new life to the church. His freedom from everything but the truth gave him the freedom of that Kingdom of Truth, which Christ came to establish on earth. As we look back, he is as one standing erect and kingly in a den of chained and cowering lions; or as one walking amid a burning, fiery furnace, seven times heated, and beside him One like unto the Son of God."

THE CHRISTIAN INTELLIGENCER,

Revs. John M. Ferris, D. D., and N. H. Van Arsdale, Editors.

"Martin Luther was God's man; selected and prepared by him for the work which was to be accomplished. He was chosen and endowed, protected, sustained and prospered, as were Moses, Samuel, David, Isaiah, Peter, John and Paul. A fulness of time had come, and he was called out to introduce a new era. The night was far spent, and he was appointed by the King to herald the coming of a new day—a day of light, of triumph, and of joy.

"Certain characteristics of this man may be profitably considered now, when the attention of the world is turned upon the Reformer. Is it providential that men have been moved to celebrate the birth-day of the man after four centuries have passed away? It has not been the custom of the Church to observe the anniversary of his birth. Why now? What has occurred to give this present prominence to the great Protestant? Does any such event occur that is not providential? Surely, there are lessons to be learned from the character and life of Luther that will prepare the Church for greater devotion and efficiency. It is possible and probable that there are characteristics in

7

this apostle that the Church of this day needs to consider, to desire and obtain.   What was he?

"He was heroic, confident, aggressive.   His boldness held his enemies in check.   His courage arrested and unnerved the arm raised to smite him.   His heroism won admiration and confidence, and led men to follow him.   The foundation of his courage was faith in God, faith in the Word of God as the supreme, infallible truth.   Rome was mighty, had her hand on the thrones of Europe.   Kings and princes served the Papacy because they feared it.   Rome had armies, money, learning; had possession of the social, political, commercial life of Europe.   She ruled in the courts, in the universities, on the exchange, in the shop, and in the homes of men.   Other men had challenged her and been destroyed.   Excommunication meant no trade, no social intercourse, no friendly offices; meant poverty, starvation, and death.   To stand up before, to defy, to assail such a power, demanded a courage such as the world has seldom seen. Luther nailing his theses to the church door is the incarnation of moral courage.   Luther going alone to Worms is the perfection of heroism, is a spectacle unsurpassed in the world's history.   *   *   *

" God's man was aggressive.   He made the attack, did not wait to be attacked.   He smote the iniquity about him, laid hold upon it, exposed it, condemned it in the name of God, gave it no rest, and did not wait for it to smite him.   His warfare was not defensive, but aggressive.   He invaded the enemy's country and subdued it.   Has not the Church need to-day of this spirit?   Are not many waiting for favorable opportunities, for providential indications, so called, for invitations from the perishing, for iniquity and falsehood to bear such fruit that men shall cry out and plead for relief? Is not the world ripe for a bold, energetic, enthusiastic assault upon delusions and superstitions and worldliness, and all the forms of sin.

"Luther was not only confident, heroic, aggressive; he was also joyous. God's man was a singing man. God selected as the herald of the new bright day a man who delighted in song, whose joyous spirit expressed itself in song. He was happy, glad, exultant. Why not? He was God's son, justified by faith, at peace with God, an heir of God, doing God's work in confident reliance on God's promises, and doing it with God's supreme, infallible truth. Why should he not be exultant, full of praise? Why should he not go singing on his way! Why did God select a singing man to overturn the thrones of error and sin, and bring in the best, the freest, the purest, the brightest, the happiest period of the world's history? Was it not because it was such a period? It was a period to be welcomed and introduced with song.

"Ought not the Church of to-day to be an exultant, happy, joyous Church, filling the air with songs of praise and triumph? What wonderful results have followed the Reformation! What a new world this world of ours has become! How have men been divinely endowed in the fulfilment of the exceeding great and precious promises! What poets, what historians, what statesmen, what merchants, what a host of noble men and women, has the Church of the Reformation had through these four hundred years! What a host it has now! What a mighty change has been wrought! How dark the world was when the cheerful, joyous, full-toned, confident and exulting voice of Luther was first heard proclaiming liberty and life and everlasting joy! How light the world is now! What a change has been wrought in governments, in education, in social life, in the comforts and conveniences of life, in charities, in provision for the sick and poor and unfortunate! How the truth has spread, what conquests it has won, what countless thousands have been enlightened, purified, cheered, saved by it! How much better the world is than it was four hundred years ago! Ought not the Church to go about its work as Luther did, singing, joyous, rejoicing, exultant, hopeful, praising God and filling the earth with thanksgiving! Why not?"

THE CHRISTIAN UNION,

Rev. Lyman Abbott D. D., Editor, in its issue of Nov. 8.

"Providence always has some great and masterful soul made and developed to meet and master every great emergency. As often as society prepares its molds, God fills them; pours himself into them in a divine fullness that brings to pass an epoch of history. It was pre-eminently so with Martin Luther. He was the upheaval of the thought and life of his century; ay, of the thought and life of the preceding centuries. He was the child of terrific struggle and conflict—the one mighty mind which was the 'whispering gallery' of the still, small voices of enslaved spirits, and which spoke for freedom, million-tongued, in tones that thundered round the world and down the ages. 'His mind was made convex, to receive the scattered rays of God's sun which had fallen into the souls of men during fifteen centuries; and in him they were 'focused' and made to blaze and burn so as to set the moral and spiritual heavens aflame with a new life and a new hope for humankind. He found his age ' *de-*formed,' and set himself to the task of its reformation.

"To understand and estimate Luther as a reformer, as a mighty spiritual force for all time, we need to note the twofold direction and power of the work that was wrought—his own spiritual transformation, and the transformation that was wrought through him upon society.

"Look at him in his personal struggle for freedom and peace of conscience.   *   *   *   *   Find his God he would: if not in the school, then in the monastery; if not in the monastery, then at Rome; if not at Rome, then in the depths of his own conscious nature, enlightened by the Word of God and quickened by the Divine Spirit. He fell into the most depressed state of mind. He cried 'Mary, help!' It was not any peculiar transgression, nor youthful excess, that filled him with 'dread of the wrath of God,' it was his own nature struggling like an imprisoned giant to be free. The church, the sacraments, the austerities, the fastings—Rome, with all her equipments—could give him no relief. As if God would concentrate in one soul the spiritual yearnings of the race, He took this man to St. Peter's in Rome, and while he was climbing the holy staircase on devout knees He put the spirit of the old Apostle into him, which broke forth in the speech of divine liberty:

'The just shall live by faith.' After the long and dark night, the light broke forth. He stood before God emancipated by faith. He came into the glorious liberty of a child of God. Gathering up all his energies, like a Domingo, he tore off the toils that the Papacy had wound round him, and declared that a 'Christian man is a free master over all things, and subject to no one.' The new, inner, spiritual man bounded upon the plane where he had communion with God. 'God,' he declares, 'will not and cannot permit any one to rule over the soul but himself alone.' 'By means of faith he ascended far above himself into the divine.'

"When Luther had fought this great spiritual battle for himself, he was prepared to stand up, in the might of the old Apostle to the Gentiles, and demand freedom of conscience for all men. He then had that divine authority in his own reason which enabled him to say to the hierarchs of the imperial Diet at Worms: 'If I had a thousand heads I would allow them all to be cut off rather than recant a single word.' He dared to say to prelates and kings, 'Councils have often erred,' and 'to act against conscience is unsafe and dangerous.' There is nothing in history grander than this; and there is nothing that is simpler or more natural to such an experience as Luther's. With God enthroned in the conscience, what are men, or armies, or kings, or popes? What terror is there in prisons, and fagots, and the cross? When he had refused to have his own manhood crushed, he dared to say, and he had the authority to say, to the proud, corrupt, and enslaving Church of Rome, 'You shall not crush the manhood out of my fellow-men'—to say it with an authority that tore from the Papal Church one-half of her communicants.

"Luther stands before us as the exponent of true Reformation."

THE NATIONAL BAPTIST,
Of Philadelphia, Pa., Nov. 22.

"As we review the commemoration of the fourth centennial of Luther's birth, we find a good many impressions left with us as the lessons of the event. For one thing, we realize deeply the might and endurance of spiritual forces. Here is this man, Martin Luther, who held no office, who was poor, who according to the prevailing standards of human greatness was a very humble man; and yet, because he represented spiritual truths and forces, his name awakens unbounded enthusiasm; millions have risen to do him honor; crowned heads, as well as the masses, have been moved to joyful tears at the return of his birthday. Who cares for the birth-day of Charles V., who in his day ruled nearly all the continent of Europe, wielding a power not paralleled till the days of Napoleon? Who of their contemporaries would have dreamed that the poor obscure son of a miner, the simple monk, would in the coming centuries so overshadow the Emperor that the two would hardly be named together? How much real enthusiasm could be aroused over the birth-day of Columbus, of Michael Angelo, of Thomas Aquinas, of Bacon? But this man wielded spiritual forces, and spoke to the hearts of men, and hence his enduring sway.

"And not less to be remembered is the illustration of our Lord's saying, ' He that loseth his life shall find it.' In an age when position, honor, earthly greatness, were bestowed by the Church, this man broke with the Church. He might, no doubt, have been a Bishop, an Archbishop, perhaps a Cardinal, or what not. But when he was so rash as to confront and oppose the Pope, men must have felt that he was throwing away all his chances; he was dooming himself to obscurity. And yet, by that very act, he has secured such lasting fame, such immortality of glory, as no other man of his century gained. The Augustine monk towers aloft above prelates and popes, like an obelisk in the level desert.

"And as we consider the past and the present of Protestantism, we realize something of the falseness and the foolishness of the talk about the Decline of Protestantism. Four centuries ago, Protestanism had not an existence as an organized power. To-day, it leads the world. The intelligence, the wealth, the force of arms, the morality, the civilization, is with the Protestant nations.

"If we reckon the population of the Protestant nations, including Great Britain, America, Germany, Scandinavia, Switzerland, Holland, Australia, East ' and West Indies, and the British colonies, it is quite within bounds to say that the Protestants number not less than 150,000,000. If the line should be drawn, and the Protestant nations should be ranged against the Catholics, we believe that the Protestant nations could buy the Catholic nations out twice over, could beat them in war, could outdo them in argument, could show a superiority on any field that might be assigned. If this is the failure and decline of Protestantism, then we can only say that a few more centuries of such decline and failure will leave Protestantism the unquestioned ruler of the world, and Romanism only a name in history.

"The Protestant nations are the only colonizing nations. With Protestantism goes liberty of speech, of the press, of thought, of worship, an open Bible, the morals of the New Testament. We are not aware of any really first-class nation which is Romanist, for France is far from Romanist. And the Protestant nations are growing more Protestant each day; the essential Protestant principles are becoming more dominant. On the other hand, the Romanist nations are, for the most part, becoming less Romanist; Austria, Italy, are not Romanist as they once were.

"The story of Luther reminds us that often, in order to a true reform, one must go outside the body which is to be reformed. It was by breaking away from Rome, that Luther so emancipated himself as to inaugurate a reform which has immeasurably benefited Rome itself. It was by going out of the Anglican Church that Wesley awoke that church from its deep slumber, and made it a living church.

"Of course, there are plenty of small men to look back on a movement and belittle the greatness needed to produce it. It would not be very hard to-day for any of us to nail 95 theses, or 195, on a church door, if the sexton did not object. It would not be difficult to-day to burn a bull of the pope. It is the old story of Columbus' egg over again.

7*

"We fully believe that the fourth centennial has been a blessing, recalling the memory of one of the noblest characters in history, and making Protestantism once more conscious of its powers and of its history. We believe that the next centennial of Luther will find his name and his principles more honored and more dominant than ever."

THE CHRISTIAN ADVOCATE. N. Y.,

Rev. J. M. Buckley, D. D., Editor, in its issue of Nov. 15.

"His genius was phenomenal; a p et, a linguist, a musician, a philosopher, a historian. He was one of the fathers of historic ecclesiastical criticism. In industry he was a prodigy; his translation of the Bible would have been enough for a life-time. In courage he was unsurpassed. To find parallels of Luther before the Legate, the Emperor, and the Diet, we must go back to Paul before Felix and Agrippa. Elijah, Paul, and Luther, make a trinity of similar moral heroes. Luther's eloquence at times was of the ighest order, his zeal equaled that of Peter; and he was a statesman as well as a theologian. In the work of the Reformation he was led on from step to step, and wonderfully protected by Divine Providence.

"By no means perfect, he was a great and good man, a 'chosen vessel' for the work he accomplished, as really as David was when Samuel called him. His end was peace. January, 1546, he went to Eisleben on a work of reconciliation, preached four times in bad weather, caught cold, and died February 18. When dying he prayed thus: 'Heavenly Father—eternal, merciful God—thou hast revealed to me thy dear Son, our Lord Jesus Christ. Him have I taught. Him have I confessed. Him I love as my Saviour and Redeemer, whom the wicked persecute, dishonor, and reprove. Take my poor soul up to thee.'

"The Romanists are much disturbed at the honors now paid him. Some of their papers call him a lunatic, a blasphemer, a wretch. Since Luther fought the battle of civil and religious liberty for us and all men, we have no disposition to do more than give them this passage from John Bunyan; whom also, doubtless, they consider to be a wretch, a blasphemer, and a lunatic.

"'Now I saw in my dream that at the end of this valley lay blood, bones, ashes, and mangled bodies of men, even of pilgrims that had gone this way formerly; and while I was musing what should be the reason, I espied a little before me a cave, where two giants, Pope and Pagan, dwelt in old time; by whose power and tyranny the men whose bones, blood, ashes, etc., lay there, were cruelly put to death. But by this place Christian went without much danger, whereat I somewhat wondered; but I have learned since, that Pagan has been dead many a day; and as for the other, though he be yet alive, he is, by reason of age, and also of the many shrewd brushes that he met with in his younger days, grown so crazy and stiff in his joints that he can now do little more than sit in his cave's mouth, grinning at the pilgrims as they go by, and biting his nails because he cannot come at them.

"'So I saw that Christian went on his way; yet, at the sight of the old man that sat in the mouth of the cave, he could not tell what to think, especially because he spake to him, though he could not go after him, saying, "You will never mend till more of you be burned." But he held his peace, and set a good face on it, and so went by and catched no hurt.'

"Not one in the long catalogue of their popes, nor any man since St. Paul, ever exerted as great a moral and intellectual force as Luther; and so long as the world stands, the principles for which he contended will be maintained."

LUTHERAN STANDARD,

Edited by the Faculty of Capital University, Columbus, Ohio,
November 10, 1883.

"Luther was a man that well deserves to be called great. Some men are called so without sufficient reason; but he was truly great in intellect, in heart, and in deed. His mental endowments were extraordinary, and he used them well in the acquirement of knowledge. He was genial and generous and true-hearted. His labors for the welfare of man were many and valuable. As instances may be mentioned his noble translation of the Bible into the German, and the preparation of his incomparable Catechisms. His literary labors were such as to secure for him a high place among the greatest authors. But that which renders him conspicuous above all other men, was his work of restoring the Gospel to men and thus reforming the Church. To this all his labors tended, in this they all concentrated. He was the great Reformer, and we who enjoy the fruits of his reformatory work thank God for the great gift of this truly great man—all the more great because so unconscious of his greatness."

November 24th it says:

" How little is to be found against the great Reformer, Dr. Martin Luther, is evinced by the great
efforts and small success of the Romanists to find
something in history that would prove damaging to
his noble character. A man so frank and honest
might be expected to say and do things which ill-will
would use for his disparagement; but that the most
pronounced hatred of the man can find so little with
which to reproach him, must tend to raise him still
higher in the esteem of right-thinking men. Romanists
hurl vile epithets at him, it is true; but when they try
to furnish any ground for their abuse they must resort
to such silly proofs as that he once spoke reverently
of the pope, and therefore was inconsistent when he
afterwards made attacks upon him, and that he once
took upon himself monastic vows and subsequently
spoke with contempt of the whole business of monkery, wherefore he must have been a bad man. Why,
it is true that Luther was once a papist as benighted
as any other subject of the papal power, and that by
the grace of God he was led to the glorious light of
the Gospel, and ceased to be a papist. Romanists
seem to forget that if he had remained a devotee of
the pope he never would have been the great Reformer
whose praise all the world is singing."

THE NEW YORK EVANGELIST,
Henry M. Field, editor,

Notices the 400th anniversary of Luther's birth in the
following abridged editorial of its issue of November
8, 1883:

"On the tenth of November we celebrate the four hundredth anniversary of the birth of Martin Luther, the man raised up by the divine hand to be the master spirit of the modern world.   Athanasius, Augustine and Luther, are the names which stand out before all others in Christian history, to mark the epochs of its advancement since the apostolic age.   The Reformation burst forth at the same time in independent movements in England, France and Switzerland, as well as in Germany, yet they were all influenced and determined to a great degree by the mightier movement which sprang from Luther, and were shaped by his masterly influence.

*   *   *   *   *   *   *   *   *

"The Church had assumed the place of God, and presumed to control men in faith, worship, and conduct.   Luther broke through the obstructing Church to find God.   He forced his way through the masses of traditional dogma and ecclesiastical institutions and ranks of authoritative priests, and gained the presence of his Saviour, and learned from God himself the rule of faith, of worship, and of conduct.   This was the Reformation at its core.

" It is the unique position of Luther that he was made the providential specimen and miniature of the entire reform.   He fought the Reformation through in his own self before he fought it out as the chieftain of the nations.   Luther was born of sturdy German peasants.   He was honest and brave from the cradle to the grave.   The battle of the law with sin was waged in his inner man.   A second Paul in self-discipline, he learned the vanity of human righteousness, and was constrained to cast himself without reserve on the mercy of God. His apprehension of the divine grace of forgiveness was life from the dead. A vital principle from God took possession of him and mastered him. It was the principle that made him the master of the Reformation when the supreme hour arrived."

THE ILLUSTRATED CHRISTIAN WEEKLY,

Published by the American Tract Society, under the editorial management of Rev. O. A. Kingsbury, in its issue of Nov. 10.

"Two things, we think, stand out with especial prominence in the history of the great Reformer—the man; the truth which he preached.

"There was the man. Luther's was a grand personality. As Dorner says of him: 'He is one of those great historical figures in which whole nations recognize their own type.' And as the Roman Catholic, Döllinger, says of him: 'It was Luther's overpowering greatness of mind and marvelous many-sidedness which made him to be the man of his time and of his people.' We naturally associate the work that was done in striking off the bonds of the Papacy with the man Luther. He rises preëminent among the men of his time as a great character. It was, most certainly, the truth which he proclaimed which broke shackles and brought in spiritual liberty. But in the good ordering of the divine Providence there was a man behind the truth, a man whose whole being was possessed by the truth. Men saw the truth, as it were, incarnate in one of their fellows. They felt the power of the rugged nature of the man. Dr. Martin was no carpet-knight. He was a warrior whose blade fell with grim

and terrible earnestness at every stroke.   Granted that
he was vehement and rough and uncouth.   It needed
a man whose nature was composed of the elemental
powers to awake a slumbering nation and make spiritual freemen out of the slaves of superstition.   The
zephyr is very pleasant, but there is need sometimes
of the tempest to clear the atmosphere of murky
miasms.

"There was this tremendous personality in Luther,
because in part of natural endowment, and also because
of his deep experience of the truth that saves.   God
raises up such servants as He needs for His special
work.   As has been well said, ' Men do not make times,
any more than times make men; but there is a soil in
the ages, continually husbanded by divine Providence,
from which grow in their seasons the progressive
harvests of humanity.'   The man, Luther, in his rugged
and strong nature, was of God's providential making.
Then upon this nature was superinduced the power of
the truth *experienced*.   He had felt the sting and tor-
ment of sin.   Church, pope, ceremonies, penances, had
brought no relief.   But faith had brought the sense
and assurance of pardon.   Henceforth this naturally
strong nature was clothed with the 'power of an end-
less life.'   He was a man on fire with the love of
Christ.   But it was a *man* who was nailing up theses
against indulgences, and burning pope's bulls, and de-
fying cardinals and councils, and translating the Scriptures, and preaching and writing and teaching; and the
man moved with tremendous weight.

"This man had a message—'The just shall live by
faith.'   It had brought peace to his own soul.   It fired

his zeal, it nerved his arm, it sustained his courage. This truth, brought into prominence, broke fetters and set souls free. It was the truth that men needed. The church had wandered from it. Superstitions had overlaid it. In the rubbish that the hierarchy had for long ages been piling upon it, it had become hidden out of sight. Brought once again into view, it showed men the way to God, each for himself. It was the divinely-revealed truth that the way of salvation is not through sacraments or orders or priests; that however helpful these may be when rightly used, they are simply impertinent when they stand in the place of simple individual trust in Jesus Christ.   *   *   *"

THE EVANGELICAL MESSENGER,

Cleveland, Ohio, chief organ of the Evangelical Association, in its issue of November 13.

"Martin Luther was a mighty man of faith, worthy to be enrolled among the ancient heroes on the shining muster-roll of the eleventh chapter of Hebrews. He, too, 'through faith subdued kingdoms, wrought right-eousness, obtained promises, stopped the mouths of lions, quenched the violence of fire, escaped the edge of the sword, out of weakness was made strong, waxed valiant in fight, and turned to flight the armies of the aliens.' He went through Gethsemane agonies up to his sublime victories. He fought and conquered on his knees. On one occasion, in the darkest period of the Reformation, after a season of supplication in his closet, Luther came out into the presence of his family, with shining face and uplifted eyes, exclaiming, 'We have overcome! We have overcome!' It was God's answer to the soul of the suppliant—the prophecy and token of the great victory to come out of the long struggles of the ages in the noon-day of the nineteenth century.

"At this distance of nearly four hundred years from that supreme and awful crisis of Luther's life at the Diet of Worms, we are still permitted to hear the echoes of that wonderful prayer, through whose travail of anguish the great Reformer climbed up, on his knees, to the sublime, serene height of one of the grandest moral triumphs of human history. It was one of the darkest hours of his life. God's face seemed for the moment to be veiled: his faith was under an awful strain; his soul was tossed to and fro like a ship in a furious storm; and 'he threw himself with his face upon the earth, and uttered those broken cries which we cannot understand, without entering in thought into the anguish of those deeps from whence they rose to God.'

*   *   *   *   *   *   *   *   *

"In that thrilling scene, in the city of Worms, on the 18th of April, 1521, and in the immeasurable results of the accomplished Reformation in all lands, behold God's answer to Martin Luther's prayer! * * He gave himself to God in loyal devotion, and God used him. He was a pen, a trumpet, a light, a sword, in the hand of the Lord. The glory of his character and deeds belongs to God, and the fruits belong to us and our children. To God we will be thankful for his gift to the world and to us, for 'all things are ours; whether Paul, or Apollos, or Cephas, or Luther, or the world, or life, or death, or things present, or thi ngs

to come; all are ours, and we are Christ's and Christ
is God's.' "

THE RELIGIOUS TELESCOPE,

Of Dayton, Ohio, main organ of the Church of United Brethren in
Christ, J. W. Hott, Editor.

" Martin Luther belongs to all ages. His spirit and
thought and life projected into the following centuries.
Luther honored manhood when breaking away from
the dogma of the papacy. He laid aside the monastic
dress in 1524, and in 1525 married Catharine von
Bora. Ten months a prisoner at Wartburg, he left
the prison in March, 1522, and soon issued his translation of the New Testament. Twelve years later the
Old Testament, translated into the German language,
was given to the world. The beauty and forcefulness
of the language in Luther's German Bible almost made
the German language. His literary labors, as well as
his public preaching, were of a most important character—hundreds of works issued from his pen, many
of them small, to be sure, but adapted to the times and
necessities of the Reformation.

" To Luther the Christian world owes more than to
any man who has lived since the days of the Apostle
Paul. He belongs to all churches, and the fruit of his
toil to the ages. He is the father of Protestantism,
the Nestor of free thought, and the uplifted hand
which holds an open Bible before the gaze of the
world.

" The celebration of the four hundredth anniversary
of the birth of Martin Luther ought result in great
good. He was not perfect, but his virtues and char-

acter, rising above the horizon of his times so full-orbed, presents a scene which we all need a thousand times to gaze upon.

"We need a revival of the spirit of Luther. His supreme devotion to the word of God is an example to be followed in our times. His heroism and courage are great needs of this day. Luther does not need to live over again. So profound, so undisguised, so transparent, so fired with enthusiasm, *en theos*, God in him, that his life flows down through all Christendom. He belongs to the nineteenth century as certainly as he did to the sixteenth.

"We hope our preachers will take advantage of this occasion to discourse upon the character and fruits of the Reformation. A better appreciation of the blessings of our day, and a feeling and act of fuller consecration to Christ, should be the results of such meditation. No one of us should have been what we are had there not lived, and thought, and suffered, and written, and preached the Saxon monk, Martin Luther."

THE CHRISTIAN AT WORK.

"The voice of Christendom pronounces the name of Martin Luther to-day, not only with admiration, but with the profoundest feelings that can stir the human heart. The significance of his name, however, and of the innumerable celebrations held in honor of the four hundredth anniversary of his birth, lies in the fact that he represented more than any other one man the principles of the great Reformation of the sixteenth century. In what did this mighty upheaval of human thought consist? It was more than a Revival of Letters, although this revival was one of its powerful aids.   *   *   *   *   *   *   *

"Again, the Reformation was something more than the result of the invention of Printing. True, the quickening influences of the Press—one of the mightiest of agencies—just then burst upon the world.

  *   *   *   *   *   *   *   *

"Nor is the Reformation to be identified with the astounding development at this time of the vernacular tongues of Europe.   *   *   *   *   *

"Once more: Let no ardent lover of liberty claim that the Reformation was the offspring of the free cities, and struggles for national independence that then asserted their ability to regenerate and ennoble the human race.   *   *   *   *   *   *

"What, then, was the Reformation? It was the free proclamation of the Gospel, the glad tidings of Jesus Christ as the only balm for the sin-sick soul. The supreme source of the Reformation was the discovery and circulation of the Bible as the only infallible guide in doctrine and practice. The papacy had built its huge foundations on tradition, on the authority of councils and on the sole word of the pope as the Vicar of Christ and only irresistible aid of God among men. The battle shout of the Reformation was, Down with the pope; up with the Bible! In the words of Chillingworth, 'The Bible, I say, the Bible is the only religion of Protestants!' Exactly. The Reformers received the name of Protestants after the diet of Spires in 1529, because under the influence of this Book of Life they protested against the imperial decree, which

would have closed the Bible and destroyed freedom of
worship. They had been protesting all along against
the authority of the pope as infallible; against the
meritoriousness of good works; against the abominable sale of indulgences to commit sin; against the
idolatrous worship of the Virgin Mary, and of saints
and relics; against five of the seven sacraments;
against the dogma of transubstantiation and the sacrifice of the mass; against prayers for the dead; against
the use of the Latin language in services for the
people; against everything and every man, priest or
bishop, that dares to step between the individual soul
and its God. 'Catholicism,' says Schleiermacher,
'makes the believer's relation to Christ depend upon
his relation to the church; Protestantism makes the
believer's relation to the church depend upon his relation to Christ.' Protestantism knows no priest, save
the one all perfect priest, Jesus Christ; it claims the
right of private judgment against all the councils that
ever assembled, and follows individual conscience, enlightened by the Divine Word, as safer than the *ipse
dixit* of any pope, even the best that ever graced the
triple tiara. It was for these regenerative and world-
lifting principles that Luther thundered and the gentle
Melanchthon prayed in Germany; for which Calvin
and Farel labored in Geneva and France, and Tindale
was burned in Holland, and Cranmer and Ridley and
Latimer went to heaven in robes of flame from England. These principles, more than any other cause,
have helped to emancipate the human mind from ignorance, the citizen from tyranny, the worshipper from
priestcraft and the soul from every form of spiritual

thraldom. Let them be exalted. As the horse bearing the body of the dead Cid put to flight more enemies than hosts of living generals, so may the grand old name of Luther, coupled with these principles ride triumphant through the future, as it has through four centuries just closed."—Nov. 8th.

THE UNITED PRESBYTERIAN,

"'HERE I STAND; I CANNOT DO OTHERWISE; GOD HELP ME.'

"These words are familiar to every school boy. They are great in themselves, but infinitely greater when considered in connection with the man who used them, and the occasion which called them forth. Should any one read them without knowing their origin, he would conclude they came from a man who was acting in some great crisis of his life. They carry with them proof of the heated depth out of which they sprang. But all who are acquainted in any measure with the scene at Worms when the heroic Reformer, standing in the presence of so many enemies, defending himself and his books, made this final declaration, must add the effect of the splendid picture to the intense meaning of the language.   *   *   *

"Luther stood against the tradition of the ages, and against the despotism that had become the chief distinction of those who represented it. To face all the dangers suggested by such conditions required a courage that none but the hero possesses.

"In all the attitudes in which he is seen during those memorable days, none is more striking than this one at Worms. He is alone or nearly so. His cause had as yet made but little progress. He was in the presence of men who regarded him as an apostate and enemy of God. They thirsted, many of them, for his blood. But he did not falter. He spoke warmly, but collectedly. His boldness increased with his danger until he became the very impersonation of moral heroism. After justifying his works and reaffirming his determination to stand by the Scriptures and his conscience, he ended all with the words that are so sublimely linked with the immortality of his name."

THE CHRISTIAN LEADER,

Universalist, Rev. George H. Emerson, D. D., editor, says:

"Of the many peaks which make the culminating points of the White Mountain range, five have an eminence above others to a degree so marked that they are classified apart, and are honored with Presidential names. Of the by no means small company who by pen, voice and act, led in the great emancipation of Central Europe from papal bondage, five rendered such decisive and conspicuous services as to eclipse all coadjutors—Luther, Erasmus, Zwingli, Melanchthon and Calvin. Of these peaks of the Reformation range, the Mount Washington, by many degrees of elevation and grandeur, is the once monk of the Augustinian convent of Erfurt—Dr. Martin Luther."

THE RELIGIOUS HERALD,

Congregational, of Hartford, Conn., David B. Moseley editor, says
November 1, 1883:

"Luther thus rooted and grounded in the truth, not only by his intellectual conviction but also by his heart experiences, could not be frightened by papal anathemas from his steadfastness. He was a fearless moral hero. He did not quail before kings and nobles, nor yield to the imposing assumptions of ecclesiastical dignitaries. He was an orator whose magnetic eloquence enchained the masses. He was a sturdy and keen debater, whom the champions of the papacy learned to dread in a disputation. He was a scholar whose attainments no one could question. He was a writer whose tracts and books thrilled, charmed, and swayed the people. He was a poet whose sacred songs touched the most sacred chords of the human heart. This was the man whom the Lord raised up to break the papal yoke and remove it from the necks of the people. * * * * * *

"Luther was a wonderful man. He stood unabashed in the presence of nobles and princes, and was at the same time the affable companion of the peasant. He wielded the dreaded pen of the keen controversalist, and wrote sacred hymns full of sweetness. He faced his foes with lion-like fierceness, and played with his children in gleeful zest. He discussed nice points of Greek and Hebrew grammar and lexicography with Jonas and Melanchthon, and counseled the Elector Frederick on critical questions of statesmanship. Such a man is worthy to be remembered."

THE PRESBYTERIAN.

"The name of Luther is just now the most prominent name before the Protestant nations. The four hundredth anniversary of his birth has come, and sovereigns, nations, universities and venerable churches, are stirring themselves to do honor to the German monk.

8

In Germany especially, the people and the princes are alike moved to an enthusiastic remembrance of the man whose name is among the grandest on the national records. What Germany would have been without Luther no one can say, but every one is ready to concede that his influence upon the national life has been more potent than any other influence which has worked upon it in the last four centuries. In the cities of Germany they are raising monuments, carving statues, observing elaborate ceremonials, in which all the power of art, music and of eloquent speech is employed to glorify the name of the great Reformer. In Eisenach, where he sang under the windows of the houses for bread, and in Erfurt, where he was a student in the University, the students have celebrated the early life of this great student. And the Roman Catholics are adding keenness to the interest felt and expressed, by adding largely to the abusive words which they ordinarily heap upon this old and powerful foe of the papacy. Friend and foe are thus aroused alike by the recurrence of this anniversary.

*   *   *   *   *   *   *   *   *

"We do not propose to follow his upward course, nor to give any sketch of a life which is now coming under general review, but to draw attention to the fact which, we think, ought now to be specially emphasized, to wit: that the special qualifications of Martin Luther for the work to which he was called grew out of his profound religious experience. His intellectual growth and his constantly increasing acquisitions were consecrated by a baptism of the Holy Spirit which came upon him in early life.   *   *   *   *

"We hope that this great spiritual lesson will be deeply impressed upon the vast companies which will be gathered to do honor to Luther's name."

THE LUTHERAN VISITOR,

Of Prosperity, S. C., organ of the General Synod South, Rev. J. Hawkins, D. D., Editor, says:

"A Presbyterian minister, in *Electra* for November, says: 'Though Luther was shut up in the Wartburg castle, the Reformation went on. God, no doubt, intended to separate the work from the man, and establish it on the simple basis of Gospel truth.' This is a grand mistake. We can easily conceive of a Reformation without a Justus Jonas, a Bugenhagen, an Elector Frederick, or a Melanchthon, yea, even without a Zwingli or a Calvin ; but we can no more conceive of a Reformation without Luther than we can conceive of a New Testament without a Paul, or American independence without a Washington. Luther's name and character and spirit are as indelibly stamped upon every feature of the great Reformation, and of the church which grew out of it, as is the spirit and character of St. Paul upon his epistles. The *Sunday-school Times* has an elaborate article on one-man power. It says that God has always worked through one man at a time. 'He putteth down *one* and setteth up *another*.'

" 'And it is much the same in outside history. The history of the world is practically the history of individuals; and the story of one man at a time is the story of the race which for the time felt that one man's power. It is Xerxes, or Alexander, or Cæsar, or

Charlemagne, or Saladin, or Cromwell, or Napoleon, or Washington. It is Columbus, or Galileo, or Gutenberg. It is Plato or Aristotle. It is Wolsey, or Hampden, or Richelieu, or Voltaire. It is Homer, or Virgil, or Cicero, or Shakespeare. In whichever sphere of life we review the history, the one-man power is, for the time being, the chief power exhibited in that history.'

"In all this array of names, that of Luther does not appear. Here is a one-man power besides which the power of many names mentioned by the *Sunday-school Times* is very weakness itself. This name to-day sways to a greater or less extent the politics, the literature, the theology and the religion of the world."

THE VERMONT CHRONICLE,

A religious organ of Montpelier, Vt., in its issue of November 9, 1883, contains the following eulogistic editorial:

" Protestantism has never been wont to canonize its saints and heroes. It gives God thanks for them, and gives them all needed admiration and gratitude in its heart. No one among its mighty men does it more honor than Martin Luther. There was everything about the man to fill the ages with love for him. Erasmus was a prodigy of learning. Melanchthon was strong and irresistible in logic. Luther was greater than either in his immense personality, in his grand manliness, in his great human nature, in all qualities of heart and life and love. And so it was that Luther's strong nature wrought a hundred-fold more effectively than all the vast scholarship and all the keen dialectics of his illustrious co-workers, towards arresting the sinking Church of Christ from destruction, and planting it again upon the old foundation of God's Word. Germany has had a long, shining list of great men—brilliant statesmen, powerful rulers, mighty warriors, profound thinkers, renowned poets. But the one name that towers above them all in the German's pride and love, is that of Martin Luther. He stands out as no other man does against the background of history, a clear, strong figure, in human flesh, with a courage in him unequaled among men. His humanity was complete. Although he was engaged in the most serious, perplexing, and perilous mission ever laid upon man, he was full of humor, and gracious sympathy, and open to all the cheer of fellowship and the joy of life. Such a grand, warm figure as this, fills the imaginations and holds the hearts of all men. Age does not obscure it. It only clarifies it, and makes it more intense. And so we can understand the magnificent outburst of enthusiasm which has seized upon the German people in their celebrations of the four hundredth birthday of Luther. Germans with little religious faith glory in the greatness of the man, for they feel that he was the greatest German of all. Men of Protestant conviction admire more and more the tremendous work that Luther did for the Church of Christ, and for the individual believer. He tore aside a thousand barriers which the church had erected between the soul and its Maker, and let God as a Father down close to man as God's child. He thus gave such a sense of worth to the human nature, of its dignity and possibilities, which has made itself felt with an irresistible power in every sphere of man's being and activity. Civil liberty, equality of rights, all free institutions and free thoughts which belong to modern civilization, had their rise in that fountain-head of religious liberty and individual worth which Luther broke into and set a-flowing. Protestant Christians of every nationality acknowledge the surpassing work which the German monk did in all these ways. They marvel at his work, and they thank God for it. And yet it is with Protestants everywhere as it is with the Germans themselves — it is the man Luther, that holds their chief admiration. That great figure of his, that bold, fearless face, that ringing, defiant voice, that genial though cutting wit, that beaming, triumphant look — these external features and expressions of the man as he stood up, pleading for the truth in that Diet of Worms, carry men's imagination and seize upon men's homage the world over. Luther was no recluse. He was a man among men, and he could stand before kings. He could be as severe as John Knox was; but he could not be as grim as was he. His severity was human. He had no cant about him. He was honest, even sometimes to coarseness. His faith in God, was his faith in truth. He was persuaded that it must needs triumph; and so he put himself into perils, went into ventures, with a courage which nothing could shake. And with all this loftiness of spirit, he was as humble and tender as a child. The affectionateness of the man was something marvelous in one so strong and independent. Here, in these qualities of his heart, he rules men to-day. The sublimity of his faith, and the childlikeness of his nature, are the double scepters by which he still sways so many men."

THE AMERICAN WESLEYAN,
Of Syracuse, N. Y., Rev. N. Wardner, Editor.

"One of the leading characteristics of Luther was his great courage and unflinching fidelity. He was not a man to be terrified by any array of opposition, or weakened in the least by the most threatening perils. Like the great apostle, he counted not his 'life dear unto himself,' that he might vindicate the truth. Though 'devils' were as plenty as 'tiles,' on the houses, he would go to 'Worms,' or anywhere else, where duty called. This fearless devotion, which committed all to Christ for service or sacrifice, and ever trusted his almighty presence and aid, was the underlying might that gave to the world the great Reformer and the great Reformation."—Nov. 14, 1883.

THE ARKANSAS METHODIST,
Of Little Rock, S. G. Colburn, Editor.

"It was meet that the whole Protestant world should have been engaged in the celebration of this anniversary, for Martin Luther was more than a Lutheran. He belongs to the whole Protestant world; his name and the blessings of his life are a common heritage. The church of Rome could, with equal propriety, have entered into the celebration; for she, not less than other churches, is indebted to the man who defied the Pope, burned the papal bulls, withstood the whole Roman hierarchy, and thundered against its corruptions; and indeed the Church of Rome has been led to pay tribute unwillingly, to the great Reformer's work, by setting the day apart as an international day of prayer, in all the Roman Catholic churches of the world, for the

unification and triumph of the church. Such a movement was started by the Catholic church of Germany,
and though inaugurated to counteract the influence of
the Protestant celebration, it is yet a concession and a
tribute. It would be impossible to estimate the influence of his life and labors. There is no means of com-
puting the blessings to the world of the Reformation
which he, under God, was the instrument of bringing
about. The revival of learning, the disenthralment of
thought and feeling, the unchained and open Bible to
the masses, and the consequent elevation of the church
above the darkness of superstition and error, and the
dawn of our civilization, are to be taken into account,
when we would form some estimate of the value of his
life to the world. He was a grand man. The more
closely we study him, the more deeply we are impressed with the grandeur of his character. We can
scarcely conceive of moral heroism more sublime than
that which was shown in his appearance before the Diet
of Worms. With the whole Catholic world against
him, knowing not whether 'bonds, imprisonment or
death' awaited him, in spite of the protestations of
friends, he obeyed·the summons to appear before the
august body that was to sit in judgment upon his doctrines, saying in the language and faith of a true martyr:
'Though there were as many devils in Worms as there
are tiles on its roofs, I would enter.' And he did enter:
and undaunted in the presence of all the dignitaries
of Church and State, he calmly and fearlessly gave
'a reason for the hope that was within him,' closing
his famous speech with these decided words : 'Here I
take my stand, I can do no otherwise, so help me God,
Amen.' "—Nov. 17, 1883.

THE NEW HAMPSHIRE JOURNAL,

Of Concord, N. H., Rev. George B. Spalding, D. D., Editor.

"On the tenth instant will occur the four hundredth birthday of Martin Luther, and the occasion will be commemorated throughout Christendom as the birthday of no other man has ever been. This commemoration will take largely the form of discourses upon the personality and work of the great Reformer throughout the pulpits of Protestant Christendom. It is altogether fitting that this should be the case. For Luther's life stands in vital relation to the religious experience of to-day and the religious life of all coming time. His experience and his work are wrought as inseparably into Christian thought and Christian life, as were the experience and work of the apostle Paul.

"It is not the greatness of the man that will call forth such universal homage to his memory, though his heroic proportions make him the representative man of his age and his nation, and, in a sense, of evangelical Christendom of every age. But it is because his personality stands in such vital relation to Christian experience and Christian history, that Protestant pulpits will echo with his name, and Protestant thought will dwell upon his memory.

"In Luther we have embodied the Protestant Reformation; and in the Protestant Reformation we have Christianity restored to us in its primitive purity, and its beneficent influence incorporated into modern life. The Reformer stands as the champion and vindicator of the spiritual over the formal in religious experience and religious institutions. He stands as the champion

8*

and vindicator of the independence and the sanctity of the individual man in his mental and spiritual experience; as the representative and champion of the doctrine of justification by faith, which is the very marrow of the gospel, and makes it at once honoring to God and grateful to man. He stands as the champion of the Scriptures, as the exclusive teacher of divine truth, and still more as a living means of grace.

"It is because the ideas for which he stood, and stands, have become so largely incorporated into modern life that we owe mainly the different character which modern civilization presents from that which the civilization of the middle ages wore—a difference so great as to make the two seem to belong to different worlds. Christianity as restored by Luther has proved itself the salt of the earth, preserving the wholesome elements of life with which it has come into contact from the corruption which else had well nigh totally destroyed them. We owe to the Reformation the establishment of political and religious liberty. We owe to it the invigoration of the intellect, and its direction into the channels of useful knowledge. We owe to it the humanitarianism and the gracious charity of modern life, and whatever else which is lovely and pure and of good report that came from the breaking down of the separation between religion and the varied activities of life. The contrast between England and Italy of to-day, or between the United States and Mexico, is not as great as would be that presented by the Christian world at the present time without the Reformation, and the Christian world with it. For Roman Catholic Christianity has profited indirectly by the Reformation, and never has shown so debased a condition of society where it prevails, as it would were it left without the reaction of the Reformation upon itself.

"Well may the world then celebrate the birthday of him who was the central figure in the reformation of its religion, with all its beneficent influences upon the life of man. Well may it call to mind the principles for which the Reformer stood, and strengthen its resolution to maintain them intelligently and vigilantly and courageously."—Nov. 9, 1883.

THE CHRISTIAN HOUR,

The Presbyterian organ for Iowa, Nebraska, and the Northwest, William J. Harsha and Thomas C. Hall, editors, Omaha, Neb.

"There is a profound significance in the spectacle of the whole world uniting to celebrate the birthday of a humble German monk. England has the birthday of her queen to remember; France does homage to the birthday of her Napoleons, and the United States celebrate the birthday of Washington. But there are no local and sectional interests—there are no national aims and patriotism—in the united reverence paid to the four-hundredth anniversary of the birth of the great Reformer. We behold the whole world moved by a common impulse—filled with a single idea —and that not political or social, but religious. Is there not something significant in this? May not an argument be found here upon the much-mooted question: 'Is the old faith dying?'   *   *   *   *

"Of the results of Luther's work there is little need of speaking—the world is full of them, and a man can not open his eyes upon a Protestant Sabbath without being impressed with them. The fundamental doctrine of justification by faith alone has been vindicated. The right of a penitent soul to approach God through Christ, without the help of priest, or pope, or saint, was explained. Free pardon was offered to the most wretched sinner who sincerely repents. The Bible was given to Germany in German, and to England in English. Political liberty, social purity, and spreading intellectual light, followed as a matter of course. All the best institutions of this free land were made possible by the religious movement started in the penitent heart of the sturdy German monk.

"And what is our duty? It is to defend the reformed theology, to spread the glorious message of free pardon, to encourage souls to confess to God alone, and to work into our own lives, under the Spirit's blessing, the purifying principles that regenerated Luther and shall regenerate the world."—Nov. 9, 1883.

THE CHRISTIAN GUARDIAN (METHODIST).

"As Methodists, our teaching respecting personal, spiritual religion places us in direct opposition to every form of Romish ritualism and sacramentarianism. There is also an historical link connecting Methodism with Luther. It was while a person was reading Luther's preface to the epistle to the Romans, in a society meeting at Aldersgate, that Wesley found the peace of God. To give his own words: 'I felt my heart was strangely warmed. I felt I did trust in Christ, Christ alone, for salvation. An assurance was given me that He had taken away my sins, even mine, and saved me from the law of sin and death.' Millions have reason to thank God for raising up Luther. While we join in the general thanksgiving, let us examine ourselves to find out if we have the brave, truth-loving spirit of Luther, or whether we have not a something of Romish intolerance and sectarianism under the name of Protestantism."

THE CHRISTIAN EVANGELIST,

Of St. Louis, Mo., I. H. Garrison, W. H. Johnson, J. H. Smart, Editors.

"What was it, in the character of Martin Luther, that entitles him to the gratitude and the admiration of mankind? It was not his learning, for there were greater scholars; nor was it the correctness of his theological views, for others were his superiors even in this regard, and he was never free from some gross superstitions. It was not his intellectual superiority in any field of thought that makes him the hero he is in our eyes to-day. It was not in any or all of these respects that Luther looms up so grandly above all his compeers. But in this: Having learned, from reading the Bible in his cloister, that the church of which he was a member was vitally wrong in doctrine and grossly wrong in practice, he had the sublime faith and courage to denounce the wrong and proclaim the right, in the face of papal denunciation, royal disfavor, and the prospect of death, as the penalty of so doing. What God taught in His blessed word ought to be proclaimed, though it disrupt the church, overturn the decrees of Popes and councils, and run contrary to the

prejudices and time-honored usages of the great mass
of the religionists of his age.   The corrupt practices
of the church and its officials must be exposed, though
it stir up a revolution, and cost him his life.   This was
Luther's greatness and his glory.   He had the courage of his moral convictions.   He believed, and therefore spoke.   He was no miserable time-server.   He
believed that God, who had enabled him to see His
truth, would take care of him and his future, if he
would stand up bravely for that truth against the mal-
edictions of civil and ecclesiastical dignitaries.   For
that the world honors Luther, and he would be entitled to that honor no less had he fallen a victim to the
malice of Charles V. and failed to carry out his plans
for reform.   A man's greatness is not to be measured
by the world's standard of success.   *   *   *   *

" If the religious world is to be benefitted by this
revival of the memory of Luther, and this wide-spread
celebration of his virtues, it must be by our drinking
in more of the spirit of his moral heroism, and his unyielding fidelity to the word of God.   If the historic
scene of the great German Reformer confronting the
Diet of Worms and re-affirming his principles, shall
nerve any preacher of the gospel to condemn popular
evils and to proclaim unpopular truths ; if it teach us
to respect God's reformers of to-day, and to submit
ourselves anew to the sole guidance of God's word ; if
it shall rebuke our moral cowardice and qualify us, in
some degree, to bear the frowns of the world for the
smile of God, then indeed will this world-wide celebration not have been in vain.   But if, when all the
noise and parade and eloquent eulogies are over, there

has come to the Protestant world no perceptible increase of moral courage for the condemnation of the
sins and abuses of our own times, and no high resolve
to follow the light of God's word wherever it may
lead, the event will only furnish a fresh illustration of
how men may admire a virtue in another, if its exercise involve no personal inconvenience to them, while
they are wholly incapable of putting it into practice in
their own lives.

"Luther said: 'Satan is an artful orator, and his
highest art is to make a law out of the gospel.' The
great Reformer said few things more significant, and
evincing keener insight into human nature than that.
The tendency from Christ's time to the present has
been to construct an inflexible law out of Christ's free
gospel. The spirit of the gospel cries, 'Stand fast in
the liberty wherewith Christ hath made you free;' but
the spirit of the church has too often been, 'Submit
graciously to the bondage wherewith the customs,
usages and traditions of the church have bound you.'"
—November 15, 1883.

THE WATCHMAN,
Baptist.

"The approaching Lutheran commemoration makes
especially pertinent whatever pertains to the life and
career of the great Protestant Reformer. It is hence
fitting that he should be made the subject and theme
of discourse and discussion by the pulpit, the platform
and the press. The recent triennial Congregational
Council at Concord brought Martin Luther into the
foreground, where in report, followed by eloquent

speech, he had due and fitting recognition. Prof. Egbert Smyth was inspiring and impressive in his deliverance, as was also Rev. Dr. Duryea. Prof. Smyth set Luther forth as a grand motive power to holiness, and pleaded for his example to become more pervasive and potential in the Congregational body. Dr. Duryea contemplated the Reformer as an apostle of moral and spiritual freedom, and thus as largely an emancipator in the realm of religious thought and of action.

"Both the Andover professor and the Boston pastor gave expression from the standpoint which each holds respectively in viewing what was distinctive in the pioneer Reformer of Germany. There is much truth doubtless in what each urged and insisted on.

"Martin Luther in rising up in his spirit of a mighty remonstrance, in his vehement protest against the Romanism of the times, was animated first of all, it may never be doubted, by zeal and devotion to the cause of the Lord Jesus. That vocal text in Romans, 'The just shall live by faith,' was the quickening keynote of his whole ministry, and of his course as chiefest of the reformers. In the spirit with which it electrified and fired him on, it was ever with him, whether writing his commentary on Galatians, whether preaching or talking or communing by the wayside, or standing in the presence of hierarchs, of potentates, or of kings and princes. Never did he cease to glory in his protest, while in this motto-text he found enfolded the core and central principle of the Reformation. It is safe to assume that, to his far-seeing view, that Reformation itself was to stand or fall just in so far as its disciples saw clearly and held firmly its basal truth, or as they saw it dimly and held it with a loosened grasp.

"The religion of Martin Luther thus got its keynote and its inspiration from this New Testament doctrine of justification by faith in Christ—and there alone. A religion which is central and concentered there, which is anchored on this very 'Rock of Ages,' cannot be else than the mightiest incentive to holiness, as a host of consecrated men and women, heralds and missionaries of the cross in all lands, bear witness. Carey and Marshman, the Judsons, and many more, not counting their lives dear unto them, have for Christ's sake borne the Gospel as Paul and other Apostles bore it onward, until death amid peaceful scenes or martyr sufferings ended their mission among the living.

"If it is suggested that Luther came as a religious liberalizer in the sense and with the stress that is now-a-days so much assumed, there are many who will demur to this claim. Luther was no such religious emancipator as that. As insistent as Calvin on the great essentials of what is elemental and fundamental in that which is known as the system of evangelical truth, he stood sturdy as a rock to this consensus and confession 'of the faith once for all delivered to the saints.' Not more than the equally eminent and perhaps intellectually greater Genevan preacher and reformer, not more than Paul himself, would Luther at any time have blanched, or departed from the purpose to 'know nothing among men save Jesus Christ and him crucified.' It was this 'banner displayed because of the truth' under which the battalions enlisted by the Protestant Reformation of the sixteenth century went forth before trembling Rome to their achievements and to their triumphs. As there would have been retrogression rather than progress under any other banner, as there would have been defeat in room of victory, so must it be for four hundred years later; so must it be to the end."

THE CHRISTIAN INDEX,
Of Atlanta, Ga., M. B. Wharton, Editor.

"During our residence abroad, we lived in the very cradle of the Reformation, and in the midst of scenes forever memorable because associated with the name of Luther. * * * We have seen many of his relics —his garments, books, manuscripts, drinking cups, bed, writing desk, and writing materials. We felt, though nearly four centuries divided us, that we were near him, and tried to drink in some of his inspiration. He was a wonderful man. With his gigantic intellect, iron will, and persevering industry, he broke the papal power, and gave light and liberty to an empire. Though the Germans have in many instances departed from his teachings, it is yet fitting that they should honor the man who did such a mighty work for his people."—Nov. 15, 1883.

THE AMERICAN,
Philadelphia.

"No other German celebration could excite so much interest throughout the rest of the world; for no other German occupies such a position in the world's history

as does Martin Luther. His name is a household
word throughout Protestant Christendom: *i. e.*, among
the most progressive, enlightened and prosperous peoples of the world. To his initiative as a Reformer
those peoples in great part owe the qualities which
give them their preëminence in the present and their
prospects in the future; to his memory is due the
tribute of respect which mankind must pay to the great
leaders and benefactors of mankind.

" But whatever Luther may be to the people of other
countries, he always must be more to Germans than
to other Protestants. He is *the* German man—more
distinctly such than any other in German history.
The best qualities of the Teutonic character—staunch
truthfulness, loyalty to wife and home, childlike simplicity, cheerfulness, happy humor, fervent devotion to the
Fatherland, fearless faith in God, and joy in the truths
of the Gospel—all these are united in Luther as in no
one else. He is not the less dear to German hearts
because he was not a faultless man. * * * But
after all allowance is made for his scars and wrinkles,
he remains one of the grandest figures in religious history—a figure of mountainous bulk, in whose outline
scars are hardly noticeable.

"The central point in the man's character was his
profound and unshaken faith in the living God. Of
Moses it is written that 'he endured as seeing Him
who is invisible.' It might be written of Luther also.
That vision went with him through his life. God was
the first of realities with him. Hence his personal
contempt for danger when the fate of Huss seemed to
impend over him at Worms. * * * He stood un-

shaken and as on a rock amid the shifts and changes
of his time, always believing that a higher power than
emperors, princes and nobles had a hand in the making of history, and would fail in nothing that the
good cause required. 'If our Lord God will have His
Church,' said he, 'then we tell Him plainly that He
must uphold it. We could not do so for an hour, and
if we could we should be the proudest asses under
heaven.' *   *   *   *   *   *   *   *

"Luther is dear to his countrymen as the vindicator
of the sacredness of family life as the best and most
Christian kind of living. * * * What their family
life was, in cheerful devoutness and constancy of faith,
we know from the letters that passed between him and
his wife, from the accounts left us by those who visited
him in Wittenberg, and, above all, from that most in-
discriminate and often blundering, but still admirable
record of what passed at his own table, the ' Tischreden' (Table-Talk). It seems that we have in this huge
congeries of his sayings little more than the record of
the year 1534. Yet it exhibits the overflow of a mind
large in its intellectual and moral interests, richly
stored with the fruits of study and observation, and
heartily devout in all things. We should have known
Luther less intimately had no such Boswellian zeal
been busy with him, in spite of his resistance and his
protests. Some of his finest sayings are in the 'Table-
Talk;' and while it contains much that his enemies
love to quote, it remains a remarkable monument to
the household piety of a great and good man. His
Christianity was not an official dress; he never laid it
aside. His heart was full, and his mouth ran over
with good thoughts.

" From the first day of his appearance as a Reformer, the family and marriage held a lofty place in his thoughts. Divesting himself of scholastic sophistications, he fell back on the old Teutonic ideas of woman's worth and of the family's dignity. He hated monkery, he said, because it debarred men from bearing rule in the house, the State, or the Church. In the family, he told his people, they would find the true monastery, full of crosses and trials as many as the soul needed, but full also of joys and blessings such as the monks never knew."

THE PHILADELPHIA PRESS.

" The world has seen all sorts of reformers and a great variety of reformations. Some have been mighty, while others have been ridiculous. The success of some has been followed with beneficent and lasting effects, while on the other hand there have been reformations of considerable value whose effect has soon passed away.

" The reformer, whose reformation of four hundred years ago we now celebrate, differed from most other reformers in his complete unselfishness and the absence of any plan for setting himself up as a leader. Moved by a conscientious conviction that there were wrongs in the Church which ought to be righted, Luther commenced, on a limited scale, an agitation of the possible extent of which he had very little conception. He knew the world only as he had seen it in his association with the scholarly men of Germany and the students who listened to their teachings. When he first saw society in Rome, he was bewildered. Returning from the sumptuous fare of the ecclesiastics in the Eternal City, he betook himself to his plain diet and his hard work with renewed convictions of the importance of the responsibility he had undertaken. Regardless of consequences to himself, he pushed ahead in the face of the fiercest opposition, not caring for a period of retirement and rest before he should die, and not concerning himself about the honor to be bestowed on his memory after his career should be ended.

"One of the most noteworthy features of Luther's reformation was that there was no money in it for Luther or his friends, nor was there any of the fame or popular applause with which the ambitious souls of reformers are sometimes stirred. Luther put on no airs. He made no pompous publications as to what he intended to do. He asked no testimonials of esteem at the hands of his followers or of the public. Peculiar, eccentric, impulsive and enthusiastic, was Martin Luther. Yet not the bitterest of his enemies could call him a mere hobbyist, nor could they successfully impugn his motives. Of course, he was sneered at, and joked about, and cursed: but for that he cared nothing.

"There is a wide gulf between the character of Martin Luther and that of some of the hobby-riders who have paraded themselves as reformers. There are some whose mere announcement of intended efforts at reformation are enough to brand them as cranks or self-seeking promoters of their own fortunes. Both in the church and in politics, quack reformers have been plenty. Their demonstrations are generally more like the pompous performances of Tetzel, with gorgeous equipage and polychromatic parade, than the steady work and the hard knocks with which Luther achieved such phenomenal success.

"Of sham reformers and quack alleviators of misery and wrong, we do well to be wary. Such people are plenty wherever an honest penny is to be turned, or a penny of any kind. In bold and honorable relief, in letters of gold, above all these men and their efforts, stands the name of Martin Luther, the man pure in purpose, honest in convictions, unflinching in the face of enemies, and true to the very end."—Nov. 11, 1883.

THE BALTIMORE AMERICAN.

"A bond of union among all Protestant churches is the Lutheran memorial which was celebrated yesterday all over the Protestant world. In Europe the ceremonies began some days ago; but yesterday, being the Sunday nearest to the birthday, was everywhere the day for church services in honor of the day. In this city yesterday all forms of Protestantism— Episcopal and evangelical—improved the occasion. There were many eloquent sermons preached upon this inspiring theme.

"Protestantism, divided and subdivided as it is into sects, is prone to dwell upon the points of difference in the creeds rather than upon the points of resemblance. It is, therefore, well for Christian fellowship that at times there come occasions like this, when all are united. Luther was the greatest spiritual leader that has lived since apostolic times, and his life seems to be the heritage of all Christians, as is St. Paul's. It is an ennobling thing to study such a life as his was. There is a benefit, too, in recalling the times in which he lived. One of the good results of the Luther festival is that it stimulates the study of one of the great eras of history. The sermons that are preached will awaken a desire to know more of this grand personality and of his epoch. The religious awakening was one of the symptoms of the general intellectual stir that animated the sixteenth century. The study of the ancient literatures, the renaissance in art, the dawnings of physical science, the discovery of America, and other similar things, marked the daybreak of modern-mindedness in Europe. A grand type of men came at that epoch. A love of adventure and of heroic deeds survived from the knightly mediæval times ; but along with this courage and enterprise came a higher intellectuality. Luther was the leader in religious progress, as Columbus was in discovery, and Michael Angelo in art. The time was ripe for casting off the fetters from free thought, and if Luther had not come, there would have been some other leader; but the chance would have been slight that so grand a leader as he would have come at the call of his epoch."—Nov. 12, 1883.

THE CHICAGO INTER-OCEAN.

"Of the grand total of Christendom, 400,000,000, not less than 120,000,000 are Protestants, and by common consent, Luther is regarded the father of Protestantism.   *   *   *   *   *   *   *

"To Luther the Bible was not simply the sacred Scriptures of the Jews. It was rather the veritable word of God.   *   *   *   *   *   *

"It is inconceivable that the 400th birthday of any other man could be celebrated so widely and with such profound interest. * * * * *

" The Catholic church is one. The Vatican with its forty or fifty thousand apartments is the veritable capitol of a veritable empire, and one as autocratic as Russia. The Protestant church has no such unity. It is none less true, that over them all, the scepter of Luther is held with a potential sway. * * * *

" Luther was hardly less the Reformer of Rome, than the father of Protestantism."

" The celebration of the four hundredth anniversary of Luther's birth was certainly the largest and most inspiring known in this city's (Chicago) history, where so many religious gatherings of great size have been held."

9

PART III.

WHAT EMINENT DIVINES AND OTHER SPEAK-
ERS HAVE SAID OF LUTHER DURING
THE RECENT LUTHER QUARTO-
CENTENARY FESTIVITIES.

THE LUTHER CENTENARY.*

Adapted from Whittier's Centennial Hymn.

BY. W. H. S.

Our fathers' God! from out whose hand
The centuries fall like grains of sand,
We meet to-day, Thy servants, free
And loyal to our Church and Thee,
To thank Thee for the era done,
And praise Thee for the opening one.

Where'er of old, by Thy design,
Our fathers preached that Word of Thine,
Whose echo is the glad refrain
Of rended link in error's chain,
Let every land in concert sing
Glad anthems to our God and King.

Thou who hast here in concord furled
The banners of a Christian world,
Beneath our western skies fulfill
The angel's message of good will,
Jehovah-nissi still our song—
To Him the praises all belong.

O make Thou us through centuries long
Secure in God our fortress strong!
Around our homes of freedom draw
The safeguards of Thy righteous law!
Then, kept by Thine almighty hand,
Thy holy Church will ever stand!

* Can be sung to music of Centennial Hymn by J. K. Paine.

PULPIT TRIBUTES.

THEODORE L. CUYLER,

Pastor of Lafayette Ave. Presbyterian Church, Brooklyn, N. Y.

" LET us take one more look at what Luther was, and what he gave to Germany and the world. In the first place, he gave the world a prodigious *personality*. He 'bulks' largest, and casts the longest shadow, of any man of modern times. Napoleon's genius was more splendid; but in sixty years it has gone to ashes. Four centuries hence that comet will require the telescope of history; Luther, after four centuries, still rides the heavens as a primary planet. Great men are the greatest hand-work of the Almighty; and since the Apostle Paul stood on Mars Hill, the most majestic personality this world has seen was Martin Luther before the Diet of Worms. Look at the stout Saxon monk as he stands there before Cæsar, squarely in his peasant shoes. His shoulders are broad enough to carry off the gates of the Vatican ; he has a neck like a bull, and an eye like a falcon's. Those coal-black eyes ' flash like a demon's,' said the pope's underling at Worms; they pierce through the soul of every beholder.

" All the world was listening for his answer to Emperor and Pontiff; never since Pilate's judgment-hall had so much depended upon an answer. If Luther had turned white in the lips that day and betrayed his Lord, then awakened Europe might have sunk back 'nto night, and the whole history of the world been altered. The immortal answer which bolted from the lion's mouth is the best-known sentence outside of the Bible—'Here I stand; I cannot do otherwise; God help me! Amen.' That sentence unbarred the gates of the morning, and in streamed the *Reformation!*

"When Luther began his revolt against Rome, his eye did not look beyond the confines of his native country. His patriotism was as profound as his piety. The peasant's son of Eisleben was, in every fibre of him, a *German*, as Nehemiah was a Jew, and William the Silent was a Hollander. His soul had waxed hot within him, when at Rome he had heard his countrymen reviled as 'stupid Germans' and 'German beasts.' Popish tyranny was more intolerable to him, because it was the tyranny of the Italian over the Teutonic race; and he demanded a spiritual independence for his Fatherland. To this hour Martin Luther is the ever-living Emperor of the Teutons. Luther's Bible —the noblest version in the land after God's own version, the Hebrew—remains as his richest bequest to his country. Luther's Catechism trains every Protestant German child for admission to the church. To Martin Luther's hymnal the German nation has marched to battle; and to-morrow his magnificent 'Ein feste Burg' will make the rafters roar from Hamburg to Bohemia. When, a few weeks since, the Kaiser William dedicated that colossal statue 'Germania' to keep its watch on the Rhine, he might fitly have carved on it the name of the great Reformer, above even the brilliant names of Von Moltke and Bismarck. The dead hand of Luther led the armies that swept the fields of Saarbruck and Sedan; the ghost of Gustavus Adolphus rode in the ranks of the Protestant conquerors.

"Luther's peasant origin was one element of his power, for it gave him his racy Saxon dialect. Like our own Lincoln, he understood 'the plain people,' and had Lincoln's homespun wit and idiomatic directness. A scholar himself, he yet translated the Bible into the language of the fireside and the market-place, and thus made God's Book the people's book. Sometimes, when his soul was roused to righteous wrath, his words were bludgeons. There are a few letters of his yet extant which are rather too coarse for publication. The howlings and chantings of the monks, he denounced as 'tongue-thrashing;' he addressed Emser as the 'he-goat of Leipsic;' and of malicious gossips he sharply said, 'they are exactly like hogs, who do not care for the violets and roses in the gardens, but only to stick their snouts into the garbage.' The bravest thing Luther ever did after his defiance of the Papacy, was his marriage to the fugitive nun, Catherina von Bora. When questioned for his reasons, he answered in his racy Saxon fashion: 'I wanted to please my father, to tease the Pope, and to vex the devil.' Without this practical protest against the abominable doctrine of celibacy, he would have left his life-work incomplete.

"The consummate gift and glory of that life-work was, of course, the Protestant Reformation. That was (under God) as truly his as the discovery of America belonged to Columbus. Other heroic men— Wycliffe, Huss, Jerome—started a revolt; Luther

9*

alone achieved a revolution. To his eye 'Popery was a Satanic institution, the worst calamity that devils ever devised,' and he made it forever impossible for Popery to continue what it had been; he smote off its horns. Other men have pulled down, and left only *ruins*. Luther pulled down, and then built up the magnificent structure which bears on its dome the name of *Protestant* underneath the name of Christ Jesus. 　　*　　*　　*　　*　　*

"When Luther was laid in the Schloss-kirche, Protestantism scarcely extended beyond Germany; now it controls the destinies of four hundred millions of the human family. It runs in the blood of the strongest races—the races that invented steam-engines and the telegraph; the races that rescued Holland from the sea and America from the savage; the races that have given birth to John Knox and John Milton, to Newton and Leibnitz, to Washington and Lincoln and Gladstone. It runs in the blood of the races that shall rule the world.

" Under God this was Luther's work; it stamps him as the foremost character since the Apostolic era. Martin Luther's hammer struck the first strokes in the building of the Reformed Church of God. Martin Luther's bonfire kindled the flame of freedom, which has lighted four centuries of religious progress. Martin Luther's heaven-sent message—'The just shall live by faith'—ushered in a second Pentecost of spiritual power. The Omniscient Eye foresaw all this; the Omnipotent Arm therefore made strong the solitary Saxon monk, so that in the decisive hour he could ring out his defiant answer to the powers of darkness,

—'Here I stand; I cannot do otherwise; God help me! Amen!'"—*Memorial Service at Princeton College.*

FREDERIC H. HEDGE,

Of Harvard University, and author of " Prose Writers of Germany."

"The power which presides over human destiny and shapes the processes of history is wont to conceal its ulterior purpose from the agents it employs, who, while pursuing their special aims, and fulfilling their appointed tasks, are, unknown to themselves, initiating a new era, founding a new world.

"Such significance attaches to the name of Luther, one of that select band of providential men who stand conspicuous among their contemporaries as makers of history. For the Protestant Reformation which he inaugurated is very imperfectly apprehended if construed solely as a schism in the church, a new departure in religion. In a larger view, it was our modern world, with its social developments, its liberties, its science, its new conditions of being, evolving itself from the old.

"It would be claiming too much to assume that all of good which distinguishes these latter centuries from mediæval time is wholly due to that one event; that humanity would have made no progress in science and the arts of life, but for Luther and his work. Other contemporary agencies, independent of the rupture with Rome—the printing-press, the revival of letters, the discovery of a new continent, and other geographical and astronomical findings—have had their share in the regeneration of secular life.

"But this we may safely assert: that the dearest

goods of our estate — civil independence, spiritual emancipation, individual scope, the large room, the unbound thought, the free pen, whatever is most characteristic of this New England of our inheritance—we owe to the Saxon Reformer in whose name we are here to-day.   *   *   *   *   *   *   *

"I have presented our hero in his character of reformer. I could wish, if time permitted, to exhibit him in other aspects of biographical interest. I would like to speak of him as a poet, author of hymns, into which he threw the fervor and swing of his impetuous soul ; as a musical composer, rendering in that capacity effective aid to the choral service of his church. I would like to speak of him as a humorist and satirist, exhibiting the playfulness and pungency of Erasmus without his cynicism ; as a lover of nature, anticipating our own age in his admiring sympathy with the beauties of earth and sky ; as the first naturalist of his day, a close observer of the habits of vegetable and animal life ; as a leader in the way of tenderness for the brute creation. I would like also, in the spirit of impartial justice, to speak of his faults and infirmities, in which Lessing rejoiced, as showing him not too far removed from the level of our common humanity.

"But these are points on which I am not permitted to dwell. That phase of his life which gives to the name of Luther its world-historic significance is comprised in the period extending from the year 1517 to the year 1529; from the posting of the ninety-five theses to the Diet of Spires, from whose decisions German princes dissenting received the name of Protestants, and which, followed by the league of Smalcald, assured the success of his cause.   *   *   *

" Honor and everlasting thanks to the man who broke for us the spell of papal autocracy; who rescued a portion, at least, of the Christian world from the paralyzing grasp of a power more to be dreaded than any temporal despotism—a power which rules by seducing the will, by capturing the conscience of its subjects—the bondage of the soul! Luther alone, of all the men whom history names, by faith and courage, by all his endowments—ay, and by all his limitations—was fitted to accomplish that saving work—a work whose full import he could not know, whose far-reaching consequences he had not divined. They shape our life. Modern civilization, liberty, science, social progress, attest the world-wide scope of the Protestant reform, whose principles are independent thought, freedom from ecclesiastical thrall, defiance of consecrated wrong. Of him it may be said, in a truer sense than the poet claims for the architects of the mediæval ministers, ' He builded better than he knew.' Our age still obeys the law of that movement whose van he led, and the latest age will bear its impress. Here, amid the phantoms that crowd the stage of human history, was a grave reality, a piece of solid nature, a man whom it is impossible to imagine not to have been: to strike whose name and functions from the record of his time, would be to despoil the centuries following, of grains that enrich the annals of mankind."—*Mass. Hist. Soc'y's Memorial Meeting*, held at Boston, Nov. 10, and published in Dec. No. of *Atlantic Monthly.*

THOMAS ARMITAGE,
Pastor of Fifth-Avenue Baptist Church, New York.

"It would require a volume to detail the changes that the gigantic power of the man has wrought in the religion and institutions of the world. He was not the father of the Reformation, but he was much the mightiest spirit that shaped its course and destiny. At the time he began his work, cupidity, ignorance and profligacy marked the clergy from the papal throne down. John Huss, Savonarola, John Wycliffe, and others had risen to repair the ruined fabric, but their labors had been prostrated. The age demanded that the man whom God had provided for the age should step forth in his own original greatness, arouse his own master-spirit, and lead the nations. Such a soul must not be formed by the age or he would bear its image. No genius, but only a special creation of God, could free and consecrate a world. Public opinion has stopped a conqueror, broken a tyrant, overthrown a corrupt institution; but more frequently it has advocated, not oppressed, virtue and defended vice. Public opinion—in the church or out of it—on religious questions is of very little consequence. To this point Luther had to be educated before he could undertake the leadership in such times as he lived in. The public opinion of that empire which Luther made great denounced him as a madman filled with blasphemy; as not a man, but Satan with the form of a man. But Luther had the qualifications necessary for the work before him. He began the Reformation by reforming himself. He made the Bible the first agent in the Reformation; he himself was the second. Blot out

Luther's name from history, and you must write another destiny for Holland, England and America, as well as Germany."

ROBERT COLLYER,

Pastor of the Church of the Messiah, New York, chose as the subject of his discourse on Sunday, November 11, " *Our Saint Martin.*"

"These are the three things I love to find in my good Saint Martin Luther. *First,* there is so much pure manhood in him that he could be in his one life a vast and sure believer, and deep and dire doubter; gentle as a mother with her little children, and angry as Michael with his sword; able to fast until you could count all his bones, and the threads of life began to snap, able to feast royally when that was the order of the day, but still to be a man and not less than a saint in his feasting. *Second,* he held as brave a soul as this world ever had, in a coward's body, or something very like it—a body that would shake and tremble in the presence of shadow of death, but durst not give way and follow the white feather in clear sight of the rack and the flame. *Third,* with the instincts of a bigot uppermost now and then, not always able to stand free and walk free in the way of truth, at the innermost center of his heart he was a free-thinker and a free man, and would have no man follow Luther, but only God and his Christ; would not let the Bible, even, become an object of blind idolatry, but would have all men bring their minds to its study and distinguish between the wheat and the straw. There is still another quality I love in my good St. Martin—my Saint of the new tenor and the new life. * * *

He began by taking his oath on all the sacraments that he would never marry nor have a home of his own and children. The day came when he saw that he had lied against his own nature and his own soul in doing this, found a woman who had also taken this oath and found that she had forsworn herself, married that woman, and they made a home, and had children born to them. And with all his doubts and fears, misbeliefs and unbeliefs, I have not found the day or the moment of his life when my good saint said he was sorry for that—else he should not be my saint, after all I have said for his canonization. In one word, he loved all things lovely, and so he is for this last lovely reason my good Saint Martin."

JOSEPH A. SEISS,
Pastor of the Church of the Holy Communion, Philadelphia.

"The central element of Luther's greatness was his amazing *faith*. What Samson was in muscle, Luther was in soul. He was another Hannah's son in the strength and victory of his prayers. That mighty principle, which looks at things unseen, which launches out unfalteringly upon hidden realities, which joins men to omnipotence and transfigures them into sacred heroes, rose to sublime proportions in him. He lived on the Word of God. His perpetual and close communion with the Eternal Spirit, whose instrument he was, enabled him to lay his hands upon the throne, and lifted him into a wealth of light, energy, endurance and command, which made him one of the phenomenal wonders of humanity.

Out of his faith sprang his prodigious daring; and

daring, especially in the name and strength of God, is the life of power, the soul of heroism, the impulse of new creation. The guiding-star of human advancement is *daring*. Paul *dared*, and a world-wide classic paganism received its death-wound. Columbus *dared*, and the earth gloried in a new hemisphere. And that the Reformation should come, it was not enough that Huss should anticipate it; that Savonarola should preach it; that Reuchlin should write about it; that Erasmus should advise it; that Frederick should desire it; that Zwingli and Calvin should hail and help it; that the soul of suffering Christendom should yearn for it; there had to be a Luther to *dare* it. To brave all risks, to persist, to be self-faithful, to grapple with destiny, to surprise defeat by despising its terrors, to confront unrighteous power, to defy intoxicated triumph, to hold on hard amid tempest and thunder —is the example nations need, and the light that electrifies them. And such was the puissant fire in Luther's bones, kindled and fed by the clearness and transcendant vigor of his faith, making *the man* of the modern ages.

" As the impersonation of one of the greatest revolutions of time, we look in vain for another with whom to compare him. Nor is it too much to say that he was a Peter and a Paul (inspiration excepted), a Socrates and an Æsop, a Chrysostom and a Savonarola, a Shakespeare and a Whitfield, all condensed in one.

"A lone man, all whose days were spent in poverty; who could withstand the mighty Vatican and all its flaming bulls; whose influence evoked and swayed successive diets of the empire; whom repeated edicts from the imperial throne could not crush; whom the talent, eloquence, and towering authority of the Roman hierarchy assailed in vain; whom the attacks of kings of state and kings of literature could not disable; whose teachings the greatest General Council the Church of Rome ever held, sitting 18 years, could not counteract, nor adjourn without conceding much to him; and whose name the greatest and most enlightened nations of this earth hail with glad acclaim; necessarily must have been a wonder of a man.

"To begin with a minority consisting of one, and conquer kingdoms with the mere sword of his mouth —to bear the anathemas of church and the ban of empire, and triumph in spite of them—to refuse to fall down before the golden image of the combined Nebuchadnezzars of his time, though threatened with the burning fires of earth and hell—to turn iconoclast of such magnitude and daring as to think of smiting to pieces the gigantic idol of principalities and powers —nay, to attempt this, and to *succeed in it*—evinced a sublimity of heroism and achievement explainable only in the ordination of God, set to reform the ages.

"Many and glowing are the eulogies which have been pronounced upon him; and yet we hear the philosopher of history, even from the side of Rome, giving it as his conviction that 'few of his own disciples appreciate him highly enough.' Genius, learning, eloquence, and song, have volunteered their noble efforts to do him justice; centuries have added their light and testimony; half the world, in its enthusiasm, has urged on the inspiration; but the story, in its full dimensions, has not yet been adequately told. The skill and energy of other generations will yet be taxed to give it, if, indeed, it ever can be given apart from the illuminations of eternity."

RICHARD S. STORRS, (*Congregationalist*)
Of New York.

" Luther's common sense was vast. He had wonderful sagacity in reading political conditions. He had a poetic spirit, which wrought itself out in actions rather than words; also a power of rugged eloquence, and an immense capacity for labor. All these were combined with varied and extended learning in Hebrew, Greek, Latin, and German. He was a man of the people; humorous, fond of music, and affectionate, and without the least sanctimoniousness; fond of gardening, fond of games. Associated with this was a devoutness of spirit and great courage. He was a typical German ; he loved the common people. All his personality went into his work. He never could write or preach so well as when he was angry. Now think of the results. Civil and religious liberty in Germany, widening in France, and extending over all the world."

PHILLIPS BROOKS, (*Episcopalian*)
Of Boston.

" The noblest monument of modern Europe stands in the old town of Worms, erected fourteen years ago in memory of the man who was born in Eisleben at nine o'clock on the evening of the 10th of November, 1483, four hundred years ago last Saturday night. In the centre of the group stands the stately effigy of

Martin Luther overtopping all the rest, and around
him are assembled the forerunners, the supporters and
the friends of him and of the Reformation which must
always be most associated with his name. Savonarola, Wickliffe, Huss and Waldo, Frederick the Wise
and Philip the Magnanimous, Philip Melanchthon and
John Reuchlin; the city of Augsburg, with her palm-
branch; the city of Magdeburg, mourning over her
desolation, and the city of Spires, holding forth her
famous protest—all of these sit or stand in imperishable bronze around the sturdy Doctor who was the
master of them all.

"That monument at Worms but represents and utters the vivid memory in which the great Reformer is
held not merely in Germany, but through all the world
of Protestantism. The approach of the anniversary of
his birth has been greeted with an overwhelming wel-
come. The old German towns in which he lived have
reproduced in pageants and processions the pictures
of his life. His unforgotten face has come back once
more to a thousand homes. His books have been re-
read. His faults and virtues have been re-discussed.
His place and power in history have been estimated
anew; and the whole great portion of the world which
has been blessed through him has thanked God once
again that he was born.

"At such a time the voice of the Protestants of
America could not be silent. It has not failed to
speak in many ways, and now to-night we have assembled at the summons of the Evangelical Alliance to do
honor to the memory of Martin Luther, and to think
together of what he was and did.

"We are to think of one of the *greatest men* of human history. I say advisedly one of the greatest *men;* for at the outset we ought to realize that it is the personality of Luther, afire with great indignations, believing in great ideas, writing books which in some true sense are great books, doing great, brave, inspiring deeds; but carrying all the while its power in itself, in his being what he was—it is the personality of Luther which really holds the secret of his power. It is *he* that men hate and love with ever fresh emotion, just as they loved and hated him four centuries ago. His books were burnt, but the real object of the hate was he. His pamphlets, scattered broadcast over Germany, were read, and praised, and treasured; but the real love and loyalty, and looking up for power, was to him. Indeed, the name and fame of Luther coming down through history under God's safe-conduct, has been full of almost the same vitality, and has been attended by almost the same admiration and abuse, as was the figure of Luther in that famous journey which took him in his rude Saxon wagon from Wittenberg to Worms when he went up to the Diet; and at Leipsic, Nurnberg, Weimar, Erfurt, Gotha, Frankfurt, the shouts of his friends and the curses of his enemies, showed that no man in Germany was loved or hated as he was.

" It is this vigorous and personal manhood which is the strength of Luther, and if we analyze it a little we can see easily enough out of what two elements it was made up, or more properly, perhaps, in what two channels it ran and made its strength effective. Both are distinctively religious. There are two sentences out of two parables of Jesus which describe indeed the two components of the strongest strength of all religious men. One is this from the parable of the vineyard: 'When the time of fruit grew near the lord of the vineyard sent his servants to the husbandmen that they might receive the fruit of the vineyard;' and the other is the cry of the returning prodigal: 'I will arise and go to my father.' Put these two together into any deep and lofty soul (you cannot put them into any other), and what a strength you have! The consciousness of being sent from God with a mission for which the time is ripe, and the consciousness of eager return to God, of the great human struggle after Him, possessing a nature which cannot live without Him—the imperious commission from above and the tumultuous experience within—these two, not inconsistent with each other, have met in all the great Christian workers and reformers who have moved and changed the world. These two lived together in the whole life of Luther. The one spoke out in the presence of the Emperor at Worms: the other wrestled unseen in the agonies of the cloister cell at Erfurt. The broad and vigorous issue of the two displayed itself in the exalted but always healthy and generous humanity which, with pervasive sympathy, filled and embraced all the humanity about it, not as persuasions or convictions—that would not have worked any such result— but as the living forces which exalted and refined, and consecrated and enlarged, a nature of great natural nobility and richness. So it was that the sense of the divine commission and the profoundness of the human struggle created the Luther who shook the thrones of

Pope and Cæsar, and made all Europe new. You need only look into the faces of Hans Luther and his wife Margaret, which hang, painted by Lucas Cranach, in the Luther Chamber at the Wartburg, and you will see how you have only to add the fine fire of a realized commission and a remembered struggle to the rugged German strength of the father and the human sweetness in the mother's eyes, and you will have the full life of their great son.   *   *   *   *

"Some men are events. It is not what they say or what they do, but what they are, that moves the world. Luther declared great truths; he did great deeds; and yet there is a certain sense in which his words and deeds are valuable only as they showed him, as they made manifest a son of God living a strong, brave, clear-sighted human life. It is thus that I have spoken of him so far, feeling his presence still through the deep atmosphere of these four hundred years. It is not certainly as the founder of any sect; more, but not mostly, it is as the preacher of certain truths; but most of all it is as uttering in his very being a re-assertion of the divine idea of humanity, that he comes with this wonderfully fresh vitality into our modern days.   *   *

"But there is more to say than that. These centuries of Anglo-Saxon life made by the ideas of Luther answer the question. The Protestantism of Milton and of Gœthe, of Howard and of Franke, of Newton and of Leibnitz, of Bunyan and of Butler, of Wordsworth and of Tennyson, of Wesley and of Channing, of Schleiermacher and of Maurice, of Washington and of Lincoln, is no failure. We may well dismiss the foolish question, and with new pride and resolve brighten afresh the great name of Protestant upon our foreheads.

"Have we not seen to-day something of what Protestantism really is—the Protestantism which cannot fail? Full of the sense of duty and the spirit of holiness, there stands Luther—moralist and mystic. Conscience and faith are not in conflict, but in lofty unison in him. Through him, because he was that, God's waiting light and power stream into the world, and the old lies wither and humanity springs upon its feet. Ah, there is no failure there. There cannot be. The time will come—perhaps the time has come—when a new Luther will be needed for the next great step that humanity must take; but that next step is possible mainly because of what the Monk of Wittenberg was and did four hundred years ago. There is no failure there: only one strain in the music of the eternal success—fading away but to give space for a new and higher strain.

"It may be that another Luther is not likely. It may be that the freer atmosphere in which the world is henceforth to live will give no chance for such explosions as in the sixteenth century burst open the tight walls of papal power. Perhaps not by the apparition of one great leader, but by the steady upward movement of the inspired whole, the future · great advances of humanity are to be made. No man can say; but this at least is sure, that the great principles of Martin Luther's life must be the principles of every advance of man on to the very end. Always it must be by a regeneration of humanity. Always it must be by the power of God filling the soul of man

Always it must be religious. Always it must be God summoning man, man reaching after God. Always it must be the moralist and the mystic, conscience and faith meeting in the single human hero or in humanity at large, which makes the Reformation. And however it shall come, all human progress must remember Martin Luther.

"Every reformation until man comes to his perfection will be easier and surer because of this great Reformer whom we have been honoring, for whom we have been thanking God, to-day. Every return of man, rebellious against sin or worldiness or false authority, into a more simple and devout obedience to the God to whom he belongs, will remember with gratitude and find strength in remembering brave Martin Luther. The echo of the shouts which rang at Wittenberg while the pope's Bull was burning, the echo of the trumpets which the watchman on the tower blew when Luther entered into Worms, will be heard, if men listen for them, in the farthest and latest of the ever-repeated chimes which, until the Light and the Lord have perfectly possessed the earth, shall again and again

> " Ring out the Darkness of the world,
> Ring in the Christ that is to be."

CHARLES DUDLEY WARNER,
The celebrated New England literateur and humorist.

" The city of Hartford, the State of Connecticut, the United States, Great Britain and its world-encircling colonies, Holland and its dependencies, the German empire, are to-day what they are largely because of the

10

life of Martin Luther. 'Had there been no Luther,' says Mr. Froude, 'the English, American and German peoples would be thinking differently, would be acting differently, would be altogether different men and women from what they are at this moment.' This city of Hartford, supposing it in existence without the Reformation, would have been a different place from what it is—different in its social, literary, religious and civil economy. There is not a person in this audience who is what he would have been but for the influence of Luther. We may say this at any time of all preceding influences, of all great writers and actors in the world —they change human life after them more or less; but no man I think has affected it so largely since the fall of the Roman Empire as Luther. There would probably have been a Reformation, though not at the time it did occur, without him; but it would have been different in its character. Without him at that time it would probably have resulted in a compromise, and a compromise which years would have shown surrendered that which we now regard as vital in the Reformation. It needed exactly such a fighter as Luther to win the battle in the great movement of the 16th century, and such a conservative as Luther to keep the movement within bounds.

"Fortunately Luther was endowed with physical force and moral courage equal to his spiritual. For it is a lesson of history that evil and force often triumph, that persecutions of good causes are often pushed so far as to crush them, that progress is stayed by violence. The success of good movements depends often on physical force. Protestantism lost its chance of making Bavaria Protestant by the defeat at White Hills in 1620. The Reformation was stifled in France by the strong hand. There come times when the right, or what men deem to be right, moral and spiritual freedom, has to be fought for with cruel weapons, or at least with the forces inherent in the physical nature. The struggle of the Reformation in Germany demanded other qualities beside learning and spirituality. And it found them in Luther.

" Hosts of men have been great in certain directions; not more than one or two in a generation great all round. When such an one does appear in human affairs he needs room, he takes it, he profoundly influences his age, and makes an indelible mark on the race. Luther seems to me, looking not only at what he accomplished, but studying the man himself in his individual qualities, to be the greatest force, perhaps the most completely developed man, in modern times. He was like a magnificent iron steamship, with the engines adequate to the hull. His genius had the physical basis necessary to make him the complete man. He was strong in his energy, strong in his passions, in his affections, in his love, in his spiritual aspirations, in his will, in his convictions. There were greater scholars, poets, men of affairs; but Luther was so evenly developed in his powers that success might be predicted of him in any special direction he chose to exert them. He had the capacity to have made himself the preëminent man of letters and the national poet of his time. In the few words I have to say of him, I have been asked to consider his services to literature. *   *   *   *   *

"The Table Talk is full of originality, common sense, individual character, and not seldom noble elevation of discernment of things spiritual and mundane. It is the overflowing of a man of genius, whose brain was never idle, but to whom literature and the fashion of this world were only incidents in his stormy and glorious struggle to clear a place for a free man to stand in Germany, and to break the bondage imposed on the Christian world."—*In Park Church, Hartford, Conn.*, Nov. 11, 1883.

DAVID SWING,
The celebrated preacher of Chicago.

"But what shape did the Christian church assume under the touch of Luther? Under the persistence and force of this one monk, the religion of the sixteenth century opened its old iron and rusty doors to admit three new ideas, and to exclude ideas enough to make room for these. The first in the order of time and excellence was salvation by faith instead of by works. It is said by some writers that in some hour of deep anxiety over the way of salvation, there came into his mind as a lightning flash the revelation that the just shall live by faith. Faith being something within, it was the opposite of the idea of indulgences —that man could be saved by something from without. Salvation by paying money to the pope was the exact opposite of the new thought of purity and charity within. God in the soul was to take the place of the pope on the outside. Having visited Rome, and having found a city of external religious splendor, but of internal vice and crime, Luther's already burdened heart gave way, and his day of opposition and heroism began. It was at this point the piety of the monk came to the help of the world; for had not this discoverer of an internal religion been also a lover of it, little would have come of the new truth. Many mentally perceive the need of a God-like character, but do not love holiness enough to make a struggle to acquire it and lead others in its pursuit. Our great Webster perceived the value of universal freedom, but he did not love the thought enough to die for any emancipation of slaves. Washington and Jefferson perceived that the blacks should be set free, but this mental perception did not burst forth in a flame of love and action. Their liberty was on a canvas as a beautiful picture, or in marble as an impressive image, but it did not imitate the marble of Pygmalion by beginning to breathe and move. It was in the later years of Lincoln, and Chase, and John Brown the fanatic, and a million soldiers, that the love for man arose as high in the heart as the thought of liberty had risen in the brain. Luther combined the thinker and the lover: and while he perceived the logical value of a spiritual religion, he bowed daily in prayer and girded himself for battle. He surpassed our Webster, because to the intellectual grasp of a great idea he added the storm-power of a hero. The reformation came, not from the superior mind of Luther, but equally from his inflamed heart. *   *   *   *

"A second idea which came into the church in the sixteenth century was personal liberty. *   *   *

"The third great blessing which followed the storm of the sixteenth century, was the exaltation of learning." *   *   *   *   *   *   *   *

SAMUEL DOMER,

Of St. Paul's Evangelical Lutheran Church, Washington, D. C.

"Some think the scene at Worms, when Luther stood before that imperial parliament in his royal response to the papal demands, the sublimest one in the history of the Reformation. I do not know that it is. There are many stirring scenes in that history, and Worms is grandly tragic; but the Wartburg in its intimate connection with that scene, and in its sublime significancy to the new era, the spiritual renaissance, can hardly be secondary to that of Worms. The Wartburg is literally a mountain summit; and, meaningfully, it is one of the highest peaks of human achievements and influence. There Luther rises into the imperialism of his lofty mission. He stands face to face with the Angel of the Apocalypse, and the 'pure word of God,' laid into his hands, is sent down through Germany and the world, setting kingdoms aflame with the new evangelism, and lighting up the pathway of salvation to the millions that were sitting in the darkness and shadow of death. Paint the two pictures; put into that conclave of kings, princes, and ecclesiastical nobilities all the grandeur and glamor of pomp and power; then, central in the picture, place the solitary man, and arm him with more than Ithuriel's spear, as he stands in sublime defiance of imperial and papal power, and the hoary heresies of a thousand years! The picture starts our wonder and admiration. But the Wartburg—paint that! Let that mountain loom up before us high and towering; let the dark forests of Thuringia around its base and on its sides type out the darkness of the Middle Ages, out of which the great Reform is now emerging; cover those mountain slopes far up to summit with the blackest clouds, in which the lightnings dance and the thunders make their home; let these be types of the tempests in which the Reformer lifts up his head and stretches forth his hands; make the dark clouds inky black with ignorance, superstition, bigotry, religious hate, and every envenomed passion of political and ecclesiastical malevolence;—but overhead, where the bold, brave man stands, calmer far than Ajax in the storm, let the clouds be riven; let a glory of amber and gold bathe that mountain peak with a heavenly radiance, then crowd that glory with the angels of God singing as they shine, a new-born version of the old anthem brought from Judean hills, 'Glory to God in the Highest!' This the Wartburg. It lies along the march of victory! Luther in veritable apotheosis, through the reflected glory, which the Word of God flings back upon him as he sends it flaming down the ages!"—November 11, 1883.

C. F. W. WALTHER,

President and Professor in Concordia Lutheran Theological Seminary at St. Louis, Mo.

"We have no reason to be ashamed of the person Luther. On the contrary, we have the strongest reasons to glory in him, in defiance of the slanders of the papists. His unfeigned piety, his invincible trust in God, his dauntless heroism in the presence of danger, his unremitting diligence in prayer and supplication, his genuine meekness and simplicity, his transparent disinterestedness far removed from avarice and the love of money, his tender sympathy for all the sorrowing, his beneficence ever flowing freely for all who were in need, his sincerity utterly averse to the ways of the flatterer and of the hypocrite, his candor that marked his intercourse with the lofty and the lowly, his sobriety, his abstinence, his purity, his self-consuming diligence, his faithfulness as son, as husband, as father, as preacher, as professor, as friend, as counselor, as citizen—in a word, his full exemplary piety, all together present a model of true Christianity that may command the admiration, and is worthy of the imitation of all subsequent times. Further, we have abundant reason to boast of Luther's exalted gifts, and of the use he made of them; of his profound wisdom, his extraordinary learning, his penetrating judgment, his commanding eloquence, his fine poetic inspiration, his incomparable services to the Church, the State and society at large, to art, to science, to our German name and our glorious German speech, and above all to the gigantic work of the Reformation, the triumph of which, under God, the Church owes to the faithfulness of Luther."

A. L. FRISBIE,

Pastor of Plymouth Congregational Church, Des Moines, Iowa.

"If there were any doubt as to whether the influence of Luther be race-wide and world-wide, current facts would go far to satisfy the doubt. To-day Germany is swept by a tidal-wave of joyful recognition of what the child of Hans Luder became. She could not bring forward a name which represents so much to the German mind of the commanding, illustrious, and dear, as does the name of Martin Luther. Sweden, Norway and Denmark are scarcely behind Germany in enthusiastic observance of his anniversary; France, Holland, Switzerland and Italy join to honor him. England sets his name among those of her own most renowned. And North America, which has come out of the sea since Luther died, reads, and thinks, and sings of Luther. These facts show that the child Martin Luther has grown to be a mighty influence in the Christian lands of to-day. Protestant Christendom, forgetting sect and division, unites to honor one of the mightiest factors in the development of Protestant Christianity. So his birthday quickens the heartbeats, and sets thrilling within us, and vibrating upon the air, the songs, and prayers, and battle-words of the Reformation. The birthday of no other man born within the last 1500 years could suggest so much of that world's birthday at Bethlehem."

A. J. HERR,

Pennsylvania State Senator from 16th District.

" Luther was not a religious reformer only; he was also a liberator of thought. Learning, then, was a sealed book to all but the rich, and those who intended to enter the Church. While it is true that many schools and universities were established and flourished, yet the favored few only could gain admission to them. Learning was claimed to be the special property of the superior class; it was believed to be the best thing to keep the common people in fear and ignorance, and that man was looked upon as dangerous who thought that they had any right to the know-

10*

ledge of the truth.　But that was not Luther's way of thinking.　He believed they had a right to education, and was untiring in his efforts to establish schools for their benefit.　His translation of the Bible into his mother-tongue unlocked a storehouse of wisdom and poetry and sacred story which the common people received with gladness and surprise.　It brought to their very doors what they had long yearned for.　It did more to clarify the intellectual atmosphere and to stimulate the growing desire for learning which was sweeping over the nation like a wholesome influence, than perhaps any single circumstance of that age.　His labors were incessant and almost incredible, throwing off letters and lectures and pamphlets and sermons with the ease and facility of a machine.　He never stopped to polish a phrase or to veneer a thought. His heart was in his work, and that was the reason why he never wearied, but went straight on, uttering in strong, homely Saxon the intense convictions of his soul, and hurling his metal-like arguments through the ranks of his opponents like cannon balls crashing through the trees of a dead and dying forest.　One of the consequences of this prodigious energy was to liberate the human mind, for it is true as Michelet, the French historian, said: ' Who can estimate the gratitude we owe him?　We can not think or write an hour without remembering him ; for to whom do I owe it that I can send forth what my pen has been recording, if not to Luther, the liberator of modern thought?' And this judgment is confirmed by an illustrious line of thinkers, orators and poets of every age.　It would be a matter of profound astonishment if a man endowed with such qualities of mind and heart had not been a patriot in the truest sense of the word. But he was a patriot, and no self-seeking one either. He felt deeply for the people and with the people, in their suffering and distress, and sought in every way to lift them out of the mire into which they had been plunged by the rapacity of Church and state. In hot displeasure he exclaimed, 'What benefit would it be to the poor man if his field bore as many florins as grains of wheat, if everything is to be taken by his master to be squandered on fine castles, fine dresses, fine eating and drinking?' With the sure instincts of a statesman he predicted the revolt of the peasants a year before it occurred, and warned the authorities that 'Government was not instituted for the benefit of the rulers, but for the advantage of the people.' That sounds as if it had been taken from the Declaration of Independence; but it was uttered three hundred years before that document was written or the first foundation-stone of this republic was laid. If he had lived here in 1776, his blood would have stained the snows of Valley Forge with the rest of those immortal heroes.

"Across the gulf of four hundred years Luther sends greeting to this generation. The events of his life are fast and secure in the irrevocable past; nothing can wrench them from the order they hold in the history of the progress of mankind.   *   *   *

"An old writer once wrote: 'On the theatre of the world there have been many great men, some good men, but only a few both great and good.' It is the eminence of Luther that he was both great and good, his life-work striking everlasting roots which leave perennial blossoms on his grave. His monument is the memory of mankind. Wherever conscience is free; wherever man, poised on the axis of personal responsibility, limited by nothing but the curve of moral law, lives to fulfill the possibilities of his creation; wherever there is deliverance from the tyranny of the past and hope for the future; wherever art, culture and religion make a trinity of virtues to refine and exalt true manhood—there, there will be found the imperishable fame of Luther, the Reformer and Patriot."— Harrisburg, Pa., Nov. 23, 1883.

M. RHODES,
Pastor of St. Mark's Lutheran Church, St. Louis.

"In no event of the Reformer's life do the great elements of his manhood and the excellence of his character appear to better advantage than before the Diet at Worms.

"There was an illustration of animalism, a dominance of the lower faculties there: but not in Luther, nor in his righteous protest. He bore himself as became one whose cause needed no help from passions and methods that could only have proven a reproach to the truth, and paralyzed his claim. He was there to speak for God and the race, and he acted in clear view of his final account, which, to him at least, seemed near at hand.

"His appeal was to the noblest faculties of the human soul, a tribute alike to that Word which is supreme, but not of any private interpretation, an acknowledgment of entire dependence upon the Holy Ghost sent to discover to the human soul the truth as

it is in Jesus, and a proper recognition of the endowment which God has conferred on rational man.

"Never was there a man more utterly unselfish, more
sincere, or more entirely a martyr to the cause of God
and the good of men. In the largest sense, Luther
saved his life by losing it, and in the sixteenth century
he towered above 'the sovereigns and warriors,
statesmen and divines who were his contemporaries,
his antagonists and his disciples;' and to-day, after the
wrestle and triumphs of four centuries, Luther's name
and work constitute the mightiest and best pulse in
the progress of the race.

"I do not propose now to enter upon any defence of
Luther's moral character. He was not faultless, and
no one was so conscious of it and deplored it so much
as himself. He did not live in an age eminent for
godliness, but his own pure life was so marked an
example in his time, that we may well leave others
straightened for a stronger weapon to smirch his
memory.

"Luther's work—a tree of life whose leaves are healing the nations to-day—is sufficient on this point. I
speak only of those great moral faculties rooted in and
inwrought with the truth of God, which made him the
force he was in his great battling life, and more than
ever is to-day. He had abundant and flattering opportunity to gratify any selfish interest he might desire
to serve; his distinction was great, his influence unbounded; but in no single instance did he turn these
to any selfish account. Rare man! Magnificent manhood! Could he honor God? Could he lift up the
defamed cross of his Lord? Could he promote the

best interest and purest happiness of his fellow-creatures? It was what he desired, and for this he lived
and died. What he wrought under God was not
nearly so much any earthly reward of his as it is the
splendid and imperishable heritage of the Church and
the world to-day. What with his great yearning heart,
and the tenderness that comes of the discipline of trial
along with his masterly faith in, and communion with
God, was it strange that he won the hearts of princes
and people, and that his most formidable foes were
abashed and awed before him? Great thoughts beat
on that brain. God's inspiration charged that princely
soul.

> " ' Chief o'er all the galaxy of lights,
> Which stud the firmament of Christian fame,
> Shone Luther forth—*that miracle of men!* '
>   *   *   *   *   *   *   *

"I do not ask—Do we owe something to the Reformation? I say, rather, that through the mercy of God
we owe all to it. There are those who look upon that
movement as a rash, defiant, and expensive venture,
meriting only the execration of the race ; there are
others who can only regard it with indifference, and
whose limited vision see only what they term its mistakes.

"Thousands and millions of voices roll upon us to-
day, bearing a nobler and truer testimony. Luther
uncovered and reset the foundations of every kingdom
that makes our civilization the wonder of the world,
and we shall serve our day and generation in some
part as Luther served his, if we build thereon as we
should. The Reformation was no calamity, still less

a crime, as some would have us believe. It was one of the conquering events in the world's march to the final ripening. * * * * * * *

" When Luther stood up at Worms, he struck for the highest liberty of the race. He it was who made the triumph of the American Revolution possible."— Nov. 10, 1883.

GEORGE DANA BOARDMAN,
Pastor First Baptist Church, Philadelphia, Pa.

" Luther's mission was manifold. First, it was his mission to emancipate the Bible. For, practically speaking, the Bible had been for centuries an imprisoned book. Luther's recovery of it, like King Josiah's recovery of the Pentateuch which had been lost for centuries, was a startling event. His translation of it into matchless German (a version which has won the highest praise even from Roman Catholic writers), laid the foundation for the reformed theology, ethics, and polity. Hitherto, through the mediæval period, the canon of doctrine and the rule of life had been the decrees of councils and the decretals of popes; henceforth the one supreme authority in these transcendent matters was the Word of God.

" Again: It was Luther's mission to emancipate doctrine. For the Scriptural theology had become well nigh lost in the perversions and traditions and excrescences of ecclesiastical deliverances. Not that Luther was eminent as a theologian; the systematizing faculty was not his forte. But while Melanchthon arranged and Calvin constructed, Luther brought the blocks, or rather, by removing the overlying rubbish of centuries, showed where the divine quarry lay. His restoration of the apostolic theology has its most signal illustration in his recovery of the doctrine of Justification by Faith. We are all so familiar with this 'article of the standing or falling church' (*articulus stantis vel cadentis ecclesiæ*) that I need not dwell on it.

*　　*　　*　　*　　*　　*　　*　　*

"Again: It was Luther's mission to emancipate conscience. It was one of the baneful fruits of the middle-age theology that it captured the individual conscience, turning it over into the custody of the Church, appointing the priest its jailor. Luther it was who opened the prison doors. The Spirit of that Lord before whose face he went forth in the power of Elijah was upon him; and so he proclaimed deliverance to the captives, setting at liberty the oppressed, announcing the acceptable year of the Lord, even the jubilee of our God. Trained in the bitter school of a personal struggle and personal victory, he issued forth from the cloister of Erfurt, the assertor of an individual conscience, the champion of a personal morality. And if our excellent friends of the Roman Catholic Church enjoy to-day, in this Protestant land of their adoption, the privilege of building their own sanctuaries, and having their own clergy, and worshiping God according to their own consciences, with none to molest or make afraid, it is because that same Martin Luther, whom their own pope excommunicated as a heretic, but whose triumph no papal bull could avert, taught and maintained the Protestant, Apostolic doctrine of personal conscience, and so of personal freedom.

"Again: It was Luther's mission to emancipate the laity. For centuries they had been virtually taught to believe that no layman could approach God except through the mediation of a priest, and, therefore, that the distinction between layman and priest was a distinction in essence as well as in form; a distinction on which the whole hierarchical system of Rome rests. But Luther, remembering how he himself, in his own bitterness of soul, had come directly to God without any intervention, save that of the one Mediator between God and man—the man Christ Jesus, and had found peace in believing, struck a Titan blow at the distinction between priest and layman, declaring that the veil of the temple is still rent in twain, and that all believers, whether ministers or laymen, men or women, adults or children, are alike priests before God, having equal right of entrance into heaven's holy of holies.

"Again: It was Luther's mission to emancipate worship. The prescribed liturgy of the church was in Latin; a form of speech which in many countries was a dead language, and therefore unintelligible. Luther provided a liturgy in the mother-tongue, with his wonted clear sense expressly declaring that it should ever be pliable to circumstances. He also made special provision for the public reading of the Bible, preaching or expounding, and congregational singing. Himself both poet and musician, Luther was the father of the modern hymnology and psalmody, giving the people an opportunity to worship God for themselves and in their own vernacular, and thus resuscitating worship from the tomb of a dead language.

" Once more, and comprehensively: It was Luther's

mission to emancipate the latent or imprisoned convictions and yearnings of awaking Christendom. He
was both the child and the sire of his epoch. For he
lived in a great era, and was just enough greater than
his age to be able to interpret the great Christian heart
longing to achieve, it knew not how, a reformation, or
rather a return to the purity of apostolic doctrine and
life. And in organizing and guiding this return, his
moderation was as marked as his dash. For it is a
great mistake to conceive Luther as a reckless reformer or wandering iconoclast, bent on nothing but
destroying. In respect to what was merely speculative or rubrical or incidental, he was too intensely practical, and even traditional in his tendencies, to be a
general iconoclast, saying, with characteristic quaintness, 'I am never for throwing away the old shoes till
I have got new ones.' In fact, it was this very moderation, born of his naturally conservative instincts,
which saddened his later years, as in the painful affair
of Carlstadt. While fighting most uncompromisingly
and to the very death every doctrinal and practical
error of the Roman Catholic Church, he still believed
that this Church was the lawful heir of the Apostolic;
and so, in respect to all that was incidental or kept the
impress of the apostolic original, he to the very last
clung to the Church of his fathers. Nevertheless, sur-
veying his mission as a whole, it was a mission of reformation, and so of destruction. Luther's true symbol, like that of his reforming prototypes John and
Elijah, is the axe, evermore famous as the lifter-up of
the axe in the thicket of the forest. And for this
special mission he was, as we have seen, by nature, by

training, and by circumstances, specially fitted. No
man ever illustrated more finely the poet's saying :—

> " ' Great offices will have
> Great talents, and God gives to every man
> The virtue, temper, understanding, taste,
> That lifts him into life, and lets him fall,
> Just in the niche he was ordained to fill.' "

S. A. REPASS,
President of Theological Seminary of the Evangelical Lutheran Church,
at Salem, Va.

"Among all the periods this side the Apostolic age,
none stand out so prominently as the Reformation of
the 16th Century; and in the firmament of the Church
through all these ages, there is no name that shines
with such a singular lustre as that of Martin Luther.
A patient study of the times in which he lived, of his
personal character and qualifications, of the work he
accomplished, of his peculiar adaptation to all the
varied circumstances of the age, leave no more place
to doubt his election and commission of God than that
of Isaiah or John.

" The statement may occasion surprise, that next to
· that of the Divine Author of Christianity, Luther's
birthday holds more prominence in the Christian world
than that of any amongst its thousands of heroes, and
that during this year of 1883 more emphasis is being
laid upon his life and work than has been upon any
man of God since the age of the Apostles. The statement, we repeat, may excite surprise; but it is a fact,
and a most significant one.

" There must be some solid underlying reason for

this unanimity of sentiment and action. A people may embrace a delusion, and for awhile follow 'a vain imagination;' but surely, after four hundred years, and these too embracing the most highly civilized and enlightened in the history of our race—centuries marked by the most skeptical and thorough-going criticism of men and principles—after such a period, the general readiness to honor and to recognize the Leader and the principles of the Reformation is surely the most triumphant vindication of the man and his work. And at this late date the endeavor to impugn either is only surpassed in folly by those, who, after eighteen centuries, undertake to prove that Christianity is itself a delusion.

"Luther presents himself to us, in the highest and best sense a truly representative man. He stands identified with the Reformation in a manner wholly unique. The movement gathered about him in a way at once so real and intimate that you cannot in fact separate the one from the other. * * * * His life and work sustained much more than a near relation to civilization and human liberty. It gave a living beginning, as well as a real impetus, to that slumbering germ, and placed it out in the clear warm sunlight of a pure, personal, renovated Christianity. Standing upon the threshold of the era of modern history, his name and life are inwoven with all the growth of the subsequent period; and in the midst of his gigantic and successful struggles with the multiform errors of the papacy, Luther appears the true hero of the ages— a very man of God and friend of the race.

"Luther not only found and restored the truth, but

he *lived* it.   In him the Christian son, husband, father, citizen and pastor, were embodied.   In studying his character, or that indeed of any representative man, we cannot unduly emphasize the fact that he was the truest exponent of his work, and that in him the Reformation had its best living embodiment.   Melanchthon was the superior theologian, and surpassed him in the Christian grace of gentleness.   He was inferior to Calvin in logical acuteness and consistency.   But combined in him, in a manner wholly unique, were all those qualities of mind and heart which preëminently marked him the leader of men.   Whether we study him as the patient translator of the Holy Scriptures on his Patmos, or as the earnest preacher and teacher; whether in the sick-room administering consolation to the afflicted and dying, or before the assembled power of the pope at Worms, he appears all in all the grandest name in uninspired history, one whom the ages delight to honor."

HENRY C. ROBINSON,

Of Connecticut.

"This man stands, in my thoughts, as a great emancipator of his race.

"It is difficult for us of to-day, girt with freedom as by an atmosphere, and protected by the sweet majesties of constitutional law, to appreciate, even when we read of them, the chains and oppressions of that other day, tied upon human hands and human minds and human hearts.   The assumptions of imperial princes and imperial pontiffs were unlimited, and were only endurable because of their jealousies of each other.   Four

and a half centuries earlier the great Gregory, Hildebrand, had claimed for the head of the church the
power to depose emperors and to absolve from their
allegiance the subjects of wicked princes.   At the end
of the Fifteenth century the ecclesiastical machinery of
the church was shot through and through with the
lust of power.   Bishoprics were no longer located in
counties, but counties in bishoprics.   The canon law
was getting to be the supreme law of Christendom.
In Luther's address to the German nobles he asked
for these four things: Germany for the Germans, civil
government uncontrollable by ecclesiastical authority,
a married clergy, and a national system of education.
Into the same places where he cast the pontifical
decree, which was written to make him an outlaw, but
which made him the first citizen of his world, was
thrown a volume of the canon law.   His doctrine of
justification, whether philosophically true or not,
hurled from the catapult of his raging eloquence, went
far to break down the hierarchical and sacramental in-
termediaries, which stood, as in solid masonry, between
the individual soul and his God.   Step by step, and by
ways of overwhelming surprise to himself, but always
following his ideas o truth, Luther at last reached the
inspiration of Jesus for individual rights; and, though
his scientific theology never apprehended the Father-
hood of God, and the Divine heritage of man, which
Jesus taught, his great soul, broader and nobler than
his education, wa ked u.der the benedictions of the
one truth and in the nobility of the other.   *   *

"And now, where was the great personal power of
this man ?   This question is too far-reaching.   Let me

give but one of the many answers. It was because he was in all respects a man. He was full to the brim of human nature. Man is naturally patriotic, because he is born into government, and it is so within the universal consciousness: Luther was a patriot of patriots. Dominion of Germany by Italy or Spain or France was to him intolerable. Man is naturally domestic, he is born into the family: Luther was intensely domestic, and sang the sweetest songs of home. Man is naturally religions, for he is born with a spiritual, trustful nature: Luther carried his reverence to obedience to the throne of the Infinite, and walked under His shadow in the burning sun and in His light by night.

"And his courage, and faith, and enthusiasm, and sociality, and love of music, were manly. And his pugilism, and violence, and ill-temper, and other weaknesses, were all human, too. The demonstrations of his violence seem to us shocking, but they were in the dialect of the age. The controversies of the great men of our age, of Newman, and Wesley, and Stanley, and Bushnell, and Swing, are in the dialect of a century whose manners are much nearer Gospel. Luther's grandeur is in his being a great, rough, noble piece of humanity. And here he takes hold of the whole family of man, for he touches the universal. The cynics and the unnaturals may be but partially great, but Shelley was in many senses a great poet, but Robert Burns, warbling his sweet lyric of pure husband-and-wife love, in the sixteen lines of 'John Anderson My Jo,' has reached a wider world than the other can ever touch. He told the universal story of true human nature, and if we go higher up to the supreme in literature, to the banks of the Avon, we shall find in Shakespeare a larger illustration of our thought. And once more, let us go to Palestine. Listen to the story of the Prodigal Son and of the publican at the temple ; to the sermon on the mount. Follow that career of love! Lo! we are at the feet of the Universal Man, whom no race nor age can call its own, for He fulfilled the humanity of all ages and all races."—*Union Memorial Meeting, Hartford, Conn.*

E. C. GORDON,

Pastor of the Presbyterian Church, Salem, Va.

" He was a mighty river—not like the Nile, issuing from a single source; rather like the Mississippi, enriched by a hundred streams having their springs in the countless hills and valleys of a continent. All the influences for good which had come down from the past served to swell Luther's greatness and power. From his parents he received a vigorous body, an unbending will, a capacious intellect, and a temper easily moved towards piety. The discipline of the times was harsh to severity. By this discipline he was hardened for contests from which men more delicately reared instinctively shrank. His peasant's blood brought him into full sympathy with the difficulties, trials, sorrows and cares of the masses. His clerical profession brought him into intimate intercourse with the most cultivated men of his age. His dangers threw him much with soldiers.

" In him met the coarseness of the clown and the high tone and bearing of the knight-errant. The pure stream of Pauline doctrine which had come down through Augustine, gave him religious back-bone. The mystics fed him with their tender, imaginative piety. He was a celibate and a man of family. He practiced all the arts of the ascetic, and was developed and strengthened by the duties, joys, anxiety of marriage and domestic life. The revival of learning enriched him with the stores it brought from Athens and Alexandria, from Constantinople, Jerusalem, Antioch, and Rome. The schoolmen taught him their methods, and his constant intercourse with the wisest men of action showed him how to use yet not abuse the arts of the scholastic and the refinements of the logician. Court and camp, cloister and school, peasant and priest, politics and religion, all helped to make him what he was. Above all, and under all, and encompassing all, God's grace, the Baptism of the Holy Ghost, gave him strength and movement.

" Luther was no gentle meandering stream, gliding softly through banks crowned with flowers. His was the spirit and power of Elijah. Enriched, made great, by all these mighty influences, his love for God and man forced him on with headlong speed—a rushing torrent, sweeping much away, but also bearing in his resistless course untold blessings to the ends of the earth.

" He is the first in time of that long line of learned commentators who have made the Word of God plain to the masses of the people.

" He is the first in time and in power of that long line of eloquent preachers who, in modern times, have brought the truths of the gospel home to the hearts and consciences of men.

11

"He is the first of that long line of reformers, who, taking the truth from him, have learned and taught that all reformation in the church consists essentially in a revival of true religion in the lives of God's people.

"He is the first of that long line of modern witnesses who have proclaimed the supremacy of God's Word, the right of private judgment, the sacredness of a man's conscience, as he must answer for himself at the bar of God.

"And because he is *thus first*, the whole Church in this four hundredth year of his birth honors his memory and thanks God for his life and work. He belongs exclusively to no country, to no party, to no denomination. God gave him to his redeemed saints. To them he belongs. He is their minister. If the chief of all, it is because, like his Master, he has served them all.

"It was once my privilege to stand on a hill-side in the city of Geneva, and look across the lake to Mount Blanc. On the right I saw the church in which Calvin preached, and below the church the school he founded. In front was a landscape as lovely as the eye of man ever looked upon. As I gazed in admiration, the sun sank slowly behind the western horizon. The hills and valleys across the lake were shrouded in gloom. Farther on, the mountains were still tinged with purple and gold; while in the distance Mount Blanc lifted his head grandly towards the heavens, and from his glistening summit flashed the glorious sunlight far and wide.

"So on this occasion, I stand upon a Genevan platform of theology and ethics. Born and reared in the church and school organized by John Calvin, I look back over these four centuries to the age which is now rapidly receding into the darkness of the past. The common men no longer appear. Time in his onward flight has left them dead, buried, and forgotten. They lie like the valleys after sunset in the gloaming. But as I gaze, I see the great men, like giant mountains, still living in the consciousness of this busy age. They still glow in the light which they continue to reflect across the years to us. There are Melanchthon and Calvin; there are Zwingli and Knox; there are others of lesser mould and stature standing out against the sky. But there is one higher, grander, nobler than the rest. His form is rugged; his character deeply furrowed by his contests within and without—with sin and the devil; with Pope and Emperor; with fanatic and worldling; with skeptic and sensualist. It is getting late. Four hundred years have passed; but the outline of this man is still clear and distinct, and he is yet flashing the glorious light of the gospel of the grace of God down the ages.

"May that light continue to shine, reflected by men as good and as true, if not so great as Martin Luther, until the Lord come!"

CHARLES W. SCHAEFFER,
President of Philadelphia Theological Seminary (Lutheran).

"No good picture of Luther can be drawn without presenting the lowliness of his origin, the splendor of his natural talents, the rigor of his early training, the hardships of his youth, his tender conscience, his

strong passions, his thorough acquaintance with all
the teachings of Rome, his prayerful struggles to find
salvation in those teachings, his utter and hopeless
failure, his discovery of the Word of God, his accepting it as a voice from heaven, his indomitable courage
in maintaining it at the peril of his life, his exhaustless
enterprise, his unwearied industry in spreading abroad
the knowledge of the Word among all people, so that
the people's hearts might be everywhere aroused and
enlisted for the truth, and thus the triumph of the
truth be assured.

"All these and other similar items are essential
features of the man; and with each separate element,
so interesting in itself, the harmonious combination of
the whole, in one single character, gives that character an extraordinary prominence in the first rank of
illustrious and extraordinary men."

WILLIAM L. GAGE,
Of the First Baptist Church, Hartford, Conn.

"It is no Christmas which we keep, no advent of
one born without sin and living without offence, it is
the birthday of a man strong in all that he was and
did, so rough in speech, so violent in temper, so controversial in tone and pugnacious in opposition, that
we never think of him as we do of the gentle and po-
litic Melanchthon, but have a full sense of that which
made his frailties. Yet we always think of him as
wonderfully adapted by God for the hard piece of
work which was laid out for him, and which he alone
could do; and we as distinctly see that he had a place
in the Redeemer's kingdom as marked as that of
Peter or Paul.

"Others will speak to you of this man's influence in literature, the beauty and strength which he gave to his mother-tongue, the impulse which he gave to free and independent thought, the value of the individual conscience and the individual life; the honor which he claimed for music and poetry; the impulse which he gave to education and to classical learning; the great humanity and heartiness of the man endearing him to all men. Luther has an hundred claims on us, and able men here and in other lands will voice them and honor them. For me in these introductory words, it remains to speak of him in what he was first and foremost, a man of God. When he was professor of Latin in Wittenberg for a year and a half, he did not deem that he had reached his true work; not until he was in his theological chair did he conceive that he was where God placed him. And amid all that Luther was called to do that was great and commanding in relation to art, education, letters and free thought, I deem that the first place must be what he was to the church in rescuing and restoring certain great dogmas of religion.

"We must not forget of Luther that he gave back to the church the great truth that man must approach his God empty-handed and soul to soul, God's grace flowing forth freely to a repentant heart, and giving life and strength and peace and full forgiveness for the past. A doctrine like this, so large, so deep, so rich in its results in life, cannot be covered up without infinite loss. Luther found it hidden in forgotten books, in St. Paul's epistles, in the writings of St. Augustine and St. Bernard, but as good as lost to the experience of living men, and he tested it by a personal trial as searching as the 7th and 8th of Romans, and set it on high and made it again the great life principle of a living church. He found the Bible covered up and hidden by disputations which seemed to him trivial and peculiar. He took it out from the great rubbish heap and opened it, spreading its treasures out in the tongue of the peasant and not in the dialect of the learned, and gave to the world a book so fresh and inspiring, so exhaustless in its life and wisdom, that from that day to this it has been peerless.

"We often speak of Luther's influence as limited and registered by Protestantism; and because the boundaries of Protestantism remain to-day precisely what they were when Luther died. It is often said that his work has not gone over them and beyond them. It would be a most interesting inquiry how far the Roman Catholic church has been modified by the Reformation. Doubtless very much in all respects. Its standard of doctrine may remain the same; its doctrine of papal infallibility, accepted in 1871, would appear to imply that Luther's work was all in vain. But we know that it is not so. It is vain to imagine in our time any such recoil from the Roman Catholic church as was felt in the sixteenth century. We are all of us constantly discovering good things in that church. All religious ceremonies have a most powerful reaction upon each other; and it would not be surprising if under disguises which we cannot penetrate a work of reform is going forward as rapidly as in the old days of rough words and fiery onslaughts. I trust that it is, and that the work begun by that great, brotherly man four hundred years ago may go on and on long after we shall have passed away, and when the great name of Martin Luther shall have faded into that dimness which awaits all names save that of the Lord Jesus Christ."

LUTHER A. GOTWALD,
Pastor of St. Paul's Lutheran Church, York, Pa.

" No blood of indolence flowed in our great Luther's veins. No idle moments filled up his life. No buried napkin of selfish ease held wrapped within its folds even the least of his high talents. Energy, activity, incessant planning, busy thinking, ceaseless doing, writing, speaking, giving, going, coming, working and putting others to work; now in this way and now in that; here to-day and there to-morrow; now translating the Scriptures, now preaching, now writing a letter to his little boy Hans, now one to Melanchthon, now one to the Elector, now dozens to others; now devising plans for the improvement of the schools; now counseling with kings and princes concerning great questions of State; now seeking to direct an awakened and anxious soul to Christ; now tenderly weeping and sympathizing with the sorrowing; now hurling his thunderbolts of invective and defiance against Pope, Turk and Devil; now studying the Catechism; now composing a tract, now a book, now a hymn* with

---

* Luther's enemies declared that he did more harm by his songs than by his sermons. Coleridge affirms that he served the Reformation as efficiently by his hymns as by his translation of the Bible. And another writer says: " The children learned Luther's hymns in the cottage, and martyrs sang them on the scaffold."

which, on wings of melody, to sing the new faith of the Reformation into the homes and hearts of the nation of the world: such is a single leaf from the book of our grand Luther's busy life—brain, tongue, hands, pen, all were ceaselessly busy and consecrated to Christ. A man was he in red-hot earnest in the work of the Lord; the fire of love to God and man glowing at white heat in deathless flame upon the altar of his heart!"—*From his published ordination sermon.*

A. K. YOUNG,
Pastor of First M. E. Church, Des Moines, Ia.

"What does human freedom owe to the German monk? His hand never touched a carnal weapon in the interest of his cause. His voice was never heard in the halls of legislation. He championed no measures that looked to governmental reform. With only the Word of God in his hands, he stood against the corruptions of the church, and demanded purification. To that purpose he steadfastly adhered. But we know that this work outran his purpose, and the Reformation once started overleaped ecclesiastical boundary lines. Modern civilization is one of its offsprings. Liberty of conscience and freedom of thought began in the sixteenth century. The revival of learning dates from the birth of Protestantism, and civil liberty dawned when Martin Luther nailed his ninety-five theses against the doors of the Wittenberg church. * * * Trace modern civilization to its source— you will find it on the borders of the sixteenth century. Follow the stream of popular learning to its fountain head—it began to flow when Luther gave the people

the Bible in their own language. Find the birth-
place of liberty—Wittenberg. There was the world's
'Declaration of Independence' written, and Martin
Luther's Reform is the prophet and apostle of human
freedom."

E. GREENWALD,
Pastor of Trinity Lutheran Church, Lancaster, Pa.

"*What does the world owe to Luther?* Of course,
Luther was but an instrument in the hands of God.
We thank God for Luther. In every expression of
praise of Luther, we glorify God for the blessings
which he bestowed upon the world through him. We
are not guilty of Lutherolatry, as the Romanists are
of Mariolatry. We do nor worship Luther, nor pray
to Luther, nor invoke Luther as a saint, nor pray to
Luther to pray for us. We make no mistake like this,
and are guilty of no such sin as this. At the same
time it is right and profitable for us to commemorate
his birth, and to recall the benefits we have through
him, as one of the world's greatest benefactors.

"What are the benefits that inure to us through the
instrumentality of Luther?

"We have *sound doctrine.* False doctrine lay at the
root of all the evil of the time. That evil consisted
not merely in empty forms, and idle ceremonies, and
unmeaning genuflections; in pictures, and relics, and
processions; in penances, and flagellations, and counting beads; but, at the root of all these, and as the cause
of all the corruption of practice that was the reproach
of Christianity, lay the corruption of doctrine that had
crept into the church. The head and heart were un-

11*

sound. Luther struck his hardest blows at the corruption of doctrine that prevailed. If the head and heart were healthy, the limbs would be sound. True doctrine would produce sound practice. In this respect Luther differed from the reformers that lived before the Reformation. To him we are indebted for the revival of true, sound, scriptural doctrine. We now have truth, where there was error, light where there was darkness, true Christianity where Christianity had been corrupted and false. For this we thank God for Luther.

"We have *salvation by grace.* Salvation was supposed to be by work—works consisting not of real virtue, and goodness, and benefits conferred upon mankind, but human works, observances of human rules, and self-imposed penances, often meaningless, and of no spiritual or moral value whatever. It was practically a Gospel with no grace in it; a Christianity without a Saviour. Much adoration was rendered to the cross, and the crucifix, but Christ crucified, as effecting a full satisfaction for our sins, and salvation by grace and mercy alone, without any worthiness or merit in us— this way of salvation was covered up and buried out of sight by the cumbrous mass of humanly imposed observances. 'The just shall live by faith'—justified by Christ's righteousness alone, apprehended by faith —this is the grand doctrine of grace and mercy revealed in the Gospel, and covered up by a corrupt hierarchy, which grand doctrine was exhumed and resurrected from the dust by the instrumentality of Luther. For this priceless jewel we thank God for Luther.

"We have *the right sacraments*. Sacraments are channels through which God conveys grace to us. Besides the false notion expressed by the words *ex opere operato*, and the gross carnal idea of transubstantiation in the Lord's Supper, the corrupt Church of Rome made the Eucharist an unbloody sacrifice, in which Christ, who had offered himself once for all on the cross, was daily re-offered by the priest in the mass, to save souls from purgatory. This direct contradiction of God's Word, the Reformation corrected; and whilst we have in the two sacraments, not seven, all the grace and blessings which they were appointed to convey, they are relieved of the false human additions which had been attached to them. For the right sacraments we thank God for Luther.

"We have *the pure Church*. Our Augsburg Confession truly says, the true Church is where the Gospel is truly preached, and the sacraments are rightly administered. It is not by pope and cardinals, by age or long succession, by numbers of adherents, by compact organization, by gorgeous ceremonial, or by lofty pretension, that the true Church is constituted. It is the true faith that constitutes the true Church. A corrupt faith makes a corrupt church. We have the true faith of God's Word. For the true faith, and the true Church, we thank God for Luther.

"We have *an open Bible*. The Bible had been a shut book. It was locked, and chained, and forbidden. Human tradition took the place of God's Word, as the rule of faith. Human tenets usurped the place of divine truth. The right of private judgment was denied, and men were burned for not accepting the dogmas imposed by a corrupt priesthood. The shut Bible is now an open book. Every man, woman, and child may have it, and may read and hear in their own tongue the wonderful words and works of God. The Bible, now open, will remain open, and can never be shut again. For an open Bible we thank God for Luther.

"We have *freedom of thought*. Thought had been bound with fetters stronger than iron. No man could call his soul his own. The very walls seemed to have ears. The most secret utterance of a sentiment at variance with the prevailing dogmas of the papacy, was reported to the Inquisition, was wrung out by the most cruel tortures, and exposed him that uttered it to be burned at the stake. Spies were in every house, and no man's life or liberty was safe. Worse than African slavery existed, for not the hands, but the mind was bound in shackles. The Reformation broke those fetters, and emancipated the conscience from the thraldom that enslaved it. Men, thenceforth, could think their own thoughts, and speak their own minds. For the inestimable blessing of freedom of thought, we thank God for Luther.

"We have *an untrammeled Church*. The Romish hierarchy is the most absolute despotism on earth. It boasts of unity; but it is the unity of the tyrant's heel that presses upon its victim's neck, and crushes out all power of free action. In Italy, it was only when its temporal power was wrested from it by Cavour's well-known maxim: 'A free Church in a free State,' carried out by the Italians, themselves, and announced by Cadorna's cannon battering down the gates of

Rome, that the fetters that bound the people were broken in that dark and priest-ridden land. But that principle was only a repetition of the principle that was enunciated in Germany more than three hundred years before. It was Luther that first announced it. For a 'free Church in a free State,' we thank God for Luther.

"We have *civil liberty*. Civil liberty before the Reformation was unknown. Kings and popes, and lords, and priests, claimed to own the world and to rule it, whilst the people had no voice either in the choice of rulers or in the making of laws. There was despotism in the Church, and despotism in the State. The Reformation appealed not only to kings and princes, but also to the people. Their emancipation from ignorance, and error, and superstition—from the dominance over their minds and hearts, of priests and monks, was the first elevation of the masses; the first assertion of their right to choose the doctrines they ought to hold, the first movement toward independence from despotic rule. It revealed to them their power, and made known their capabilities. The echoes awakened by the hammer that nailed the ninety-five theses to the door of the castle church at Wittenberg, are reverberating among the nations still. The Augsburg Confession and the Smalkald Articles in Germany, made possible the confirmation, extension, and popularization of the Magna Charta in England, and the adoption of the Declaration of Independence in America. If there had been no Luther in Germany, there would have been no Washington in America. For the invaluable blessings of our civil liberty and free institutions, we thank God for Luther.

"We have *our modern church civilization.* No event in modern times has had a more marked influence upon the age, than the Reformation. The great English historian Froude has well said in his recent articles on Luther: 'The traces of that one mind are to be seen to-day in the mind of the modern world. Had there been no Luther, the English, American, and German peoples would be thinking differently, would be acting differently, would be altogether different men and women from what they are at this moment.' * * * * For these inestimable blessings we thank God for Luther, through whose instrumentality, He has brought it about.

"For these, and many other blessings, let choir and orchestra, let young men and maidens, let old men and matrons, let pulpit and pew, let heaven and earth, ring out their glad anthems to-day, and thank God for Luther."

MYRON W. REED,

Pastor of First Presbyterian Church, Indianapolis, Ind.

"The advice of George Eliot is, 'Never cross the threshold of a reformer.' It is a good general rule. Quite commonly the man who is busy in public in saving the world, goes home and puts on his slippers and rests himself by making it dismal for the children. It is possible to have compassion on the multitude and have no care for the individual. We admire the great reformers and heroes of the world, but many of them we do not love. As a rule they are not the people we would drop in upon of a quiet evening. There was no better man in the Senate than Charles

Sumner, but there was better company. John Knox was a gloomy man, and John Calvin was not amiable. They hardened to their hard work. John Brown seemed to have no sense of humor. But it is well to cross the threshold of Martin Luther. He is as admirable at home as anywhere. He was as gentle to children as he was rough to the Pope. He was greater than his work, and the boy survived in him.   *   *

"Martin Luther was a man who laughed. He had read the Scripture 'Be not righteous over-much,' and taken it to heart. He had tried the plan of pleasing God by being painful—tried it faithfully by being a monk—tried fasting, vigils, hair shirts, and all sorts of self-torment, and he found God was not pleased; so he fell back on his healthy German common-sense and the Bible, and ceased to manufacture pain for himself or others.   *   *   *   *   *   *   *

"An American actor, dying, sent out for a minister, and when he came he looked at him and said to him: 'Your religion does not seem to agree with you.' Luther had that without which man is helpless to do good—human nature—and he kept it whole.

"This German organ had all the stops. He wrote a song to sing babies to sleep with, and the song was sung going into battle by the army of Prussia. He wrote a good letter to his little four-year-old son Hans:

"Grace and peace in Christ, my dear little boy. I am pleased to see that thou learnest well and prayest well. I know of a pretty garden where are merry children that have gold frocks and gather nice apples and plums and cherries under the trees, and sing and dance and ride on pretty horses with gold bridles and silver saddles. I asked the man of the place whose the garden was, and who the children were. He said, 'These are the children who pray and learn and are good.' Then I said, 'I have a son who is called Hans Luther: may he come to this garden and eat pears and apples and ride a little horse and play with the others?' The man said: 'If he says his prayers and learns and is good he may come, and Lippus and Just may come, and they shall have pipes and drums, and lutes and fiddles, and they shall dance and shoot with little cross-bows.' Then he showed me a smooth lawn in the garden laid out for dancing, and there the pipes and drums and cross-bows hung. But it was still early, and the children had not dined, and I could not wait for the dance, so I said, 'I will go straight home and write all this to my little boy. But he has an Aunt Lene that he must bring with him:' and the man answered: 'So it shall be: go and write as you say.' Therefore, dear little boy, learn and pray with a good heart, and tell Lippus and Just to do the same, and then you will all come to the garden together. Almighty God guard you. Give my love to Aunt Lene, and give her a kiss for me. Your loving father, MARTIN LUTHER."

"It is a rare talent for one hand to be stern enough to burn the Pope's bull and tender enough to write such a letter as that. You have heard, as a child, descriptions of heaven, I suppose, given by visitors to the Sunday-school. How do they, as you remember them, compare with this of Luther's? As I remember them, they made the place not nearly so attractive to a little child as 'Charley Mayer's.' Nothing for a child to do! This letter of Luther's was written nearly four hundred years before the books 'Gates Ajar,' and 'Beyond the Gates.' So long ago it seemed to Martin Luther that a God Almighty and all-loving Father prepared a heaven that would please his children; not poorer than the earth—richer; not less variety of sight, and sound and employment, but more; a heaven in which no little child should ever be listless and homesick!

"The best book of Luther's is his 'Table Talk.' He did not bolt his dinner like an American Protestant. He mixed it with stories, good ones. I suppose there are Christians in Chicago who have not seen their children on a week day by daylight for a year, except it may be in the long days in June. They can not keep still long enough to have a photograph taken. They will have to be taken by the instantaneous dry-plate process, and be remembered by their children as running to catch something. These affairs of our people that consume the mind and wither the heart, and write their pitiful stories on the face, are not great affairs; they are not affairs that must bless the world. * * * * * * * *

"He was a great servant of God, as busy a man in great affairs as ever lived; but he loved and had sympathy with a little child—had a religion that included him. His religion included home, and friends, and games, and music, and pictures, and all that is good in the life that now is. He did not wait till he died to be pleased or to please others. He began right here and now to take in the good of life. The great God has made the face of the earth. It must please him to see a mortal make a faithful copy of it. To worship God will hinder no artist in any art. If ever a man could have excused himself from social duty and pleasure, Luther could. He had business, and 'king's business, and it required haste.' But he absented himself from no human felicity. He was a good father, and friend, and neighbor. He attracted humanity of all sorts and conditions. He 'adorned the gospel.' * * * * * * *

"'O Douglas, Douglas! tender and true.' It is possible to get that combination. 'Whatsoever things are just;' we are told to think on these things. We are also told to think on 'whatsoever things are lovely.' We strive for a religion that shall stand like its founder. You see Jesus doing the will of Almighty God, but little children are close about His feet. It is the divine and human both in one person, that, being lifted up, draws all men. And it is this mingling of strength and sympathy in Martin Luther that has to-day, four centuries since his birth, made his name to be honored in every civilized street on the face of the earth."

PHILIP M. BIKLÉ,

Prof. of the Latin Language and Literature in Pennsylvania College.

"And now, in looking at him, what a many-sided man Luther was! How well adapted for the work to which God had appointed him! There have been other men of as rich religious experience as his; others who have been as strong in their convictions; others as earnest in prayer; others who have trusted as implicitly in God's promises, and placed as high value on His holy word; others who have had as remarkable intellectual gifts, as great courage and strong will-power, or as much conservatism in reformatory movements; others who have written as precious hymns; others who could as well sway the masses by their eloquence; and others who have had the spirit of nationality and the better characteristics of their people as highly developed. But, while this is true, there is no one in whom these elements were ever so combined as in Luther. This combination is what gave him his special fitness for the work of the Reformation. God selected him and fitted him for it. He was a well-rounded, complete man. There was no one-sided development about him, either mental, spiritual, or physical, but a symmetry and harmony altogether exceptional. He was not all cold intellect, nor warm emotion, nor strong will—the one to the exclusion of the others—but a well-balanced combination of all three. With all this he had a deep insight into human nature, an appreciation of its wants, and the practical tact and skill to meet them.

"Coming to the light of the truth through an agonizing spiritual experience; endowed with a courage indomitable; proclaiming his convictions without fear of papal emissaries, the pope himself, or the emperor; a man of humble, earnest prayer before his God, but of bold defiance before raging adversaries; holding up the Word of God as supreme; setting at naught in the face of danger and death the decrees of the pope and councils when unscriptural; spreading the truth broadcast among the people by commentary and translation; proclaiming freedom of conscience and the right of private judgment, he was the leader, under God, of the Church's deliverance from error and of the world's freedom.

"With the cross in one hand—the cross, not the crucifix—the symbol of the Lamb slain for the sins of the world, but now deprived of its victim who is in the midst of the throne, ever living and highly exalted as our great High Priest and final Judge, and the Bible in the other—the Bible not with lids clasped with lock and key, but unbound and wide open, not chained to a desk but free for every one, not in a language unknown but in the people's own tongue—with the cross of Jesus Christ uplifted in one hand and the open Bible in the other, Luther stands before us as the great missionary of the truth, towering higher and higher as the centuries roll on, and becoming more and more the hero, not of the German people alone, but of the world."—*Lutheran Quarterly,* January, 1884.

DOCTOR BAYLISS,

Pastor of Walnut Hills Methodist Episcopal Church, Cincinnati, Ohio.

"John Wesley was converted to God on the evening of May 24, 1738, at a meeting in Aldersgate street, where one was reading Luther's preface to the Epistle to the Romans, and therefore there is a sense in which Methodism is one of Luther's children; for his preface helped Wesley into a new phase of religious life, and Methodism as an organized force is the embodiment of a new form of religious life, not known in Luther's time.

"It is fitting then that Methodism should add its voice to the swelling chorus, for no seed of truth planted by the monk of Wittenberg has brought forth a more wonderful and luxuriant harvest than that which found its way into the heart of John Wesley, and so we join the song which this morning gladdens the world. One of the marvels of human history is that so much of the world's greatness and light have been born of its weakness and might.　　*　　*　　*　　Luther gave to the world an unchained Bible, and prepared the way for a spiritual epoch.

"The religious thought of Europe was like an eagle in an iron cage, his wings and head drooping in sad captivity. Luther walked up to the cage and shook the bars. The eagle lifted its head and looked at Luther and drooped again; but Luther shook the cage again, and then the imprisoned bird lifted its head and wings, but there was no room to soar. Luther then said: 'Melanchthon, bring me a hammer;' and then the strong, brave man hit blow after blow, and battered, while the bird fluttered and fumed to be free. At length he destroyed the prison cage, and the eagle lifted its proud head, poised its powerful pinions, and, as Luther eagerly watched it, bore itself upward and soared away to the sun.

"Luther opened the door to the Holy of Holies in religion, and then out of the spread of truth and freedom was evolved civil liberty, making the world forever his incalculable debtor."

REUBEN WEISER,

Lutheran Pastor of Denver, Colorado.

"*No man in the whole history of the world has ever called out such a wide-spread, spontaneous and universal storm of praise and eulogy!* Luther's name for the last twelve months has been on the tongue of every Protestant from Tasmania to Iceland, and from Norway to Nova Scotia! More than one hundred millions of Protestants, and they the most intelligent, pious, and the freest people under the heavens, have rendered their praises and homage to this *illustrious champion* of civil and religious liberty in unstinted measure. Looking at the honor paid to this great man, we may well inquire, what has he done to endear his name to posterity? Single-handed and alone, he produced the greatest moral and intellectual revolution in the history of the world—he liberated the human mind from the bondage of papal error and superstition—he republished the gospel of Christ that had been buried under the rubbish of tradition—he gave the Bible to his countrymen in a language they could understand—he started all the mighty moral and intellectual machinery that is now moving the world." —November 11, 1883.

C. H. SPURGEON,
Of the Metropolitan Tabernacle, London, England.

"Yesterday four hundred years ago there struggled into the world one who was to make unlimited noise in it—Martin Luther. Blessed was the day among many of the days that had gone before—the day when he was born, whose brave spirit should shake the nations and put an end to the tyranny and error which held millions of men in bondage. The whole of human history from that time was more or less affected by the work of that man. *   *   *   *   *

"There are very few men like Luther in the present day. Most of us have not so much faith in our whole bodies as Luther had in his little fingers—not so much faith in us as in the hair on his head. Yet even that little faith will make us live. I do not say it will give us the strong and vigorous and lion-like faith that such a man as he had. But we shall live. *   *   *

"Luther put down his foot every time his friends begged of him to desist. He was a Titan, a giant, a man of splendid mental calibre, strong physique, and a man who suffered much and could suffer much. And still, while suffering so much and so often, he believed and was sure of his belief. He did not want their words when he had once got the word of God. This man lived by his faith because he was a man of strong will. This strong excitement of his body brought on him afterwards fearful depression of spirit. If you read an accurate life of him, you will find that he had hard work sometimes to keep his soul alive. He was desponding and despairing sometimes at his weakness, and this great weakness made him feel as if it would burst his mighty heart. How often he and John Calvin longed to die, for they loved not the strife in which they lived.

"But Luther always had a pledge of Christ's atonement, and he got safe and happy again after he had looked Christ and God in the face. He was comforted by the precious blood of Christ. When he came to die they asked him if he held the same faith. He said: 'Yes.' They need not have asked him that. And now, to-day the name of Luther continues to be preached, and will be until Christ Himself shall come, and they shall need no candle, neither light of sun, because Christ Himself shall be the light of the people. Brethren, let us say, 'As Luther lived by faith, so do we.' God give us some more of that faith. Amen and amen."—November 11, 1883.

A. SPAETH,

Professor in Lutheran Theological Seminary, Philadelphia, Pa.

"Luther has often been called the most German of Germans, the chief representative of the best union of the German and the Christian in one person; and again he has been characterized as the very embodiment of the Church of his name, the very type in his own person of that sound form of Christian life and theology called Lutheranism, over against other forms and other names. We admit, most willingly, that in all this there is a great deal of truth and significance; and yet this way of looking upon Luther falls short of doing full justice to the true meaning and import of his place in the history of the Church and of the world. His is a position of much more comprehensive and widespread influence. He is not the man of a single generation, or of a single nation. He does not belong, and was not meant to belong, to the Germans exclusively, or to the sixteenth century, or to that particular church which by the choice of her enemies bears his name, in distinction from other churches and denominations. Luther belongs to all Christendom. His influence reaches down to our present time, and his voice, and the impulses given by him, are just as much needed in this nineteenth century as they were in the sixteenth, and just as well suited to the Christians in the valley of the Mississippi and on the Pacific coast, as to those on the banks of the Rhine and on the hills of Thuringia. *　　*　　*　　*　　*

"These few points, which have thus been briefly indicated, will suffice to show that we are perfectly justified in calling the sixteenth century the opening of our modern era. And in the midst of the downfall of mediæval life and institutions, at the very time when the first powerful pulsation of the spirit of modern times was felt, Luther was called forward by God's providence and charged with the most important life question, that of personal salvation. It was the most critical period in the history of the world, since the end of ancient Rome and Hellas, and the foundation of the Christian Church. And, as fifteen hundred years before, Paul had been pre-eminently the apostle and missionary who carried the seed of the new life through the ruins of the ancient and heathen world, so Luther had received a similar call in his own day. He is truly the apostle and prophet of the modern era. Not in the sense of his Romish defamers, who mis-represent him as the father of all the negative and destructive tendencies of our present time, and hold him responsible for all the mischief done in church, and state, and society, by an unbounded individualism and subjectivism. The very opposite is true. In the midst of the storms and upheavings of his time, it was Luther's work to snatch from the wreck of the past, and to hand over to the rising era, the one greatest treasure, the jewel of God's pure, everlasting gospel. (Cf. the sixty-second of his ninety-five theses: ' The true treasure of the Church is the most holy gospel of the glory and the grace of God.') Reformation or no Reformation, the time of the middle ages was past. The new era was peremptorily knocking at the gate. It *must* enter. The question was only whether it should enter Christless, faithless, desperate and de-structive, a time of conflict and negation with ruin on

12

all sides, or whether it should come with the one power for the healing of the nations, the gospel of God's grace in Christ alone. But there stood God's chosen servant, firmly planted on the Rock of Ages. In the midst of the greatest convulsions and transformations, Luther was the strongest, and, in a certain sense, the only conservator of all that was really worthy to be preserved."—November 9, 1882.

S. J. McPHERSON,
Pastor Second Presbyterian Church, Chicago, Illinois.

"There was never a more formidable opponent or more manly man to fight the devil, to bless men, or serve God, than this Luther, whose deeds are praised. Being a genius, he was too discerning to find refuge in either a monastery or the Romish church; the warning that 'the just shall live by faith' was voiced to him by Jesus Christ, and marked his every step. Luther's conversion was the fountain-head of the Reformation, and every one desirous of becoming converted must do as did this zealous worker and Reformer when he followed the impression made upon his mind by Christ. He discovered that it was the duty of every one to render prayer, and that it was not the exclusive and paid privilege of the priesthood to exact the offering. His translation of the Bible was a work of such masterly finish and accuracy that it was said of him he therein made God speak German. It is owing to his discovery of the fundamental laws and facts of religious reform that he so faithfully labored for the cause, and met all opposition with a cheerful spirit; and when he boldly and courageously posted the ninety-five theses upon the door of the cathedral at Wittenberg, the world reëchoed his sentiments, simple and pure, and the Romish church shuddered at the aspect of the crushing religious phalanx commanded by the master-reformer of all ages. He bowed to no one, and was truly the mightiest man of all in the field of religious reform. It is true, that at times he was too vehement and brusque. This is not attributable solely to his temperament, but also to the time at which he lived and labored. That he was human and humane is evidenced by his 'Table Talk,' and many other productions. He loved children and music. These two fondnesses are singularly indicative of a true man. He was a veritable lion, not unlike the lion of Judah, brave and courageous. He believed in devils, perhaps more so or to a greater degree than we of to-day; but he was less afraid of a genuine devil than we are of ghosts. It was Luther who was the great emancipator of modern times, who unloosened with his own hands the many ritual obligations buckled by the Roman Catholic church around the ankles of mankind."

JOHN JAY,
President Exec. Com. Evangelical Alliance of the United States.

"We are assembled to-night, at the call of the Evangelical Alliance of the United States, to commemorate the four hundreth anniversary of the birth of Luther. This reminder of the great Reformer has stirred the hearts of the nations whom his teachings have helped to bring from the noxious mists of ignorance and superstition into the pure sunlight of

Christianity. His memory is lovingly cherished in his own land as the moulder of the German mind, and almost the creator of the German tongue—the Reformer by whose voice, in that tumultuous movement for mental and moral emancipation, God awakened the people, and the echoes of whose voice still resound throughout the world. He is the chief figure in an historic picture which will be contemplated by the thoughtful of all lands to the end of time. He still lives, in the words of Coleridge, 'an antagonistic spirit to Rome and a purifying and preserving spirit to Christendom at large.' *   *   *   *   *

"It seemed fitting that this Alliance, on which has devolved in part the work of maintaining the great truths proclaimed by Luther, against the self-same forces with which he contended, and against all other forces, foreign or domestic, which threaten our religious liberties and the purity of American institutions, should call on Americans to join with the rest of Christendom in commemorating the birth of the great Reformer. No country has more reason than this Republic to recall with joy the blessings he assisted to secure for the world, in emancipating thought and conscience, and impressing the stamp of Christianity upon modern civilization. Although America had not been discovered by Columbus when Luther was born, Luther's far-reaching influence, which to-day is felt from the Atlantic to the Pacific, helped to people our Northern Continent with the colonists, who laid the foundation of its future liberties on the truths of the Bible. He recommended the oppressed people of Europe to take the teachers of their choice, and with

the Bible in their hand to follow the star of freedom
to lands where religious liberty could find a home.

    *   *   *   *   '   *   *

"It would be easy to cite Roman Catholic tributes
—the more significant because paid perhaps uncon-
sciously—to the Christian civilization to which Luther
so largely contributed; but let me quote in closing a
few words eloquent and touching from an eminent
English pervert, Mr. Faber, of the personal value of
the Bible which he could no longer read, and the circulation of which Rome now, as in the days of Luther,
denounces as 'a pestilence.'

"'Who will not say that the uncommon beauty and
marvellous English of the Protestant Bible is one of
the great strongholds of heresy in our country? It
lives on the ear like music that can never be forgotten,
like the sound of church bells which the convert
hardly knows how to forego. Its felicities seem to be
things rather than words. It is a part of the national
mind, and the anchor of national seriousness. The
memory of the dead passes with it, the potent traditions of childhood are stereotyped in its verses; the
power of all the griefs and trials of man are hidden
beneath its words. It is the representative of his best
merits, and all there is about him of soft and gentle
and pure and penitent and good speaks to him forever
out of his English Bible. It is his sacred thing, which
doubt has never dimmed and controversy has never
soiled. In the length and breadth of the land there is
not a Protestant with one spark of religiousness about
him whose spiritual biography is not in his Saxon
Bible.'

"When the frankest warning has come to us from a Brownson, of the danger threatened to our country from foreign influence and foreign schools, and of the necessity of saving our high American civilization from the deteriorating influences of what he called 'the foreign colony;' when a Faber can thus describe with touching plaintiveness the priceless blessing of the Bible which he had lost, have such utterances no significance for this occasion? While they indicate the path to be pursued if we would preserve the blessings we enjoy and maintain in its purity the civilization which we inherit, may they not also justify the hope that our reasons for thankfulness at the life and work of Luther may find in the future yet wider scope, in the enlarging number of those who, whatever their faith or their unbelief, shall come to recognize in the open Bible the divine teacher of the world?"

WILLIAM M. TAYLOR,
Pastor of the Broadway Tabernacle Church, New York.

"In the prosecution of the excavations at Pompeii, the workmen laid bare an ancient spring of water, which, as soon as it was set free, flowed forth as copiously as ever, and carried refreshment with it wherever it went. For centuries it had been buried beneath the ashes of the volcano, but the moment it was again uncovered it sent out its stream of blessing with all its pristine fulness and wholesome influence.

"Something like that was the work which Martin Luther did for the fountain of truth in the Sacred Scriptures. For many generations that had been virtually stopped up by the rubbish of tradition, and entombed beneath the weight of authority ; but by his sturdy strength, his steady persistence, and his dauntless courage, he dug it clear again; and it became once more, as at the first, the well-head of the river of progress among the nations. That is the reason why his name marks the beginning of a new epoch in history; and why four hundred years after his birth so many nationalities on both sides of the Atlantic are uniting to do honor to his memory. There was in him, indeed, the might of a unique personality. He had a massive intellect, a glowing enthusiasm, a tender heart, a strong imagination, a masterful will, a fearless boldness, and a rich fund of common sense, all of which found vent in a vigorous eloquence and a prolific authorship to which the printing press gave the amplest range. But these things alone would not account for the place which he holds in the estimation of Protestants. Other men have been his equals in all these respects. Some have been even his superiors. But we do not hold such celebrations as this in their honor. There have been in every land philosophers, orators, statesmen, scholars, poets, who in ther own departments have surpassed him, and we give to them no stinted praise ; but yet no such enthusiasm as we feel to-night thrills us at the mention of their names, because each of them wrought with agents which had only an earthly potency and a restricted range. It was the merit of Luther that he set free the Word of God; and because that is a divine agent and touches the main springs of individual, social, and national life, his influence has gone farther, and struck deeper, than

that of any other man in modern history. Great as
he unquestionably was, his work was greater than himself, because the instrument in his hands, as in Paul's,
was that Gospel which is 'the power of God.' Hence
the celebration of this four hundredth anniversary of his
birth is truly more a tribute to the Scriptures than it
is to himself. We honor him not merely for what he
was, but mainly because he digged again the well
which for centuries had been stopped up. We cherish
his memory not simply because of the qualities which
he manifested in his great life-battle, but because by
that battle he secured for us the liberty to read and
interpret the Bible for ourselves; and so all that we
owe to it, helps to swell our tribute to him. We venerate him, but we glorify God in him ; for he would have
been no more to us than many other men, not so much
perhaps as some other men, if he had not unsealed for
us the fountain of the Scriptures.

*   *   *   *   *   *   *   *   *

"Thus the right of private judgment was with him
the abjuration of all human authority, in order that he
might keep his loyalty to the authority of God in the
sacred Scriptures. It was not, as he expounded it,
the liberty of every man to think as he liked, but
rather the inalienable privilege of every Christian to
take the truth directly from the lips of the Lord without the intervention of pope or emperor. He threw
off human intolerance that he might bow before divine
authority. He would let no man come between the
Lord and him, but when Christ spoke that was enough
for him. He accepted that at once, and would give it
up on no consideration. Now these two things—mark

it, not one thing, but two things—the repudiation of human authority in religious matters and the recognition in the same department of the authority of Christ speaking through the Scriptures, are the balancing forces that keep the life of the Christian in its proper orbit. If he yields to human intolerance there will be slavery; if he repudiates divine authority, or what is the same thing in this case, the supremacy of Scripture, there will be license; but by repudiating the one and acknowledging the other he walks in that service 'which is perfect freedom;' and in the fact that Luther insisted upon both, we have the explanation of the difference between the Reformation in Germany and the first French Revolution.

" Here, too, it was that the work of Luther touched and influenced civil liberty. He stood for freedom of conscience, and thereby also widened the area of liberty in general. He asserted the equality of all men before God, in Christ; and out of that came at length, here and elsewhere, the Declaration of Independence, which affirms the equality of all men before human law. Had he flinched and recanted like Galileo, there would have been no such result. It is to the confessor of faith, and not of science, that we are indebted for the liberty we now enjoy; and if one ask what good the Reformation has effected in national life, we point him, in reply, to the difference between Great Britain under Victoria and under the Mary who sent Latimer and Ridley and Cranmer to the stake: may we ask him to look around and see its latest fruit in the greatness of this Free Republic?"—*This, the foregoing, and that of Phillips Brooks, are extracts from speeches deliv-*

12*

cred at Evang. Alliance Celebration in New York, and published in full in pamphlet form.

M. LOY,

Professor of Theology in Capital University, at Columbus, Ohio.

"It is no wonder that the world remembers Martin Luther, and that at this time people assemble in vast multitudes to celebrate the four hundredth anniversary of his birth. Men delight to honor those of their race who are justly styled great, and among the great names in history there is none greater than that of the 'solitary monk who shook the world.' He was great in his natural endowments; he was great in his acquirements in every department of human learning; he was great in the integrity of his character and in the moral heroism which he displayed in times of trial; he was great in his marvelous labors and achievements.

> 'The brave monk who made the popedom rock,
> Champions a world to show his equal yet.'

   *   *   *   *   *   *

"In this same faith Luther performed those manifold labors by which the Reformation was spread and the Church of the Reformation was established. He never grew weary of preaching the everlasting gospel of the grace of God, and telling sinners of the unsearchable riches of Christ. In season and out of season he proclaimed the good tidings of justification by faith alone, without the deeds of the law, to the peace and comfort of thousands who heard his voice, and of millions who since have read his noble sermons in print. To the German people he gave his admirable translation of the Bible, that the Word of God might abide in them richly in all wisdom. By his teaching and powerful defence of the truth which he taught, God freed the people from the bondage in which they had been held under papal rule, so that they dared to read the book which God had given to men for their souls' eternal good, and which is 'profitable for doctrine, for reproof, for correction, for instruction in righteousness,' but which the papacy had prohibited. The translation of the Bible is an imperishable monument of Luther's industry and faith and love for the edification of God's people."

JOHN H. BARROWS,
Pastor of First Presbyterian Church, Chicago.

"Am I exalting a man into a sort of demi-god? No. God lifted him as he lifted Mount Sinai above the sandy and burning plain. After seeing the grandeur of the mountain, we may draw near and note the ragged outlines, rifts, and scars which are there. To me, considering the condition of the church in his age, Luther's virtues are the surprises, not his faults. The errors and sins of great men, exalted like the Protestant hero, afflict their own and succeeding generations. The extravagance and ferocity which Luther showed in the heat of controversy, alienated and divided the friends of reform, and are stains on his memory. His refusal to extend the hand of Christian fellowship to Zwingli at Marburg is a sad proof of his mental and spiritual limitations. His views of predestination, and the bondage of the will, he carried to fatalistic extremes. His failure in the crisis of the struggle between the peasants and the princes to do justice to the former, led to lamentable results. And yet the greatest natures have been drawn to Luther, as on the whole the most interesting and attractive Titan God ever raised up to smite a giant monster. Calvin said: 'Though Luther should call me a devil, I would still revere and love him as an eminent servant of God.' The impetuous torrent of Luther's mighty nature changes how often into a peaceful and arbored lake by which we linger with delight. He was a soul that ardently loved music and little children, and the dear Catherine—and had great hungerings and thirstings for friendship. Jovial, in the literal sense of that word,—in rough German ways at times—his heart was great and tender; and beset by devils though his life seemed, and swept by great storms of passion, and wearied and depressed and sorrow-crushed though he often was, how his faith towered up like an Alpine crag, and what great joy came to him looking over the bounteous and peaceful earth which spoke to him of God. What peace was his at times, gazing up 'into the deep heaven of worlds?'"

PERE HYACINTHE,
In St. Paul's Lutheran Church, Washington, D. C.

"It has been a habit of my Ultramontane antagonists to call me by the opprobrious epithet given to Martin Luther—that of 'Apostate Monk.' I should like to be his disciple—not in all of his opinions, but so far as these opinions are great and immortal in the work of Reformation. I salute in him the first Old Catholic. He wanted to reform according to his ideas; inside and not outside. He wanted, in fact, no division; no schism. I should like to accomplish what Luther began—a thorough reform in the Latin Church. For Luther would have kept within the church lines in a regularly constituted episcopate, if he could have done so."

Continuing, the Pere said, in substance, that Luther was animated by these principles: "First, he was to break off connection with Rome, with its errors and abuses; secondly, at the same time he was to remain loyal to the faith as taught in the Bible, and faithful to Christ as the Very Son of God. In following these two principles he traced two lines of demarcation, one of time and one of space. That of time was a new era in the Church and in society. The Renaissance was only a preparation for this Reformation, as of the Renaissance the French Revolution was only a consequence. Neither created a distinct era. That was done by the Reformation inaugurated by Luther.

" The Reformation drew a line of demarcation both in America and in Europe, between the people who were emancipated by Luther and those still holding allegiance to Rome. As regards these it was not a question of race, but of a religious system. For example, the Irish Kelts, the Slavic Poles, the Austrian Germans, all of whom are Romanists, are as surely in a state of decadence as the Latin nations. Thirdly, to practice what he preached was Luther's aim. He was courageous enough to do this, in private as well as in public and ecclesiastical life."

The Pere closed by hoping that in 1983 the whole world would be neither Protestant nor Romanist, but that humanity would be united in one great Christian Church.

Hon. Simon Wolf, Ex-U. S. Consul to Egypt, followed Pere Hyacinthe in a burst of fervid eloquence, wherein he paid a glowing tribute to the genius and character of the great German who had emancipated human thought.   He looked upon Luther as the greatest man born to humanity since time began.— *National Republican*, Nov. 12, 1883.

D. M. GILBERT,
Pastor of Grace Lutheran Church, Winchester, Virginia.

" It is not in the nature of things that a thoroughly consecrated, laborious, courageous life, like Luther's, should be lived at any time in vain.   But given to the world, in God's providence, at a period when just such qualities as his were most sadly needed, and for a work the importance of which, to his own and succeeding generations, can scarcely be exaggerated, he became, as we have seen, the hero of a deliverance grander in itself and in its consequences than any of which the annals of uninspired history can tell—the Moses of a modern exodus from an incomparably worse than Egyptian bondage.   *   *   *   *   *

" Luther's character and life have been sifted as wheat, and his worth thoroughly tested by ten generations of men.   We are not left to *suppose* anything concerning the indebtedness of our times to him whom a great Romish historian even has been constrained to eulogize as the 'Liberator of modern thought.'   His fame is secure.   His influence for good will be unceasing. As the late Dr. Krauth has felicitously expressed it,— 'Luther will abide as a living power through all time. His image casts itself upon the current of ages as the mountain mirrors itself in the river that winds at its foot. The mighty immutuably fixing itself upon the changing.'   *   *   *   *   *   *

"And as we hastily rehearse to-day something of the story of his life,—as we mark the high-souled courage with which, in the championship of his holy cause, he confronted every danger, and calmly bore himself through every trying crisis, who of us does not feel that when at last he yielded up his spirit to the God who gave it, there was no hero of a hundred battles over whom it might be more fitly said:

> "'O iron nerve, to true occasion true,
> O fallen at length, that tower of strength,
> Which stood four-square to all the winds that blew?'"

J. B. REIMENSNYDER,
Pastor of St. James Lutheran Church, New York City.

"It has been the habit of some to assert that other reformers, as Wickliffe, Savonarola and Huss failed, and Luther succeeded, because, in his case, the time was ripe for the movement. But just and acute thinkers are generally abandoning this position as untenable. For, 'if the man could have done nothing without the fortunate hour, the hour would have passed unused unless the man had appeared.' And this explains the extraordinary fact that during the tumultuous upheavals of the next thirty years, Luther never lost control of the movement. For it alone was the signal ability which had originated the Reformation, that was equal to the wise conduct of the vast forces which it clothed with a dangerous, because unwonted, liberty. Everywhere, therefore, do we see

Luther's colossal figure towering in the forefront. It is he who restrains the fiery Elector; nerves the timid Melanchthon; reproves the haughty Henry VIII. of England; represses the fanatical Prophets; reassures the wavering hosts; and snatches victory from the very jaws of defeat. His strong hand always holds the helm, and all by common consent look to him as the leader. *Without Luther there would have been no Reformation.* While he lived and his temperate counsels prevailed, there was no bloodshed between the opposing parties, and nations and millions came over to Protestantism in a day. But since his death, Romanism has held, at least, her territory. The historian Froude, therefore, truly says: 'If the Reformation had been led by Carlstadt, or Zwingli, or Munzer, it would have failed. But that it was able to establish itself was due to the one fact that there existed at the crisis a single person of commanding mind as the incarnation of the purest wisdom which then existed in Germany, in whose words the bravest, truest and most honest men saw their own thoughts represented; and because they recognized this man as the wisest among them, he was allowed to impress on the Reformation his own individuality!'" *From Synodic Sermon (pamphlet).*

CHARLES A. BRIGGS,

Prof. of Theol. in Union Theol. Seminary, New York.

"The chief merit of Luther as a professor was in his *unflinching fidelity to truth.* He was not so great a scholar as Melanchthon; but Melanchthon would have given away the Reform by his compromising policy, if

Luther had not held him fast to the truth. Luther was not so keen a critic as Carlstadt or Agricola; but these became narrow and one-sided, conceited and fanatical, and Luther could not restrain them from mischief-making. He was not a politician as were Zwingli and Calvin. He did not seize the civil or the ecclesiastical sword to battle for the Reform or to purge the church. Zwingli took the sword to perish by the sword. Calvin purged Geneva so heroically that he made hypocrites and pious exiles. Luther wielded the sword of the spirit. He grasped the truth with all his strength and made it a part of his own being. The truth of God swayed him with irresistible power. He was not controlled by half-truths and force of circumstances. *Essential* and *vital truths* and the *great unities* made him their spokesman. He held these up as the truth of God, to guide and save the nations. He impressed them so deeply upon the Germanic world, that they characterize the modern age, and will never be effaced.

"When *truth* became supreme in the university of Wittenberg, in the lecture-room of Luther, the pope and the monastic orders, the empire and the allied kings, had to contend—not with Luther and his students—but with a divine force, the eternal Logos, the living God." *Sem'y Symposiac, a Pamphlet.* (See same pamphlet for full addresses of Drs. Hitchcock, Brown, Schaff, Shedd, Prentiss and Hastings.)—New York, Nov. 19, 1883.

L. A. FOX,

Of Roanoke College, in College Church, Salem, Va.

" Prominent among the characteristics of Luther, distinguishing him from all preceding and contemporary reformers, are these three : *First.* He did not propose it. He began, as he believed, a loyal son of the Romish Church. In his simplicity, he was defending the holy Father at Rome when he nailed up the Ninety-five Theses. Duty to his congregation called him out, and he was astonished when the echo came ringing back from all Germany. In this opening he had no general plan; he was the child of Providence, and this characterized all his efforts. He took step after step as circumstances pointed out the way. When was there a great mind engaged in a grand work, a willing cheerful agent, so wanting in general plans for its prosecution? God led him, and in nothing does the grandeur of his faith come out more clearly than in his patient submission to this leading.

" *Secondly.* He was distinguished by the profound depths of his religious experience. His intense earnestness has often been noted and here is its prime reason. The Reformation took place in his own heart and was carried thence into the church. In the cloister he learned the wickedness of the human heart, its blindness and helplessness as well as its alienation from God. Not Augustine but his own inner life was his teacher in Anthropology. Our ruin and our need of a Saviour was with him not merely a doctrine but a realized fact. It was in these struggles after peace, which under the efforts of his powerful will almost destroyed him, that light came. He had tasted the bitter-

ness and found relief and now he knew how to help
others. Heart spoke to heart and his words rang
through all Europe. His own trials filled him with a
profound sympathy for toiling man, and he worked for
the people. He knew the importance of speculative
theology, but the great practical truths of religion
engaged his tongue and pen. He came up out of a
common pit and holds out his powerful hand to help
others to rise, and became pre-eminently a man of the
people. Here is the human secret of his power, the
human reason for his success.

"*Thirdly*. He has distinguished by his intense devotion to truth. Truth was to him a principle of life,
and not of mere thought, a matter of the heart and not
of the mere reason. Life had no significance to his
intensely religious eye, except as related to eternity.
He knew no means of emancipation from sin and no
source of a life in God, except in revealed truth. The
hope of the world depended on it. He was, therefore,
most profoundly devoted to it. He sunk himself in his
consecration to it. He cared not what became of himself if the truth were advanced, and he had no interest in
his work except as identified with the truth. He was
fearless in the midst of dangers that made the bravest
shrink, often reckless in the eye of his friends, courting
martyrdom apparently, and here is the reason he lost
all sight of himself in his intense gaze upon the defense
of truth. This was the power that lifted him into his
wonderful heroism. He spared no enemy of the truth.
He rejected all counsels of expediency when truth
was about to be compromised. Alliance with the
Swiss seemed a matter of the gravest importance; suc-

cess seemed to hang upon it; but he refused the fraternal hand, because he thought truth was sacrificed. God's cause and the cause of truth are one, and believing in the omnipotence of truth, he never courted any earthly power. He stood out centuries in advance of his age, holding against the ages past that truth and not force must overcome error. He corrected the errors in worship and government which the cause of truth demanded, but left all others to the determination of time and place. He grasped truth clearly, presented it plainly, arrayed not the blind prejudice of custom against his work, and where his utterances went they awakened a deep response in the hearts of the multitude.

"To-day we have the world's estimates of the importance of his work, and the grandeur of the man. Such an outburst is unknown in history. It has been said that the Reformation is a failure; but if so, what mean the vast assemblies gathered to-day in every civilized country? Luther's name is shown to be the grandest in uninspired history."

ROBERT A. EDWARDS,
In the Episcopal Church of St. Matthias, Philadelphia.

"Martin Luther, in freeing Germany from papal domination, secured blessings which have enriched and elevated peoples of every other enlightened nation on the face of the earth. His bust stands in the Walhalla at Ratisbon, among the other distinguished sons of Germany; but when Frederick, Barbarossa, Mozart, Goethe, and Humboldt, shall be known simply by their names on pages of history, Luther will remain a living power among the sons of men. * * * *

"Some years ago I entered the plain church at Wittenberg, and a modest slab in one of the aisles was pointed out to me by an attendant. It marked the resting place of Luther's ashes. There was nothing grand or imposing about the place; but an influence hangs around it more potent than ever surrounds the massive St. Peter's at Rome. Luther's enemies abused and slandered him while alive, and some prints of our day reëcho their falsehoods now; but as long as the world shall last will the name of Martin Luther be honored and his memory revered. He cared not for health and position, but lived for his fellow-man supremely. Four hundred million Protestants to-day enjoy blessings which he in part secured."

H. M. G. HUFF,
Rector of St. Mark's Protestant Episcopal Church, Johnstown, Pa.

"Little did the Church of Rome think, while Savonarola was preaching the Reformation in Florence, and a deeper piety among her children, that in Germany there nestled on the bosom of a devoted Christian mother a babe, who would in his life-time revive God's cause, and shed forth the renewed light of faith—the heritage of us all."

F. W. CONRAD,
Editor of *Lutheran Observer*, Phila., Pa. In Farwell Hall, Chicago.

"Luther gave the holy scriptures to the people in their vernacular tongue. Notwithstanding what Christ had said, the Church of Rome raised tradition above the truth. The result was what might have been expected. Luther said that until the people had the scriptures for themselves to read and judge, no great reform was possible. And so he devoted himself to the task of translating the scriptures into the German tongue. In three months he had translated the New Testament, a most herculean task. If the Bible be not in the hands of the people, no private judgment can be passed upon it. Luther saw that fact, and determined to give the people an opportunity to search the Scriptures, and to form opinions upon what they read. Luther exercised the right of judgment and the liberty of conscience. He wrote a treatise in which he declared that neither the Church of Rome nor any other power had the right to deprive people of the privilege of thinking for themselves. Luther's conduct gave rise to a conflict for freedom of thought which has gone on to the present day. Now free thought triumphs everywhere, and the triumph is that of Martin Luther; and Luther to-day is everywhere regarded as the champion of human liberty. A mistake in the translation of the scriptures occasioned the erroneous belief that except one do penance he can not prepare himself for heaven. The word translated was penitennæ, which meant not penance but penitence. The Roman Catholic church seized upon the idea, and indulgences were soon spread over all Europe, to the disgrace of Christendom. Luther heard of the indulgences. Documentary evidence of their having been granted was shown to him in the confessions. He determined to break up the pernicious system, and in his Ninety-fifth Thesis he shattered it so that it never recovered.

"To Luther we owe the bringing out in its greatest

prominence the leading doctrine of the Christian Church—justification by faith. Luther said, with regard to this doctrine, that if the doctrine be kept pure the Christian Church would be kept pure; but that if it be corrupted the whole Christian Church would be corrupted. Again, Martin Luther discarded the false sacraments and maintained the pure ones. Two sacraments were given by the Lord. The Catholic church multiplied them until there was a sacrament for nearly every ceremony. The sacraments were perverted, and reform was absolutely necessary. Then Luther, in his treatise on Babylonish captivity, showed that in the matter of sacraments the Romish church had bound the people worse than had been bound the Babylonish captives.

"Again, Luther assailed the Romish ministry as a sacerdotal body, and set up the Christian ministry instead. Luther said that the papal system must be overthrown, and he assailed it. Seeing the danger of raising into the pulpit young men who might be inflated with pride over their elevation, he made education a necessary qualification; and seeing the danger of raising up unconverted men, he had recourse to methods to determine that the ministry were of the right kind. The Romish church had taken the Word of God out of the Church; it had introduced ceremonies horrible to witness; it had put forth ceremonies in an unknown tongue. Luther prepared a form of service and had sermons delivered in the vernacular; he restored the power of sanctification; he restored the Sabbath. Martin Luther held that the Sabbath was made by nature, and that man needed a Sabbath as constituted by God. The day was to be kept holy; works of necessity might be performed, but works of necessity must not be invented. Again, when some of the Germans tried to divide the Sabbath, saying that part of the day was to be holy and part was not, he went for them. And he went for them, too, on account of their drinking customs, and in this particular he did a great amount of good. Martin Luther also proclaimed against the fancy of women for dress, and broke up many customs which had taken fast hold upon the people, and were tending to immorality. * * * * As Luther is called a successful Reformer, let us see what were the elements of his success. First, his constitutional endowments as God made him; second, his wonderful power of invention of resources under all circumstances. In twenty-nine years and four months he wrote seven hundred and nineteen works—more than one a fortnight. Third, his consummate leadership. There are few great leaders; Martin Luther was the greatest of all in his sphere. He seemed to have the power to see the two extremes, and to run the golden mean between them. Fourth, his magnetism and his modesty. All about him were attracted to him, and looked upon him as their chieftain, yet he spoke of them as equal to him, and of Melanchthon as his superior. Fifth, his great courage. When the pope excommunicated him, he excommunicated the' pope. Look at his conscientious devotion to principle and moral undauntedness. They tried to make him recant; and they all failed. At last he was brought before the emperor, and he said: 'I cannot submit my faith to the popes and the councils, for it is as clear as heaven that they have fallen into error.' Carlyle says that that was the turning point in the modern history of the world. All progress since that day owes its germ to Luther. Were it not for that day, the present civilization would bear the imprint more of Romanism than of Protestantism. We may be charged with that hero-worship of which Carlyle speaks; but, as judged from history, Dr. Martin Luther rises up a colossal figure, which to this day receives the homage of the Christian world."—*Chicago Times*, Nov. 11, 1883.

R. A. FINK,
Of Johnstown, Pa.

"The birth of Martin Luther at Eisleben, on the 10th day of November, 1483, was the most important and far-reaching event in all the ages since the birth in Bethlehem of the world's Reedemer. The child, then and there born, was destined under God to become the greatest benefactor of his age, and all the ages to follow. And on this anniversary day it is fitting that we recall, as far as possible, the memories of the man and his work. As a man he was in intellectual power, in deep and earnest piety, and in great and mighty achievements, apart from inspiration, certainly the equal if not the superior of the great Apostle Paul. As to the results of his work, it is vain to attempt to estimate their importance. It is impossible to turn round without seeing and feeling the blessings that have flowed to us and to the world from what he wrought. There is not a single bough or branch of life—religious, domestic, social, civil, or political—that is not laden with the rich and golden fruit. Had there been no

13

10th of November, 1483, there would have been no 31st of October, 1517; and had there been no 31st of October, 1517, there never could have been a 4th of July, 1776. Luther gave to perishing men an open Bible. And whatever fruit the Bible has caused to grow on the earth, 'that is pleasant to the sight,' or good for spiritual food, bespeaks our gratitude for the work God wrought through Luther in the sixteenth century. And whatever the blessings of civil and religious liberty the world enjoys, it must be remembered that the world is indebted more to Luther than to America, and that America is indebted more to Luther than to herself. A thankful jubilee, therefore, on this memorial day, is appropriate not to Lutherans alone. It would well become all Protestant churches —for they all have their life from the Reformation by Luther. It would well become our whole country— for Luther's free Bible has given its life of freedom, virtue, power and progress. It would well become the world—for the blessings of Luther's work are fast girdling the whole earth. May God cause all of us to catch the spirit of the mighty Reformer! And when we love the Church as Luther loved it, love the truth as Luther loved it, and are ready to sacrifice everything for its triumphs as Luther did, then, like him, we shall not live in vain, nor labor in vain."

E. C. SWEETSER,

In the Universalist Church of the Messiah, Philadelphia, Pa.

"There is in Worms a historic monument—Luther's bronze effigy—towering in the centre of a grand study in statuary, of which figures of Huss, Albiges, and

Wickliffe, his precursors in free religious thought, and three figures emblematic of the cities in which Luther lived and labored, are the accessories. Luther is standing with uncovered head and face uplifted, in the act of speaking the words of courageous defiance to emperor and pope, for which he is best remembered: 'Here I stand. I cannot do otherwise, God helping me.' The potent influence of the man thus commemorated was seen yesterday in the pomp and ceremony throughout Germany, and largely in every country not under papal domination, attending the celebration of his four-hundredth birthday. He was born in the despotism of Catholicism, for then the papacy controlled kings and emperors. All individual thought was crushed out by the terrors of the sword or the terrors of the Inquisition. Popes and priesthood were corrupt, and taxed the people to serve their own unworthy ends. They taught the doctrine that money could release the transgressor from more or less of the consequences of his sins. He lived in the time when abject slavery to the pope existed, in place of the liberty wherewith Christ has made us free. Journeying to Rome in search of the spiritual edification which he believed was obtainable in the Holy City, he left it heavy-hearted, after two weeks' sojourn, with the declaration: 'In Rome everything is permitted except to be an honest man.' Indulgences were openly sold; the priesthood were immoral; the Church was rotten to the core. Inspired by his high vocation, he formulated the ninety-five theses which formed the first basis of his open revolt against the papacy, and his cause blossomed out into the great achievement of German

independence.   The Romish church is indebted to
him for the purification of its morals and manners.

"Luther was far from being perfect. He was rough
in manner, but under that roughness lay a warmth of
heart that made his home a domestic paradise. He
possessed in a magnificent degree the qualities which
most command admiration—splendid courage, devotion to truth, and compelling energy.   He was to
Germany and the Protestant world what Homer was
to Greece, Washington was to America, and Ezra and
Nehemiah to the Hebrew nation."

G. F. KROTEL,
Pastor of Holy Trinity Lutheran Church, New York City.

"'And who went ye out into the wilderness to see?
—a prophet.   Yea, and I say unto you, more than a
prophet.'   So might we ask of millions throughout
the world who have come together to-day.   We could
ask them why they have gathered, and they might
have answered us as in the Scriptures: We have come
to behold a man.   He needs no picture.   He stands
before us to-day, a man standing above his fellows like
a mountain peak amongst the hills.   To look upon
such a man are we here to-day.   Four hundred years
ago a poor miner's boy was born in Eisleben.   We
may trace his steps through school, his studies at the
University at Erfurt, where he was made bachelor,
and afterwards master of arts.   He became well versed
in philosophy, the most learned Augustine in Germany.
In 1508 he was made a professor at Wittenberg, where
in 1546 he was buried.   He lived in no great cities or
palaces.   His life was spent in the smaller places, and

yet we are now in thousands of places met to remember him, because we feel that of all great men, uninspired, Martin Luther was the greatest. Thomas Carlyle once said, 'I will call this Luther a true, great man; great in intellect, courage, affection, and integrity.' He was great in intellect who could succesfully contend with such men as Erasmus; who could translate the Bible from the Hebrew and Greek into German, and do it so well that his work has lasted four hundred years. Many are his other works which are now published in this country and Germany.

" He was great in courage. When we think of him we think of a hero, and his name is synonymous with hero. When he preached against the pope's indulgences, and when he nailed up his theses in Wittenberg, and burned the papal bull, was he not courageous? He was great in affection. His private life is full of love (he had a great heart as well as brain), of love for God as well as men, for whom he consecrated his life. Children of the Sunday-school, read the home life of Martin Luther; read of his care and love for his six children; see his affection when they are taken away. You will weep when you see him leaning over the little body of the dead Magdalene. Great in integrity, another synonymous word, *integer vitæ scelerisque purus*, that Martin Luther had. He was great in one thing, which Carlyle does not speak of—faith. He trusted in God with all his soul, with all his heart and all his might. He sang: 'A Mighty Fortress is our God.' All of his inspiration came from the Bible. In the ancient pictures, St. Paul is represented with a sword in his hand; so is Luther, in that statue, shown

with his sword, not girded about his loins, but in his
hands—the Word of God.

"What are the results of Luther's work? We have
the free Bible in our homes; we have a free church,
where we can worship as conscience dictates; we have
an evangelical service; we sing beautiful hymns in our
own tongue, for you remember he was the founder of
the hymn book, the first edition of which he published
in 1524.

"In St. Paul's Cathedral, over the grave of Sir Chris-
topher Wren, are the words: 'If you seek my epitaph,
look about you.' Fifty million people in a free land,
under a free religion, make the monument for Luther.
These gatherings say to Rome: We stand to-day
by what he stood. We confess to what he confessed, and hold fast to the Scriptures, by the grace of
God, to hand down to remotest generations, saying, as
did he to his inquisitors: 'Here we stand. We cannot do otherwise. God help us!'"—*Philadelphia*, Nov.
10, 1883.

M. SHEELEIGH,
Of Fort Washington, Pa.

"In noting a few of the prominent characteristics
of Martin Luther, which were in him grand secrets of
power and success, observe that:

"1. He was a man of distinguished FAITH. No
half-heartedness could have been sufficient for the time
and the occasion. God, who had step by step prepared his servant for a work of the ages, had nerved
up the soul of this man and filled it to overflowing
with faith. I doubt whether there is *any* more promi-

nent example of mere human faith spoken of outside of Holy Scripture, or *in it either*. Such unwavering trust in the character of God, such implicit reposing upon the merits of Jesus Christ for mercy and forgiveness, such unshaken confidence in the promises of the Divine Word—oh, it is simply wonderful! * * *

" 2. Luther was a man of mighty PRAYER. With him prayer was not by any means an empty form. He took God at His word. He pleaded with heaven as a man may plead face to face with his friend. Concerning no man within the scope of history can it be more properly said that he ' moved the Arm that moves the world.' It is recorded that each day he spent three hours in secret prayer. And the more he had to do, the more he prayed. No man ever understood more thoroughly that all human exertion is vain without heaven's blessing. He cast all the interests of the Reformation work on the infinite heart of Him whose it was. He *worked* so incessantly and zealously as though all success depended on human exertion; and he *prayed* so urgently and importunately as though human agency were of no consideration. * * *

" 3. Another characteristic of Luther was that he was *utterly fearless of opponents*. He did not seem to know what it was to have any personal fear before the face of man. In him was most prominent the material of which *martyrs* are made. If at times he saved his life, on the earnest solicitation and planning of friends, he yielded only that his life might thus be spared for the sake of the Lord's cause. But when he believed that that same cause required the exposure of his life, even though it should be unto death, he would not be dis-

suaded from his purpose. Long and strongly had he to resist the solicitation of friends when his mind was made up to obey the summons to appear at the Diet of Worms. They told him that his fate would be that of John Huss, who had been burned at the stake notwithstanding the safe-conduct he bore in his hands. You remember those astounding figures of speech which he then called to his aid in expressing his determination. And you remember also those familiar words with which he closed his declaration before the assembled dignitaries of Church and State, announcing positively that he neither could nor would retract the things contained in the books he had written, which were in accordance with the Holy Scriptures: 'Here I stand. I cannot do otherwise, God help me! Amen.' At these words that assembly was startled by the heroism of this defenceless man. The land was startled. Other lands were startled. And we of to-day are startled. What forgetfulness of self — what fearlessness before the might of man—for the sake of the holy truth!" *　*　*　*　*　*　*　*
—*Whitemarsh and Dublin, Pa.*, Nov. 11, 1883.

J. B. BALTZLY,
Of Indianapolis, Indiana.

"Luther established the right and duty of private judgment, and the truths of the intelligibility of the Scriptures, the priesthood of all believers, the invisibility of the true, and the fallibility of the visible Church. He ever maintained the worth and right of the Christian man. He is the creator of the language of German literature. He suggested the incomparable

German school-system, with compulsory education. He was the earliest champion of higher education for women. He wanted to see all the arts and sciences fostered and in the service of God. He loved and composed music, prepared the first collection of spiritual songs, and introduced congregational singing. His foresight in civil and social matters was remarkable. He contended for the separation of Church and State. He warned Germany concerning her intemperance. He suggested our charity-organization societies three centuries ago. He encouraged husbandry, and spoke brave words for the common rights of the peasants. He was beforehand with anti-monopoly views. His mind was world-wide. His courage, tenderness and humor are preëminent. His moderation and tolerance seem almost a paradox in such a character. His fame is large, because he was large. He is the world's, because to so great an extent the world was his. He loved, and is loved. His sympathies went out from him like loving hands to all the points of the compass of man and life, and the world responded, and still responds, to his touch."

J. G. MORRIS,
At Union Service, in Ford's Opera House, Baltimore, Maryland.

"There were many strong men before Luther, and many powerful minds contemporary with his, but Luther was the embodiment of all of them. He was the Colossus of the noble gallery; the giant of the group. In the galaxy of stars in the Reformation Luther shone the brightest, and penetrated the gloom of that age. He was a man in appreciation of whose

13*

services the Protestant heart bows in rapture. His name and fame descend through generations. Luther was not a sectarian man, but belonged to the whole Christian church. His name and works are now more frequently mentioned, and his books more read, than ever before. In the month of October, 365 years ago, his great work was begun, and he took his stand against the corruption of the Church of Rome. Others had attacked the errors of that church before him, but they made a mistake in assailing the bad morals, rather than the unscriptural doctrine. There had been no extended exposure of the false teachings of the Romish Church until God brought out Martin Luther to do this work. Luther, who had himself been a monk and a priest, was to be the leader of the Reformation. His righteous soul was filled with holy ardor. Like Elijah, he thundered truths into the ears of princes and all the people. Instead of images, rosaries, confession and indulgences, he pointed to the Lamb of God. He made the truth triumphant, and the Gospel became free. All previous efforts had been fruitless. The cardinals and bishops had time and again promised reformation, but failed. Luther aroused the attention of the multitudes. No original faith was preached by him, but only the true doctrines of Christ. The old faith was brought out from the rubbish, from the human additions and abuses, and it was made fresh and pure. Protestantism was freshened and cleansed after the circus advertisements and the trash which had surrounded it. It had been hid under a bushel. Luther lifted it off. He raised the curtain, and let in the light of truth in all its brilliant splendor. Salva-

tion by faith was superseded by works. The light of
science had been extinguished; literature had pined in
monastic cells; the priesthood was the slavish horde
of the tyrannical usurper of God's throne; the people
were superstitious: but out of all this Luther brought
the truth triumphant. With the Bible that gave liberty to Luther, he gave liberty to the world. The
Romanists have now to believe what the church pre-
scribes, to take all on credit; we require proof from
the Scriptures. The Romanist believes what the
church teaches; we, what the Bible teaches. We re-
ject the mediation of the Virgin Mary, though we
respect her memory. We have no earthly mediator.
Above the portals of the gateway of Protestantism,
illumined by the Star of Bethlehem, is the motto,
'Believe and live.' The Reformation was not a
human work. The world was in a ferment at the
time. The people were looking for some great change
to come, and God endowed Luther with daring courage, burning zeal, devoted piety and great learning, to
accomplish this. He translated the Scriptures into his
own glorious German language. He was a genuine
hero. It was Luther's humanity that made Protestantism the religion of the household, as Catholicism
had been the religion of the state and of the cathedral.
All Christians should commemorate him by the study
of his life and work, and by studying the era of the
Reformation.

"Through him the church was emancipated from
thraldom. The mighty Luther with his goose-quill
pierced the superstitions, and God's house was purified
from all idolatry. The pulpit was brought back to

its proper purpose, and no longer was a platform from which to sell indulgences and medals. How, then, are we to account for the universal enthusiasm of the Protestants at this time? Is Protestantism in peril? No; it never stood firmer. That which did not exist four hundred years ago now controls 488,000,000 of people, and on the other hand the Romish Church controls 280,000,000. Protestantism is more powerful than ever. In the Sunday-schools the gospel is being taught to five million children. It is Protestantism that sets up free government, builds churches, stimulates thought, encourages science and business, and keeps the Lord's day. This does not look as if Protestantism was declining."—*Baltimore American.*

ASSOCIATE JUSTICE STRONG,

In Memorial Lutheran Church, Washington, D. C.

"In all times some man comes forward who, as a leader, is greater than all his fellows. Martin Luther is the most conspicuous instance of how God brings such leaders up to do his work. Luther is the father of Protestantism; he breasted the opposition of the whole world, and brought man face to face with his God without the intervention of priests. Such a man is one of the most beneficent gifts of God to mankind. Hundreds of millions to-day all over the world thank God for Luther's life and work. Luther can be regarded as the author of the civil liberty that is enjoyed to-day. At the time he wrought the world was under the dominion of the Catholic church, which claimed to rule the thoughts and actions of men, both in civil and religious things. He translated the

Bible into the German language, and spread before his countrymen the ethics and principles underlying religion and freedom of life. From the hour that this publication was made, civil liberty sprang into birth, and became a possibility for men. There can be no perfect civil liberty anywhere except it is founded on the general ethics and teaching of the Bible. The golden rule is the basis of all good government, and the admonition of 'As ye would have men do to you, do ye even so to them,' is the corner-stone upon which the civil liberties of the world rest to-day ; and in distributing the Bible so widely as has been in the United States, it follows as a natural consequence that in no country has civil liberty and that freedom which is bound to flourish reached such growth."—*National Republican*, Nov. 12, 1883.

W. A. BARTLETT,
Of Washington, D. C.   In Memorial Lutheran Church.

"Rev. W. A. Bartlett then delivered a brief address, in which he contrasted the lines of Luther and Calvin. Dr. Bartlett said that Luther and Calvin were hardly two characters that would be suggested for comparison or contrast. He had visited the birth-place of the great Reformer, the church in which he last preached, and the spot where he had rendered up his spirit to God. The place seemed pervaded by the intense spirit of that great man. At Geneva he had wandered over the ground where Calvin had performed his great works. The character of Luther was that of the largest German man, and in his sphere Calvin was the largest Frenchman. One was a man of the people, working with brawn and brain. The other worked in narrow lines, but to the same great end by different means. The criticism that Luther was a narrow theologian was an absurdity, for with all his rich German blood and intellect he would have seized the Greek language even as he would have seized the devil to make the Bible plain to his people, and his work at Wartburg bore testimony of his indomitable energy and rare intellect. At the age of twenty-seven Calvin had produced the clearest system of divinity ever published to the world. Calvin and Luther were alike in their courage; each feared only to do wrong. At Worms before Charles V., and in every situation that surrounded him, he had hurled his defiance at all who opposed his life-work. Calvin worked under other conditions, which involved the giving up of every worldly prospect, and a life of sacrifice and self-denial. Yet he had organized the theological body of the Reformation, which up to the present moment, commanded the admiration of the intellectual world. Some deeds, it was true, could be admitted of both that in the light of to-day were great wrongs; but these were the flies in the amber of their manhood, and by the preponderance of the good showed that they were but men. These two men never met, but in their fellowship in Christ, made majestic by the great truths to which they devoted their lives, Calvin was the great theologian, Luther the great Reformer, for no one mentioned Reform but his name was the only one suggested. He was the heart, the centre, and the motive power that had sent down to us civil and religious liberty."—*National Republican*, November 12, 1883.

HENRY WARD BEECHER,

Pastor of Plymouth Church, Brooklyn, N. Y.

" The value of man is not to be estimated by what
he is worth in this world. From the standpoint of
political economy, he is worth only what he can do.
Ten thousand times ten thousand men are in the way.
They have nothing for life, and life has nothing for
them. It is a marvel why they were born. There is
another way of measuring men, and Luther had a hand
in introducing it. He gave the open Bible to the common people. They were prepared for the seed. God's
wheat was there; but there had been wrapped around
it perfumed nonsense, swathes and bandages, that shut
out the light. Luther cut it open, sowed the wheat
which he found there, and you are part of the product.
You cannot tell what a man will be by what he is here.
You cannot tell until he has come into the full possession of his royal nature. It is the value of the individual man by reason of his origin from God, and his
destination hereafter, that the Reformation brought
out. Previously he had been considered worth nothing, except to make churches and states of. Man as
a unit had no value, only organized man possessed
value. The difference between the Protestant and the
Roman Catholic faith is the difference between the individual relation in man and the corporate relation.
All our popular institutions have been founded upon
this sense of the dignity of a man not by reason of
what is in him, but because of the destiny which God
has conferred upon him. For this the Puritans strove,
and they sprang from the loins of the Reformation.
They were filled with this sense of the value of man

as an individual. What is the consequence? In every State between the two roaring oceans we have a framework of government made expressly in the interest of the individual citizen. Multitudes come to our shores disowning the Word of God out of which came the liberty they enjoy here. If there be one single doctrine that the American people cannot afford to lose, it is the doctrine of manhood as established in the genius of Christianity. Our civil liberty is the result of the open Bible which Luther gave us."—*In St. Matthew's Lutheran Church, Brooklyn.*

G. W. MILLER,
In the Spring Garden Methodist Church, Phila.

" Luther, take him all in all, like the lovely German masterpiece which exhibits in one glow of associated beauty the pride of every model and the perfection of every master, presents us with the combination of all those high and rare qualities of human nature which we ordinarily find separately in men. He was no ideal saint; he was thoroughly human, and this is the peculiar glory of him. He touched human nature on all sides, and always with the masterly touch of power. He had the power above most men of acting as a kind of tongue to human nature. The passions, the traits and the motives he pictured were always elemental, the very ground-work of human action and interest in all conditions of life; and he painted these things, not as if they were outside of him, but with that sympathy which makes the difference between a dead and a living language.

" The Romanists are trying to obscure this colossal

character, but it will stand an inspiration to all men and a glory for all time. A little water wrought into a mist will obscure for a time his native Thuringian mountains, but when the mist has cleared away the mountains will remain in their grandeur. So, when the temporary fog of detraction is lifted, Luther will stand out in his unhidden and peculiar glory, casting his 'image on the current of the ages as the mountain mirrors itself in the river that winds at its foot.'

"What made this man great? First of all, great nature. Luther is immense. There is a great deal of him, body, mind and soul, and the glory of it all is that it is all real. He had grip, the power to take hold and to hold on. He had grasp—the ability to comprehend subjects in themselves and in their relations. He had greatness—the capacity to seize and move and mould other minds and hearts, and to put his personal impress on all whom he touched. In one word, there was quantity of being, as well as quality, in which his greatness rooted itself. But nature alone never made any man really great.

"There was great personal endeavor. What a life!—genius wedded to industry! He had no idea of life apart from work. He cultivated a genius for work. Every faculty was brought into harness and every fragment of time was improved, so that his attainments were more many-sided than any man of his age, and there is hardly a problem of modern times that he did not touch. Still, we have not reached the true secret of his greatness. He might have used his vast and varied gifts and his capacity to work for selfish ends. Then we should have had to mourn that another page had been added to the record of human frailty, and yet it would have been but a specimen in larger type of the moral and spiritual failure that so many men have painted in smaller type upon their allowance of time and opportunity.   There is another element in his greatness.

"Thirdly, he had great trust in Providence.   The Emperor or the Pope might be in league against him, but there was another order looming behind the veil. It only awaited God's time.   And they who had gone out of an idolatrous church would find in the end that Christ and not anti-Christ ruled the world.   In this faith Luther lived and died, and here, at last, you have the full secret of his greatness—great nature wedded to great personal endeavor, and both alike wedded to Divine Providence—these three, but the greatest of these is Providence."

CHESTER D. HARTRANFT,
Professor of Church History in Hartford (Conn.) Theological Seminary.

"The address proposed to treat Luther, not from a logical or biographical standpoint; not from his life, but from his ideas.

" I. The first great idea and consequent force was the restoration of the true source of Revealed Theology; (1) negatively, by the overthrow of speculative philosophy and reason; by the overthrow of dogmatism, established by church authority and tradition; by the overthrow of mysticism ; (2) positively, by the instauration of the Bible as the only source.

" II. The second great idea was the instauration of the *novum organum* for accumulating the facts of the

Word; (1) exegetical theology, Luther's view of Sacred Philology, especially as to the language, grammar, lexicon; views of canonics, views of textual criticisms; laws of interpretation, overthrow of allegory, his own commentaries and his noble version; (2) historical theology, biblical, ecclesiastical.

"III. The third great group of ideas and forces was derived from the application of the *novum organum* to the source, the Bible: 1. In dogmatics eminently: (*a*) Dogma of the Holy Spirit. (*b*) The soteriological dogmas, (*a*) faith, (*b*) universal priesthood of believers. (*c*) Ecclesiological dogma: doctrine of the Invisible Church, Luther's scheme of polity, national, democratic, collegiate: his efforts at effecting fellowship; the compulsory definition of the dogmatic and ethical positions of the Curia. 2. In religion: Spirituality as the most eminent Protestant religious trait. 3. In ethics: Principally, the doctrine of Christian liberty on its human side, or genuine individualism. 4. In morality: (*a*) The Protestant idea of the family as asserted by Luther. (*b*) The Protestant idea of education as indicated by Luther's attitude towards Humanism. (*c*) Anti-monasticism, or the Protestant idea of life in the world. (*d*) The Protestant idea of State.

"IV. The fourth group of ideas and consequent forces from the reconstruction of Practical Theology, notice particularly: 1. The Protestant idea of the sermon and office of the preacher as illustrated by Luther. 2. The Protestant idea of Liturgies, especially Luther's use and view of music; the Protestant theory of music. 3. The Protestant idea of Catechetics as inaugurated by Luther.

" V. The career of Luther—a proof that there is a special Providence in History.

" VI. The career of Luther—a proof that the Kingdom of God is the kernel shaping force of human history."

J. S. McINTOSH,
Pastor of Second Presbyterian Church, Philadelphia, Pa.

" There are men who belong to a year, to a decade, to a period; there are men who belong to the ages, and live for all time ; there are men, fresh and forcible, who belong to a city, to a country, to a continent, and men who belong to the world; there are men who belong to a particular class, to a circle, to a single definite movement, to a special field of distinct struggle, and men who belong to the wide realm of our common humanity, to the round globe of varying interest, manifold thought. These men, to whom nothing of humanity is alien, are the strong, true men to gather around and to learn from.

"Art, literature, science, politics, have their universal, immortal, many-sided chiefs : and shall the Church, guardian mother of highest song and sublimest prose, friend of the truth and teacher of the perfect law, not have her imperial spirit ? Yes, verily, all down her line she has furnished these king-like children of the King of kings. And, curious enough it is, they meet us by threes, these mighty, over-topping heroes of the hosts of God—Moses, Samuel and Elijah—Peter, John and Paul—Luther, Calvin and Knox. Among these stands midmost, manly, merry, massive, masterly Martin Luther, monk of Erfurt, man of the Great Emancipation—a 'great mother man,' 'sovereign of the greatest revolution,' prophet, idol-breaker, bringer-back of men to reality, for whom these centuries, and many yet to come, will be thankful to Heaven.

"This man, whom grace made humble and God made great, belongs to the world's centuries, the broadening thought, the dominant forces, the farthest reaching influence of to-day and to-morrow. He belongs to the Church Universal; his life labors are hitting mightily within the Romish pale, as well as without. The Council of Trent and the Westminster Assembly, the wily Gant and William Carey, are all linked, though by different bonds, to the Monk of Erfurt—scholar, singer, sage, statesman, saint, a joy to real men, triumph and trophy of God's Son and Spirit. God we glorify in recalling the man. God's hand and His grace are manifest in the earnest boy of Eisenach, the ardent student of Erfurt, the God-fearing Reformer of Wittenberg, and the popular preacher of Northern Germany. Dead, he yet lives; Luther, child of the long past, and father of the fertile future, Reformer of the Reformers, poet of poets, head of the column, with Calvin, his superior in subtle analysis, on the one side, Knox, his superior in administrative statesmanship, on the other, himself chiefest of the three mighties, hero of the faith fight, with spirit resplendent, yet humble, conservative, yet radical—great man of God, we honor and glorify thy Maker!

"Great man of the centuries! we will honor thee, and glorify God in thee: for clearer than the hand of the Cæsars, or Constantine, or Charlemagne, we see thy hand, commanding thy position and controlling thy influence. This service is no secret canonization. In Luther, the popular preacher of Northern Germany, we see grace triumphant. During his boyhood he grew in reflective wisdom. When the time for the struggle came, he was already a trained athlete. God calmed him before he flung him into the battle. Luther's words were half-battles. Christ he proclaimed to rich and poor, to the scholar and to the peasant. Like the other great Reformers, he was a preacher of great sermons, of the marvelous word of God. He was a man who loved truth to the uttermost depth of his soul. He loved the truth, and it he must have.

"Every inch a man, an accurate student of philosophy, ethics, an educated lawyer, a thoroughly sound theologian, a close, conservative thinker, a skilled rhetorician, a fiery-tongued orator, poetic, historical, the common people heard him gladly, and men's souls were taxed to the uttermost by his profound thinking. Thus preaching, expounding, thus writing hymns and composing tunes, thus planting schools and fostering colleges, thus fighting papacy and denouncing despotism, for twenty years went on the genial, generous, great-hearted man. Grace marked all his years. God upheld him through life's battle, nor failed him when, smitten fatally, he lay down to die in the little town where he was born, baptized, and consecrated to God. He was a man among men. He loved the children, he knew their games; he knew the doubts of the thoughtful, the sorrows of the bereaved; and, Paul-like, he became all things to all men to win them to Christ."

THE LÚTHER MONUMENT.

BY JOEL SWARTZ, D. D.,

Pastor of St. James' Lutheran Church, Gettysburg, Pa.

Come, let us build a monument
 To Luther's mighty fame;
Let's carve upon it high and deep
 The great Reformer's name.

In this his fourth Centennial year,
 Let freemen o'er the earth
Unite to celebrate with cheer
 His own and Freedom's birth.

For who among the sons of men
 For man, as Luther wrought?
Who for the right against the wrong
 Such mighty battles fought?

He smote old Error's rusty chain,
 And crushed its links to earth;
And to unfettered Thought again
 He gave a second birth.

Now, as the mighty centuries roll
 And waft his power abroad,
Still pleads his ever-growing soul
 For freedom and for God.

How can we build to such a name?
 What shall the structure be?
It ought to be a shaft of flame
 To light the land and sea.

A marble column, mountain high,
 Tho' crowned with molten gold,
Would, to a large, discerning eye,
 Seem dwarfed and dead and cold.

But Luther *hath* his monuments—
 Not wrought of bronze or stone;

These hath he too, poor, lifeless forms,
  Not his, but ours alone.

Dost ask for his memorials true?
And what their structure be?
Lift up thine eyes, enlarge thy view,
  Sweep o'er the land and sea.

For over these a light is born,
  Whose blush the blue arch fills;
It seems as if a second morn
  Glowed on the golden hills.

Great Luther found the fettered Word,
  The lamp of light divine,
Uncased the candle of the Lord,
  And trimmed and bade it shine.

As Mary's fragrant spikenard poured
  Is her memorial true,
So the unsealed and preached Word
  Is his memorial too.

Where Faith and Love their spires uprear
  To greet the rising sun,
There Luther's monuments appear,
  For there his work is done.

But in this fourth centennial year
  Let's build a monument,
Some thankful token for the good
  The Reformation sent.

Build ye who will the bronze, the stone—
  A work which cannot grow;
Perhaps 'twill make his features known
  Whose life we strive to know.

But come and build the mighty work
  Which his brave hands begun;
Tho' grand its vast proportions be,
  The work is not yet done.

Ye who the name of Luther boast,
   And who his work would share,
Cease, first, your Babel strife of tongues,
   Your war of words forbear.

Close up the chasms which divide
   Your fierce, sectarian bands;
Your shibboleths of party hide,
   And clasp fraternal hands.

Then build in faith, but build in love,
   Build first yourselves in one;
O what a monument were reared,
   If this grand work were done!

Then with the open Bible haste
   To meet its friends or foes;
Beneath your feet the desert waste
   Shall blossom as the rose.

Build schools and churches, conscience, laws
   On every continent;
Thus, as ye build great Luther's cause,
   Ye build his monument.

Lutheran Observer, July 13, 1883.

14

INDEX.

(315)